BARGAINING FOR EDEN

ALSO BY STEPHEN TRIMBLE

NATURAL HISTORY
The Sagebrush Ocean: A Natural History of the Great Basin
Canyon Country (with photographs by Dewitt Jones)
Longs Peak: A Rocky Mountain Chronicle
*The Bright Edge: A Guide to the National Parks of the Colorado
    Plateau*

NATIVE AMERICA
The People: Indians of the American Southwest
Talking with the Clay: The Art of Pueblo Pottery in the 21st Century
Our Voices, Our Land

ESSAYS
Testimony: Writers of the West Speak on Behalf of Utah Wilderness
    (compiled with Terry Tempest Williams)
The Geography of Childhood: Why Children Need Wild Places (with
    Gary Paul Nabhan)
Words from the Land: Encounters with Natural History Writing

PHOTOGRAPHY
Lasting Light: 125 Years of Grand Canyon Photography
Earthtones: A Nevada Album (with text by Ann Ronald)
Blessed by Light: Visions of the Colorado Plateau

FOR CHILDREN
The Village of Blue Stone (with illustrations by Jennifer Owings
    Dewey and Deborah Reade)

BARGAINING FOR EDEN

THE FIGHT FOR THE LAST OPEN SPACES IN AMERICA

STEPHEN TRIMBLE

UNIVERSITY OF CALIFORNIA PRESS   BERKELEY LOS ANGELES LONDON

The author gratefully acknowledges the support of the Utah Humanities Council (2002 Delmont Oswald Fellowship in Utah Studies) and the 2004 Utah Arts Council Literature Program Non-Fiction Book Award and Publication Grant.

University of California Press, one of the most distinguished university presses in the United States, enriches lives around the world by advancing scholarship in the humanities, social sciences, and natural sciences. Its activities are supported by the UC Press Foundation and by philanthropic contributions from individuals and institutions. For more information, visit www.ucpress.edu.

All photographs are by the author unless otherwise noted.

Quotations from Bernard DeVoto, *The Western Paradox: A Conservation Reader,* ed. Douglas Brinkley and Patricia Nelson Limerick (New Haven: Yale University Press, 2001), pp. xx, 452–53, copyright © Mark DeVoto, used by permission; quotations from Marc P. Reisner, *Cadillac Desert: The American West and Its Disappearing Water,* revised and updated edition, copyright © 1986, 1993 by Marc P. Reisner (New York: Viking Penguin), p. 517, used by permission of Viking Penguin, a division of Penguin Group (USA) Inc.; quotation from Wallace Stegner, *Wolf Willow: A History, a Story, and a Memory of the Last Plains Frontier* (New York: Viking Press, 1962), p. 282, copyright © 1955, 1957, 1958, 1962 by Wallace Stegner, copyright renewed © 1990 by Wallace Stegner, reprinted by permission of Brant & Hochman Literary Agents, Inc., all rights reserved.

University of California Press
Berkeley and Los Angeles, California

University of California Press, Ltd.
London, England

Text and photographs © 2008 by Stephen Trimble
Frontispiece: Mount Ogden rises from the irrigated shoreline of the Great Salt Lake, Utah. 2005.

Library of Congress Cataloging-in-Publication Data
Trimble, Stephen.
   Bargaining for Eden : the fight for the last open spaces in America / Stephen Trimble.
      p.   cm.
   Includes bibliographical references and index.
   ISBN 978–0-520–25111–3 (cloth : alk. paper)
   1. Land use—West (U.S.).   2. Real estate development—West (U.S.).
I. Title.
HD209.T75   2008
333.73'130978—dc22   2007033571

Manufactured in the United States of America
17 16 15 14 13 12 11 10 09 08
10 9 8 7 6 5 4 3 2 1
This book is printed on Natures Book, which contains 50% post-consumer waste and meets the minimum requirements of ANSI/NISO Z39.48–1992 (R 1997) *(Permanence of Paper).*

The publisher gratefully acknowledges the generous contribution to this book provided by the Utah Arts Council.

The publisher also gratefully acknowledges the generous contribution to this book provided by the Gordon and Betty Moore Fund in Environmental Studies of the University of California Press Foundation.

FOR THE VISIONARIES AND VOLUNTEERS
OF AMERICA'S LAND TRUSTS:
ACRE BY ACRE
SAVING OUR OPEN SPACE;
COMMUNITY BY COMMUNITY
SUSTAINING OUR RELATIONSHIP WITH THE EARTH.

The cost of a thing
is the amount of what I will call life
which is required to be exchanged for it.

HENRY DAVID THOREAU, *WALDEN*, **1854**

CONTENTS

PART III: THE MIDDLE-AGED WEST

TRACK HOE EXCAVATING AUTHOR'S HOUSE, TORREY, UTAH, 2002.

BECOMING EARL

We are all industrial tourists. Physically we can take only pictures and leave only footprints. Psychically, socially, culturally, economically, and environmentally, we inexorably change all we touch.

HAL ROTHMAN, *DEVIL'S BARGAINS: TOURISM IN THE TWENTIETH-CENTURY AMERICAN WEST*, 1998

I FIRST SAW EARL HOLDING on a crisp and radiant morning in March 1999. As I walked toward the base of the new ski lift on the day of the first running of the Snowbasin Women's Downhill course during the national alpine championships, a tall distinguished-looking gentleman with thick, carefully barbered white hair was standing outside the VIP tent with a smiling older woman with wild curls. I'd seen a single photograph of Earl again and again, the one press shot he seemed to have released for use throughout eternity. I looked at the man, and my heart raced. This had to be Earl. His wife, Carol, stood next to him with one arm in a sling; she must have broken her arm—skiing? I knew she was vital: she had run a marathon at the age of fifty.

Though I'm a photographer as well as a writer, I did not pull out a telephoto and begin to shoot portraits. I did not walk right up and introduce myself. For almost two years I'd been trying to interview Earl Holding—to ask him to tell the story of Utah's Snowbasin land exchange in his own words and urge him to speak about his dreams, his legacy. People inflamed by his actions had spit words like "evil" and "lies" and "treachery" when they talked about the billionaire businessman's demand that National Forest land at the base of his ski resort be given to him in trade, to privatize and develop. His antagonists—schoolteachers and nurses, lawyers and landowners, stay-at-home mothers and Snowbasin ski patrollers—charged that he and his elite political connections had used the coming 2002 Salt Lake City Olympics as cover and that the state's congressional delegation had willingly lied to support Earl's ends.

How could I broach these accusations at a casual meeting?

I've interviewed hundreds of people over decades of book projects, but they *wanted* to tell me their stories. Though I remained as intent as ever on untangling Earl's role in shaping the destiny of my home territory, I didn't have it in me to confront him. If this reclusive self-made man was so adamant about his privacy, so intent on being a distant presence, then, by God, I would let him be a myth. I dislike conflict. Try as I might, I am no Michael Moore.

So I walked over to the Forest Service yurt and chatted with my ranger and scientist friends—and watched Earl. Within moments he strolled over and began working the crowd. "Hello, I'm Earl Holding." Soft-spoken. He shook hands with each uniformed ranger type. Then he came to me.

He was physically impressive. Imposingly tall and handsome in a clean, smooth way, he loomed over me. He had a terrific shock of white hair—considerably more than remains on my own balding head, though Earl is a generation older. I knew he could be ruthless, but his manner and voice had the same softness as the dinner rolls served at his Little America hotels. His blue eyes were anything but penetrating. They pulled you in, but where they took you was private—a still and unreadable pool.

"I'm Earl Holding."

"And I'm Steve Trimble."

He looked at me quizzically. "And who are you with?"

"I'm a freelance writer, and I'm working on a book about the mountain."

Did he remember my letters and calls—all unanswered? Had any of his minions said anything about me? I couldn't tell from the slight narrowing of his brows. I simply may have seen his leeriness of the press.

He moved on. When it came time for the ceremonies after the race, a line of dignitaries and elders trooped out onto the finish area: Bernhard Russi, the charismatic Swiss Olympic downhill skier and designer of the new Olympic racecourse; foresters uniformed in dusky green Gore-Tex, attempting to stand firm for the American people against Earl's desires even as they crystallized into inevitability; Ogden businesspeople from the little city below the mountain; ski racers, with their athlete's distillation of goofy youth, jockiness, and smiles with the high-voltage flash of orthodontic triumph and imminent celebrity; Salt Lake Olympics staff humbled by months of international scandal.

And, standing before them, Earl Holding, owner of Snowbasin and Sun Valley and a member of the Salt Lake Olympic Committee until just a month before, when he was forced to resign because of conflicts of interest. The Big Dreamer in a crowd full of dreamers. A Taos Indian woman pressed into service by the Ogden Olympic boosters performed a small blessing and gave Earl a pipe and a fistful of multicolored ribbons. She moved back, leaving Earl, as he grasped this braid of color, to deliver a short welcoming speech.

He thanked God and Bernhard Russi. Then he moved quickly into his more comfortable realm of numbers, reverting to his engineer's soul, telling us how many towers the new lifts had and how much construction had been accomplished. I photographed, burning through film, trying to capture the soul of the man in my camera and exhilarated to see him in the flesh at last. Slightly crazed, frustrated by how many things I wanted to do at once, I set aside my camera as Earl finished speaking and took out my journal.

THE SNOWBASIN LAND EXCHANGE has become an emblematic story of power and land in America. Earl Holding holds the power. Citizens band together to fight him. In theory, the mountain—Mount Ogden—stands above the fray, but privatization can destroy the wildness of the place, corporatize the charm of the beloved recreational paradise, compromise its ecological integrity, and limit access to what once were public lands.

Earl bought Snowbasin, the bankrupt ski area above Ogden, Utah, in 1984. He already owned Sun Valley Ski Resort in Idaho. He also owned the oil company, Sinclair, that generated the money required to follow his dreams. In truth, Earl had almost everything he needed to begin turning the old-fashioned ski area into a megaresort. Enormous wealth to bankroll development, political connections from a lifetime of insider status in his home state, drive and ambition. He lacked only one thing: full ownership, for though he had acquired nearly ten thousand acres of land around the mountain, the ski area base and the ski runs themselves lay within Wasatch-Cache National Forest. Earl wanted that land to develop, to control, to own.

And so Snowbasin became the scene for a dozen years of conflict. Earl called on the Forest Service to trade him the base of the mountain in ex-

EARL AND CAROL HOLDING AT THE DEDICATION OF THE WOMEN'S DOWNHILL RACECOURSE, SNOWBASIN, UTAH, 1999.

change for other land he would buy to add to the forest. This wasn't just a line drawn around random, anonymous woods. Earl was asking to privatize public land held dear by the families of citizens who had saved this high mountain basin from overgrazing in the 1930s. Utah's business community and politicians supported him, but the grassroots communities surrounding the mountain joined together to fight the loss of their common heritage. The national environmental community fought the precedent that the mountain could be subdivided at will. The Clinton administration fought Earl's assumption that money and privilege entitled him to special treatment and exemption from regulatory oversight.

When Salt Lake City was named the host for the 2002 Winter Olympics, with Snowbasin designated as the venue for the alpine speed events, the stakes increased sharply. The Utah congressional delegation, led by Congressman Jim Hansen and Senator Orrin Hatch, began legislative maneuvers to give Earl what he wanted. The fact that elected officials were serving a billionaire's whims attracted national attention and became a satellite story to the bribery scandals developing as the Olympics approached. In the months leading up to the 1996 presidential election the Snowbasin Land Exchange Bill became one more nut in the legislative shell game playing out in Congress.

While following this story, tracing how power determines the fate of land we hold dear and doing my best to penetrate behind closed doors into murky decision space, I found myself one day in a surprising place, standing with my wife on a redrock mesa in southern Utah and dreaming of building a house there—our house. We concocted a scheme that made it possible for us to purchase the land by splitting the acreage. In doing so, we would become land developers ourselves on a small scale.

I'd never owned land—except for a tiny urban lot beneath our Salt Lake City home—and the notion of owning a wild mesa made me uncomfortable. I began to look for ways to live up to this new relationship I had with a landscape I had always loved fiercely. How could I—a newly invested taxpaying citizen in Wayne County, Utah—best engage with my community, given the realities of small-town America? How do *any* of us engage with our neighbors, and how can we together successfully plan for change and wisely welcome the future? Caught between dreams, we are all greedy, and we all are generous. How then do we create a structure for our communities that expresses our altruism more than our self-interest? How do we give each other the benefit of the doubt and offer at least a moment of grace before we move on to assumptions and judgments and dismissal?

I've watched how Earl uses his power to shape our mutual home; I'm trying to influence the future of my adopted Eden in southern Utah's redrock canyon country, as well. I know where I come from—and I'm still working things out. In Wayne County locals continue to dismiss me first as a wealthy outsider, a second-home owner, a second-rate citizen. It takes years to get past that, and it takes consistent open-hearted behavior and good listening on my part to make progress.

As a lifelong environmentalist I still hold my beliefs fiercely. But in telling Earl's story and in confronting my new identity as a property owner, I've found cracks in the armor of my own assumptions. I have been startled. I have been horrified.

On some levels, I am Earl—we all are Earl.

YOU KNOW THESE PLACES WE CHERISH—the fields, the lakeshore, the park, the riverway. The homey local ski area. They ground our lives and give our communities everyday moments of beauty. You also know the threats and the hunger to speak out, to save the countryside that we remember from childhood or the wild places we discovered in times of need.

Last night your city council voted to turn over the last woods along the creek to developers. There's a heron rookery in those cottonwoods, but there is also money to be made. And your beach? New owners have closed access to South Cove, where families from both sides of town have picnicked and played for three generations. The largest coal company in the world wants to strip-mine Long Ridge, that precious public land on your horizon shielding critical winter range for the healthiest deer herd in the state. The farm that softens the views of marching subdivisions where the highway leaves town—the one with the fading mural of the black cat on an old barn? It's for sale.

Each year land trusts work frantically to preserve open space, wildlife habitat, historic sites, farmland, and rural lifestyles as these scenarios play out, as sprawl slides shut our windows of opportunity at the rate of one square mile of America lost to development every two and a half hours. The preservation tool of choice is the perpetual conservation easement, which allows private landowners to restrict development permanently while continuing to own and use their land in ways consistent with conservation values.

Each year conservation organizations inventory America's most endangered landscapes. The celebrity wildlands lead their lists: Alaska's Arctic National Wildlife Refuge; Greater Yellowstone; Utah's Redrock Canyonlands; Minnesota's Boundary Waters; Florida's Everglades and Big Cypress Swamp. All are perennially threatened with incremental or catastrophic loss. Next on the endangered lists come the fragile rivers, overextended or achingly pristine: major watersheds like the Rio Grande, the Susquehanna, the Tennessee, and neighborhood streams like the Little Miami in Ohio, the Trinity in Texas, the Big Sunflower in Mississippi. Vernacular landscapes, too, groan under the weight of haphazard development: historic Concord and Lexington outside of Boston; the corridor along State Highway 99 in California's San Joaquin Valley; the Blue Ridge Parkway viewshed in Virginia; Philadelphia's Schuylkill Marsh; Lower Marks Creek in North Carolina.

Each of us chooses our place, our issue. My stories in this book come from Utah, but the challenge turns up everywhere in America as our open spaces shrink under the combined weight of avarice, inattention, and denial. How do we live ethically on land as it shifts underneath us with changing values, exploding growth, and money and politics wielding brute force? I'm looking for answers.

We can feel these tensions thrumming across America as we fill in our open space and the twenty-first century begins to reel away behind us.

In southern Utah, in redrock canyons etched into the earth in every direction from the mesa where my family and I have sunk our roots, the drama lags by a beat, for much country remains wild. But while old-timers and newcomers squabble about wilderness and sneer at each other, corporate multinationals swoop in from backstage and hijack the story and the land.

While we fiddle, we trade "community" for "property." We trade "home" and "neighborhood" for "resort," "relationship" for "recreation." I fear for what such wholesale trading across America will do to the spirits of our communities, to the richness of our lives. We know we all are a little corrupt; we mistrust and resent the Other; we fear change. Rome is burning—the vitality of natural landscapes diminishing daily—and we must confront the crisis.

Where do we draw lines? How do we find common ground and work together? What can we do?

The people who reacted to Earl Holding chose from an array of classic American responses to change: a few withdrew into their personal refuges of peace and pastoral solitude; others fought, some by radical acts, some by engaging in the daily grind of democratic process. One even managed to outwit Earl and defeat the powerful man's drive to have it all. This duel between the personal and the communal, between greed and generosity, lies at the heart of this story.

I continued to observe Earl as a phenomenon and ultimately spent ten years trying to understand just what happened at Snowbasin in this case study of power politics. My relationship with this man remains one-sided; it is a one-way conversation with a subject I've never interviewed, a character I've imagined as much as described. But it is indeed a relationship, and so I call him "Earl."

This book—the story of a tycoon, of how we create and use power, of how we choose to place ourselves as individuals, as pilgrims, in a community, on the Earth—begins with an Olympic race on a ski mountain in northern Utah, with a man of immense wealth telling Americans what he would do with their land and proceeding to do it. The story ends in the redrock canyons of southern Utah, in Wayne County, with a community of citizens pondering together how to respond to change.

We draw our lines, Earl Holding and I, making choices determined by everything we believe, choices that balance ownership and citizenship, desire and restraint. The land's future depends on the reckoning of these decisions in every community, on the choices made by us all.

PART I: BEDROCK

LITTLE AMERICA, 1950S, WYOMING. VINTAGE POSTCARD FROM THE AUTHOR'S CHILDHOOD COLLECTION. PHOTOGRAPH BY ERIC J. SEALCH, SALT LAKE CITY.

LITTLE AMERICA

"It's my dream. Little America for life, the heart of the nation, crossroads of the world...." He knew that eventually everyone in the United States ... had to pass through Little America.

ROB SWIGART, *LITTLE AMERICA: A NOVEL*, 1977

WHEN I WAS A BOY, and Ike was president, Little America meant freedom. It wasn't Richard Byrd's Little America, the 1929 Antarctic outpost. My Little America was Covey's Little America, a truck stop hunkered low against windscour and winterblast on the rim of an eroding Wyoming mesa.

We saw the first teasers along U.S. 30 outside of Laramie: LITTLE AMERICA, WORLD'S LARGEST GAS STATION, 65 PUMPS, NICKEL ICE CREAM CONES. Black-and-white cartoon penguins and '50s signboard cursive led us to the faux-colonial buildings topping a rise.

Until 1963 those roadside ads said *COVEY'S* LITTLE AMERICA. S. M. Covey was one of three brothers from Salt Lake City who founded the place, a visionary whose story was printed on every placemat in the restaurant. *"Away back in the Nineties, when I was a youngster herding sheep in this dreary section of Wyoming, I was forced to lie out in a raging blizzard. . . ."* On that stormy night, according to the legend, Covey dreamed of surviving to build a haven for travelers in the remote spot. When he heard about Admiral Byrd's base in Antarctica he knew what he would call his Wyoming traveler's rest.

Years later the current generation of Coveys told me that the legend was more a distillation of the Covey family experience than the retelling of a single event. The name was a sales gimmick that grew out of the brothers' meeting with Admiral Byrd. They were interested and excited by his stories, and Byrd gave them models of sleds and sledges from his expedition.

Whichever it was, a dream come true or a marketing scheme, Little America, Wyoming, opened for business in 1934. Its story recapitulated in miniature the story of America, the saga of immigrants reaching a new frontier, their hope and hard work and the subsequent life of hardscrabble endurance. Like so many other Covey customers I made an emotional investment in Little America as a child, buying in to its story of survival, the romance of pioneering, the foothold in the wilderness, the intimate lonesomeness of Wyoming.

I knew nothing then about the apprentice who managed the place for the Coveys, but I now know that he was named Earl Holding.

THOSE SUMMERS OF MY CHILDHOOD reeled out as adventures, their rhythms dictated by the fieldwork assignments of my father, Donald E. Trimble, geologist with the U.S. Geological Survey. When school ended each spring my parents and I left our home in Denver and drove west through Wyoming. We traveled the Oregon Trail to a new land not once but every year. In each outpost of home in Idaho or Oregon we rented a house in the town closest to my father's mapping area.

One day out, one day's comfortable travel northwest of Denver, Little America was our gateway to three months of freedom. An escape for the three of us from the everyday challenges of life at home with its inevitable family sorrows and schoolkid yearnings. Just as the mountain men saw the West as an adventurous escape from the civilized East, our summers had the open-ended allure of a vacation heightened by the dare of being on the road.

By this time my father had already been driving the West for twenty years, and he plotted the family route from mountain to mountain and restaurant to restaurant. He loved the cool rise of the peaks as much as he loved the flake and fruit of homemade berry pies. As we drove he provided a running commentary on history, geology, and geography.

Isabelle, my mother, made sure we maintained our sense of humor and didn't romanticize the emptiness *too* much. The three of us would croon "Why-O-Why, Wyoming" and dissolve in giggles. She teased my father and me when we enthused over landscapes she saw as barren "dirt," when we rhapsodized about our love of the thunderous open spaces, no matter how nondescript.

Laramie was the first town out from Colorado: windy, railroad-dingy, a line of motor courts with cowboy neon fashioned into branding irons, bucking broncos, and buckaroos. On across Wyoming we drove, past broken-down gas stations that constituted most of the towns: Red Desert, Wamsutter, Point of Rocks, Medicine Bow. This run of the open-space West stretched as wide as the Cinerama screens in its cities, out to the limits of peripheral vision, where you knew it kept going. When something happened in that emptiness—a dust storm, a rainbow, a fleet of pronghorn dashing across the road so close I always remembered them actually leaping over the hood—it made my day.

On these long-ago evenings in Little America we would stop for the night at the motel and truck stop that punctuated the windy middle of nowhere and gratefully take our key to one of the modest red brick units. Gleeful to be out of the car, we would shower off the sweat that came from driving before air conditioning became commonplace, with the windows open and my parents smoking.

We exulted in the tight family unit of our threesome. Surely no one understood as we did the humor in Covey's self-conscious *Legend of Little America* printed on the placemats. We smirked at each other in the dining room when smiling, elderly Alice Hand played her un-hip bouncy tunes on an electric organ. I remember her benign smile, a benediction bestowed on anyone with the means to sit in the brass-studded leather armchairs and pay for hamburgers and steak and fried shrimp and soft dinner rolls.

Even today I keep meeting other middle-aged people who share my affection for layovers at Little America in the postwar years. At the time I believed my relationship with the place was special. In reality this place, with its odd charm, drew multitudes.

While my mother and father relaxed at the bar with their before-dinner gin-and-tonics, and again, the next morning, when they lingered over coffee, I was free to wander around Little America, exploring. I remember counting the gas pumps, wondering if this really was the world's largest service station. And for my tally of license plates from different states, I always censused the parking lot.

Everything about the place seemed a little askew. A gleaming shield of tile filled the restaurant bathroom with an otherworldly green—greener than any of the desert colors out beyond the cranked-open window. Across the lobby, in a glass case defending the gift shop, a penguin that had expired on its way from Antarctica to serve as a live mascot for Little America stood sentry, stuffed and mounted instead.

The penguin surveyed bins of knickknacks: rabbit's-foot key chains, ceramic jackalopes, pastel felt fedoras with *Little America* stitched on the brims. I coveted them, every one. There were fireworks, too—illegal at home but legal in Wyoming and therefore mesmerizing. Cracker balls were my weapons of choice, the little wads of brightly colored paper and gunpowder I winged at the pavement for a satisfying explosion.

I used up my allowance on the cracker balls and used up the poppers one by one on the oil-stained cement curbs. I threw them hard, venting frustration and anger stored up during the school year in my role as an outsider—the kid who loved books more than baseball. I did this without analysis. It simply felt good; catharsis followed. These little explosions gave me power.

After I turned sixteen I ferried my mother to Little America in our 1962 Dodge Dart, an ugly pinkish-tan one-of-a-kind confrontation of curves and angles, following my father as he drove the government Jeep. I was determined to drive every mile. I remember getting dangerously tired on those ups and downs of central Wyoming, but I sure wasn't going to yield the wheel to my mother. Though I was with my family, I was *on the road.* These trips were my coming-of-age rites.

I walked to the edge of the vast parking pads, where cement ended abruptly at the brink of what earnest ranchers in western movies called "Big Country." From this frontier of the mid-twentieth century I stared into empty red-desert scrubland, the tantalizing space of Wyoming, and squinted up Black's Fork toward Fort Bridger. Shrinking under too much sky, I dreamt of the time when mountain men were the only Europeans for hundreds of miles. In the beginning I needed this safe perch to confront the great North American space. I wasn't yet ready to immerse myself in it. I looked in from the edge, from the road, from the car window, from motels at the periphery of crossroads towns—bunkhouses on the rim of wildness.

AS COVEY'S LITTLE AMERICA became Holding's Little America in 1963, I turned thirteen. As a child of the 1950s I imagined that the world was evenhanded. We had triumphed over Hitler, and we would triumph over the Reds. The Powerful watched out for my interests. But now Holding, whoever he was, was fooling with my childhood—penguins, placemats, and all. Covey's name disappeared from the story; the new placemats called him simply "the founder." No longer a quirky personal statement, Little America now was a business, to be bought and sold like any other business.

I loved the romanticism of Covey, the survivor, building this motel himself, telling us his story of the Great Blizzard each spring when we returned to read his placemats. I was invested in that story, and I felt betrayed that someone could appropriate my cherished myth.

Who was this new guy, this Holding, anyhow?

———

The Holdings moved to Little America just about the same time my family began to stay there for one night each spring. On at least one windy morning in the '50s or '60s Earl surely rang up our bill.

When Earl Holding finally became the boss at Little America, he must have felt giddy with his new independence. Earl, the manager, became Earl, the owner, who began to assert control. I can only presume the details. Earl rarely speaks in public.

I've read everything I can find about him, a grand total of just six interviews published over twenty-five years. I've harvested anecdotes from dozens of people. His corporate spokesman, Clint Ensign, will speak with me about the business but never about its owner's deeper motivations. Apart from the rumors and stories that travel with the man, these are my sources.

I learned the basics of Earl's story easily enough. He started poor. He worked hard to become the owner of the original Little America. By the time he was fifty he had taken his Little America hotels into three states and acquired Idaho's historic Sun Valley Resort. He had parlayed his original remote and funky truck stop into ownership of Sinclair Oil. He had purchased his second ski area, Snowbasin, perched high on Utah's Mount Ogden.

Along the way to becoming one of the twentieth century's notable entrepreneurs, Earl Holding developed a passion for owning land—lots of land—enough to make him, according to a 1997 ranking, the fourteenth largest landowner in the country. Earl runs 50,000 head of cattle in Wyoming and Montana on his 500,000 deeded acres of ranchland. The total acreage of Earl's land measures twice the size of either Mount Rainier or Rocky Mountain national parks and about the same size as Great Smoky Mountains National Park.

Earl owns more of downtown Salt Lake City than anyone but the Mormon (LDS) Church; his five-diamond Grand America Hotel, which opened

GLEAMING WHITE GRAND AMERICA HOTEL RISING INTO THE SALT LAKE CITY SKYLINE ADJACENT TO LITTLE AMERICA, 1999.

in 2001, dominates the city's skyline. Earl's company, according to *Forbes* estimates for 2007, is the thirty-eighth largest private company in America, with $5.6 billion in revenues and 7,000 employees. On the Forbes list Sinclair appears just below the paper and wood manufacturer Boise Cascade and just above the Hearst family's media empire.

From this position of power Earl made the move that intrigued me. To fulfill his dream of transforming Snowbasin into a major resort, he asked the people of the United States to trade him the base of the mountain— long treasured by locals who had reclaimed and restored and added this high basin to the National Forest—for other lands of "equal value."

I quickly learned that Earl drove his company with an iron will and virtually single-handedly—unusual in this era of global corporatization. The Ogden Valley citizens fighting the loss of their neighborhood gem, the little ski area on Mount Ogden built on reclaimed land, were just as emotionally invested. The Olympics elevated their conflict to operatic heights and magnified the consequences of every decision.

The *Forbes 400* list of wealthiest Americans has included Earl each year since 1994, along with a one-paragraph summary of his career. Since his private company has no obligation to disclose its books, it's hard to know just how much he is worth. Indeed, for years he dismissed the *Forbes* estimates with a wink: "Just one of my refineries is worth that much!"

Over the years Earl rose in rank; his partiality to real estate, oil, and cash insulated him from the collapse of the high-tech dot.com bubble. In 2006 *Forbes* raised his numbers sharply, and in 2007 Earl Holding ranked as the sixty-third richest American, with a net worth of $5 billion. He appears on the list just three slots behind Charles Schwab and a few above Ralph Lauren, George Lucas, and H. Ross Perot. Earl Holding's wealth and power shapes the West; every dreamer who follows maneuvers within Earl's force field.

IN EARL'S WORDS, quoted in a local news story, he was "born in a bed on First Avenue in Salt Lake City" in 1926—only a few blocks from where he later raised his own family and where I live today. Three years later his parents, Eugene and Reva, lost everything in the stock market crash and went to work as managers at the Hillcrest Apartments down the street. The classic Depression mentality of saving yourself through work found a perfect seedbed in the boy. An acquaintance of Earl's describes watching from the Little America Hotel tower high above Salt Lake City as an adult Earl Holding and his wife, Carol, planted trees around the entrance. Earl looked up; my storyteller looked down. All she could think of was the image of herself as the grasshopper, fiddling frivolously, while two humorless and disapproving ants below worked, worked, worked.

At 15 cents an hour, nine-year-old Earl began his ceaseless life of work by gardening around the apartments managed by his parents and owned by the prominent Covey brothers, Almon (A. A.), Stephen (S. M.), and Hyrum (H. T.)—the brother who knew Earl best. Soon Earl was putting in three hours before school and eight hours after school, and the Coveys had raised him to 65 cents an hour. Earl's junior portrait in the 1943 West High School yearbook shows an unsmiling young man with brow furrowed and eyes narrowed, peering past the photographer at a future only he can see.

Earl's first investment was in land, a small orchard on the edge of Salt Lake City where he planted 3,500 trees. By the time he joined the Army Air

Corps, after one year at the University of Utah, he had saved an astonishing $10,000. He was a skilled poker player in his youth—a surprising talent in a young Mormon—so maybe some of that grubstake came from his winnings. His intimidating physical presence must have made for a powerful bluff. Carol Holding later made him give up cards, insisting it wasn't fair for him to take other people's money.

One generation ahead of me, Earl entered adulthood as I was born in 1950. In June 1949 he married Carol Orme, his sweetheart from college. They had met at a study table at the Salt Lake City library, where Earl discovered that she was "the only one I knew with less money than me." She was also a beauty and had been runner-up in the "Miss Utah" contest. After finishing two years of military service he returned to the University of Utah and earned his civil engineering degree in 1951.

Primed to participate in the great industrial postwar buildup of the West, Earl worked for a year as a construction engineer for the Bureau of Reclamation. He exemplified the American belief that technology can solve every problem. In 1952 twenty-five-year-old Earl was preparing to leave for Iran to build water projects for BuRec, while his old patrons, the Coveys, were wondering how to dam the flood of money leaking from their traveler's rest in Wyoming. Isolation made it hard to keep help.

The Covey brothers could tell that Earl "wasn't just an ordinary guy cruising through life," as one younger Covey family member told me with a knowing smile. They made Earl an offer: a 12 percent stake in Little America in return for his signing on as manager. Twelve seems to have been a meaningful number for the establishment: at the time Little America consisted of a twelve-pump service station and, as Earl remembered years later, "a dozen counter stools and twelve little rooms." Losses were bigger than twelve: Little America was losing $90,000 a year.

Carol was Earl's business partner from the start. "I either became part of his business or lived alone," she says. Today she is reputedly the only person who can sometimes move Earl off one of his ideas with an "Oh, Earl, just do this." That steely and sometimes unpredictable push may be the crucial opinion that leads Earl to choose between tile samples or decide to invest millions in a new ski lodge. In those early years the Holdings set the pattern for their fabled micromanaging—flipping burgers, making beds, pumping gas, operating construction machines, checking salad dressing for missing ingredients, choosing carpet and paint colors, hovering over—and intimidating—their staff.

Earl turned Little America around in one year; he ended skimming by suppliers and instituted obsessively attentive accounting. He and Carol made Little America work because overnight travelers had no choice but to eat at Earl's café and gas up at his pumps. In Wyoming the alternative lay too many miles down the road. Earl told a former college classmate that his prescription was simple: fill the beds every night, sell as many gallons of gas as possible, rotate the tables at the café constantly, and do this twenty-four hours a day. To most drivers this treeless playground for the wind appears well-nigh as desolate as Richard Byrd's Antarctica. Earl found a way to mine money from the apparently unproductive expanse.

That classmate who remembered Earl was Hal Clyde, one year ahead of Earl in the engineering department at the University of Utah and now retired from operating his family construction company. To Hal, Earl's single-mindedness stood out even sixty years ago. He remembers the earnest young man's willingness to take on visiting experts over issues that didn't yet engage others in the class.

Forbes reports simply that Earl "eventually bought out the Coveys." Several versions exist of just how Earl Holding came to be the sole owner of Little America. All involve Earl's hard work and his cleverness, and all include a legal challenge to Earl's takeover of the Covey assets that went as far as an appeal to the Wyoming Supreme Court in 1963.

The Covey family story goes like this: Earl turned Little America into a gold mine—a wonderful, profitable business—by solving the labor problems and seeing potential where others did not. The Coveys wanted him to stay and offered him part ownership. He accepted but wanted more shares; they sold him more. H. T.'s family wanted out; Earl bought them out. The court case arose when A. A.'s death led to a dispute about whether or not Earl had an agreement to buy his share as well. In the end, of course, Earl won.

One member of the Covey family told me philosophically, "You can tell it any way you want, and any story might be correct. It depends on who you are talking to." Another acquaintance of Earl's believes "there's no way that Snowbasin would be hosting the Olympics" without that 1963 court confrontation in Wyoming that gave Earl full ownership of his first enterprise. "It's a road that began in the kitchens of Little America."

LITTLE AMERICA WAS THE SPRINGBOARD. Twenty-five years after Earl and Carol moved to the failing Wyoming truck stop they also owned Little America hotels in Cheyenne (opened in 1965), Salt Lake City (1966), and Flagstaff, Arizona (1972), as well as the upscale Westgate Hotel in San Diego, which

Earl purchased in 1976. At the grand opening of the Cheyenne Little America, one of the invited guests from the town didn't recognize Earl and asked him to park his car. Earl did.

"Integrating backwards," as he put it, he had spun the expertise in gas stations acquired at Little America first into a small refinery in Casper, Wyoming (in 1967), and then into ownership of a portion of the assets of the defunct Sinclair Oil (1976). Earl borrowed heavily to pull off both deals. "When we did Casper, it was a stretch; when we did Sinclair, it was a very big stretch," he said later. Sinclair is now one of the biggest oil and gas outfits in the Rockies.

In early 1977 Earl Holding read in the *Wall Street Journal* that Sun Valley was for sale. According to a rare description of his operating methods published later that year, Earl had seen Sun Valley on a road trip three years before and been impressed. He flew back into Sun Valley and "walked the mountain from top to bottom with [owner] Bill Janss and immersed himself in the intricacies of ski-lift engineering, trail maintenance and snowmaking." He offered Janss $12 million, just enough to convince Janss to sell to him rather than to the Disney empire, which had offered $16 million.

Janss felt that "Holding seemed to care about the mountain, he seemed to care about the golf course, and he definitely cared about quality. He was the one I wanted to have the place." I suspect that Earl was more intrigued with the resort and lodge at Sun Valley than with the mountain. He must have dreamed of such luxury in those windy days at Little America in the '50s. What a treat it must have been to take over a gem like Sun Valley Lodge.

Earl has said, "I am not a developer or a promoter, but an operator." In the 1977 profile he continued: "I'm a doer, not a delegator. . . . My concept in business is that you get out of something exactly what you put in. If a place is run well, the money comes back and you put it back in again to keep getting better and better." Earl laid out his plans for a four-season resort: "I want to make Sun Valley a place that will never shut down." He had learned his economics at Little America, rotating those café tables twenty-four hours a day.

Earl spent that first spring and summer at Sun Valley "at a full gallop," fanatically supervising landscaping, lift building, and construction, just as he was to do twenty years later at Snowbasin. "We want to know everything that is done," he said. "We *do* everything that is done. We pump the gas, we make up the rooms, we plant trees, we involve ourselves with every angle of every operation. We believe that 1,000 details go together and—

if they're put together right—they will make a masterpiece." "We" means Earl and Carol, working together, always.

Describing his dream for Sun Valley at the time he took over, Earl moved quickly from the mundane to the moral. "The kitchens are terrible, the bathrooms are awful. I want to attract a family clientele. You can't run this place for a select group of 500 or 1,000 beautiful people. We love the folks with the kids. This is not a haven for hippies or yippies. We want clean-cut people to come here."

Earl "snorted" in response to a question about the impact of Mormonism on his management: "I have nothing against other people drinking. We have cocktail lounges in all of our Little Americas. There was a rumor that we were going to fire everyone here who wasn't a Mormon, that we were bussing in loads of kids from Brigham Young University to come in as a Mormon Mafia and take over all the jobs young kids usually have here. That is so wrong. I don't even know what religion half of my top people are. Honest to God, I don't know. . . . When people ask me about my religion and my business, I tell 'em, 'I'm not pious or biased.'"

His own statements notwithstanding, I believe that those conservative values permeating Earl's culture matter to him. He requires his staff to keep their hair short and their faces clean-shaven. His assumptions about class and power remain patriarchal. He wields his powerful personality and six-foot stature like weapons; when Earl arrives on site, middle management crumbles.

Earl Holding grew up and graduated from high school with Thomas Monson—"Tommy" in those days—who became the "prophet, seer, and revelator" of The Church of Jesus Christ of Latter-day Saints in 2008. His political patrons, Utah's Congressman Jim Hansen and Senators Jake Garn and Bob Bennett, together served more than fifty years in Congress (Bennett is still serving), and the three Mormon Republicans all graduated from Salt Lake City's East High School in the same class of 1950, just two dozen blocks and six years away from Earl's graduation and high school. These men cherish their membership in this tight inner circle.

In a sidebar to a 1997 article, prominent Utahns offered their take on Earl. In addition to generic praise for his hard work and attention to detail, a common thread was his complete focus on business. He is said often not to understand a joke. He makes no small talk, ever. He takes no vacations. He thinks golf a thorough waste of time.

His only motivation is the desire to own and build and accomplish and complete—at the highest level of quality he can achieve.

Attorney Jim Boud represented two clients who sued Earl over issues related to building the new Grand America hotel. He believes that there is something of Earl in anyone who "has a little drive in their life, anyone who is a little obsessive." He sees Earl Holding in himself, but he doesn't envy him. "Earl's life is his possessions. I wouldn't want his headaches."

Boud pulled a Bible from his office bookshelf, with dozens of tabs marking passages. He found what he was after, Ecclesiastes 5:12, and read it to me: "The sleep of a labouring man is sweet, whether he eat little or much: but the abundance of the rich will not suffer him to sleep."

He looked up. "That's Earl Holding."

PEOPLE FREQUENTLY DESCRIBE EARL as a "sensitive developer." Not as a raper and pillager of land. He builds top-notch structures and landscapes them meticulously. When inducted into the Utah Business Hall of Fame in 1992 his citation described him, with no conscious irony, as "a conservationist's model of the ideal manager and protector of the great outdoors." The Woodrow Wilson International Center for Scholars honored Earl with a Corporate Citizenship Award in 2004, an honor bestowed on "executives who, by their examples and their business practices, have shown a deep concern for the common good beyond the bottom line . . . at the forefront of the idea that private firms should be good citizens in their own neighborhoods and in the world at large."

Of course, not everyone sees development as positive. Not every couple wants to see high-end real estate consume their favorite picnic meadow. Not every hiker wants to see Earl's orderly blue spruce windbreaks and manicured flowerbeds replace unpredictable natives like tangy sagebrush or ragged Gambel oak.

Some see Earl's dream as an antidream, the man as a greedy despoiler rather than a benevolent civic leader. As one Ogden Valley activist said to me, "We hear all these things about Holding doing things first class; I guess that's great—if you want it done."

I admit that I don't want it done. But I do want to understand just why Earl is so intent on getting it done.

I have tried to reach him through his executive secretary, who always politely put me off, and through Chris Peterson, his son-in-law. I have called his lawyer, who pleaded lawyer-client privilege. When I stayed at a Sun Valley condo with my family, the manager turned out to be a friend of Sun Valley's longtime mountain manager and Earl's right-hand man. He said he would put in a good word for me. But Wally Huffman declined an interview.

When I heard that the Wasatch-Cache National Forest supervisor was on good terms with Earl, I asked him to vet my letter before sending it to Earl. Still no answer.

I have tried placing myself in Earl's path. I attended the Utah versus Wyoming football game at the University of Utah stadium, where Earl and Carol Holding were reputed to lead cheers each year dressed in cowboy outfits after hosting an expansive dinner for University of Wyoming fans at Little America. I went in 2001, when the Utah team clobbered Wyoming 35–0; the Holdings did not appear. Maybe Earl was too busy to attend; this was also the autumn before the Olympics.

A century ago a man of his wealth would have lived at some distinct and rarified distance from run-of-the-mill workers and professionals. In a small western state like Utah the physical continuum of class and status does not separate citizens quite as sharply, yet Earl still is out beyond the end of any chain of connections—remote, almost mythical, still living on The Hill.

As his company has grown he can no longer stay close to the people who work for him. In 2000 he told a reporter that he missed those happier days. With his 6,500 employees that year "I'm not close to anything anymore." But Sinclair is no corporation. There is no Board of Directors; there are only Earl and Carol. After years of working for the Holdings at Sun Valley, one employee summed up Earl's empire as "a very large small company," a multibillion-dollar mom-and-pop operation.

Earl and Carol divide their time among homes in Sun Valley and Utah and the split-level penthouse on the nineteenth floor of his Westgate Hotel in San Diego. At what is said to be his favorite ranch, Wyoming's Sunlight Ranch, he leaves hay in his fields as winter feed for the elk that wander across the boundary with Yellowstone National Park, just to the west.

By his actions, Earl Holding defines beauty as tamed, tidy, modern, and people-dominated, and he tries to make his properties "beautiful." He stocks grassland with sturdy cows, sprinkles homes through the woods, builds restaurants on alpine ridgelines, converts bumpy old chairlifts at his ski areas to smooth, state-of-the-art resort gondolas. He doesn't wait for snow or pray for snow; he makes snow.

Earl's empire doesn't reach far beyond his zone of comfort, the core that neatly matches the outer realm of Mormon Country. Yet even within that realm Earl rarely allows himself to be seen away from his own business properties, beyond his own small circle.

Earl Holding has no reason to talk with me. Culturally I stand in the distant outfield, far from the inner circle of pioneer Mormon Republican commercial wealth in Salt Lake City, the capital of our most conservative, most Republican state. I'm an outsider there—a liberal, an environmental activist, a member of the press, a Reconstructionist Jew who moved to Utah just twenty years ago. I attend Democratic fundraisers. I cannot identify myself by which Salt Lake high school I attended and which LDS ward house I belong to. I donate time and money and photographs to organizations that oppose Earl's projects and politics.

And so I have tried to conjure Earl's desires, piecing together his life from Gatsbyesque hearsay and from stories. Some of the stories are true, some surely exaggerated, some apocryphal. I construct a portrait of Earl Holding's public reputation—Earl as myth, straw man, character—not necessarily of Earl himself. The Wizard of Oz as magnified on the screen rather than the perspiring man behind the curtain. As in any relationship, my relationship with Earl has evolved. As I learn more about the man, as I learn more about what it means to own property myself—and even to "develop" that property—I am coming to terms both with Earl and with the Earl in me.

SALT LAKE CITY NEIGHBORS IN HIS LDS CHURCH WARD say that Earl Holding is a nice man. His contractors, on the other hand, describe him as "violently eccentric, unique, intense." When he purchased Sun Valley, he insisted that unions be disbanded. He fired the entire staff of 1,400—conditions of sale that allowed him to start fresh with his own organization and hire back only the chosen.

Earl has the reputation of begging forgiveness rather than asking for permission. He has a reputation for working his employees hard, at below-market wages. He scours the world for cheap labor for Sun Valley, bringing in waves of seasonal workers on one-year visas, packing them into substandard dorms, and giving the resort "an international flavor" with rotating staff from Cambodia, Indonesia, South America, and Europe. One year he recruited early-release prisoners from Salt Lake City whose presence contributed to a minor crime spike in Sun Valley.

In the ski patrol cabin at Snowbasin, during the transition from local ski area to megaresort, a toy Sinclair dinosaur, emblem of Earl's oil company, hung from a noose.

He owns his companies outright, and he runs his empire as a collection of businesses rather than as a corporation. He cannot remember an investment that didn't work out. The business world considers him a "bottom feeder," a buyer of distressed properties who turns them around, always with an eye on the bottom line. Once he has made a business successful, he takes immense pride in its appearance.

Earl is a huckster, too. Remember those billboards across Wyoming: world's biggest gas station, world's cheapest ice cream cones. When he purchased Sun Valley one journalist saw in him "the hyper-enthusiastic demeanor of a master salesman."

Before his death in 1999, Ken Knight, Earl's childhood friend and longtime public alter ego, made contributions to community causes in the name of Sinclair. For years Earl Holding has donated $10,000 annually to Salt Lake City's West High, his alma mater, for college scholarships. Sinclair donated a half million dollars to the Red Cross after Hurricane Katrina in 2005. Other stories occasionally surface about acts of kindness and anonymous philanthropy. More often Earl is reported to never, ever, *ever* contribute money to charitable causes. His infamous civic miserliness has helped shape public reaction to the man and his projects.

Utah Senator Orrin Hatch absolves the man for his self-involvement: "When you come up the hard way . . . you tend to hang onto everything you have. . . . Earl invests in Earl."

Earl Holding may direct his energy to work rather than faith, but the teachings of his church permeate his worldview. The scholar Harold Bloom believes that Mormonism is the very definition of "the American Religion," though no more than 2 percent of Americans are Mormon (a growing percentage, however, already exceeding that of Jews or Episcopalians). In Bloom's analysis, Americans create a spirituality different from that of European Protestants or Catholics. Mormons, who epitomize this American brand of spirituality, follow a religion of the self that celebrates the personal experience of God and a freedom from "nature, time, history, community, other selves." The consequences of this kind of freedom, in Bloom's judgment, can include callousness toward civic involvement and "exploitation of the helpless by the elite."

Harold Bloom describes an LDS reality that I see reflected in the arc of Earl Holding's life. Of the Church Bloom says: "No rival even remotely approaches the spiritual audacity that drives endlessly towards accomplishing a titanic design." Of the landscape: each free and solitary figure stands imbued with "the American experience of the abyss of space." Of the culture: "perhaps the most work-addicted culture in religious history." Of the theology: "idiosyncratic almost beyond belief" and "dangerously interesting." And of politics: the Republican Party is "the barely secular version of the American Religion."

George Lakoff comes to the same conclusion when he explores the language and values of "moral politics" in America. He could be speaking of Earl's culture when he notes that "Fundamentalist Christians view God as a strict father, and the model that structures their religion and their family life also structures their politics."

Earl is a conservative Mormon Republican power broker who is accustomed to authority and control. He takes that power for granted, and wields it with gusto. He purchased one of his corporate jets from the Sultan of Brunei. When Earl and Utah Senator Bob Bennett flew to Snowbasin one day to discuss plans for the Olympics they landed at the foot of Mount Ogden in a camouflaged Army attack chopper, arriving "like emperors," according to one amazed observer.

Earl Holding is a reflection of the past—a tycoon whose riches come not from cyberspace but from oil and land. And yet even in millennial America the wealthy and powerful still have their way. They are indeed our emperors. We obey and adore them; we fear and hate them. They are both our antithesis and our models of citizenship.

FROM THE DAY HE FIRST SAW SNOWBASIN Earl knew that the Olympic cachet lay within reach for his new ski resort. Beginning with the first Salt Lake City bid presentation in 1966, Snowbasin had turned up on all lists of proposed sites for the alpine speed events in a Utah Olympics. When Earl Holding purchased Snowbasin Ski Area in 1984 Salt Lake City had already twice attempted to corral the Winter Olympics and twice lost.

In those early Olympic bids, few questioned the notion that the Winter Olympics would be something positive for the community. Utah skiers and boosters thought only of that snowy dream of "great competition, superb showmanship, and international brotherhood," as John Jerome of *Skiing* magazine described the lingering image of California's 1960 Squaw Valley Winter Olympics. What citizens did not realize is that the event, in the words of Stephen Goldsmith, Salt Lake City's director of planning during the 2002 Olympics, is actually "a private party." As soon as a city begins to promote itself as an Olympic venue "it's manipulated from the outside in."

In the thirty years of global politicking that led to the 2002 winter games, the bid committee was corporatized, the Games became an engine to drive local economic development, and Salt Lake City became a commodity. The city spent $7 million for the bid, borrowed $56 million from state sales tax money to prepare venues, and sweetened the pot with at least another million for bribes and gifts. This marketing process reached its peak in Budapest, in June 1995, when the International Olympic Committee (IOC) chose Salt Lake City for the 2002 Winter Olympics.

In Budapest, four hundred Utah Olympic boosters presented an extravaganza of images, music, and commentary—from videos of President Bill Clinton on down. Years of preparation came down to words and images— another cleverly worded legend, spun like the Legend of Little America, but aimed at a new audience, the International Olympic Committee.

The future depended on language. Each competing country strove to make its words resonate, to play virtuoso cadenzas to move each voting IOC member. Salt Lake City spoke with the gold-medal voice of American skier Picabo Street narrating a videotape of Snowbasin in which she promised a challenging race on Mount Ogden: "This downhill will become legendary." Earl was there, but bid manager Tom Welch did the talking and played to his audience, more concerned about marketable mythmaking than cultural precision: "From the traditions of our first citizens, the American Indians, through legends with names like Buffalo Bill Cody, Butch Cassidy and the Sundance Kid and the Hole in the Wall Gang, we forged out of the Wild West a society that blends the character and spirit of the early fur trappers, miners, and settlers."

Interesting choices, elevating showmen and Hollywood outlaws over frontiersmen. The common folk at least believed Butch Cassidy to be a Robin Hood who stole from the rich and gave to the poor. Like corporate America, Butch Cassidy believed his ends justified his means. But he moved money in the opposite direction.

FROM 1993 ON SNOWBASIN'S AND OLYMPIC INTERESTS MESHED. The Salt Lake Olympic Bid Committee needed Snowbasin; the committee members needed Earl Holding. Earl joined the Olympic Committee board in 1995 and eventually contributed $100,000 to the campaign. This wasn't so much a donation as a good investment. Of the $13 million raised to finance the bids, $12 million came from corporations or business-based philanthropies. Olympic politics became Utah politics in the 1990s, and no one knew this better than Earl.

In a 1997 deal worth $13.8 million to Holding, the committee designated Snowbasin as the 2002 venue for the downhill and super-G races and Earl's Salt Lake City hotels as the official housing for Olympic dignitaries. Earl abstained from the vote. He could remain quiet at board meetings; he had secured what he needed from the Olympics.

The International Olympic Committee members bought the myth presented to them by Salt Lake City, and, as we now know, Salt Lakers bought the Committee. The romance receded as the Salt Lake Organizing Committee (SLOC) descended into scandal and chaos after the 1998 exposé of bribes to IOC members. Earl Holding resigned from the board. Mitt Romney came from Massachusetts to replace longtime local organizers (and then after the Olympics Mitt went home to Boston to be elected governor and run for president). The world moved on. Earl rejected any suggestion of wrongdoing: "I don't know of anything that I have ever done, in any way, shape or form, that I need to be ashamed of with the Olympics."

Salt Lake City, however, had plenty to be ashamed of. Caught wooing IOC members with hundreds of thousands of dollars in cash payments, college scholarships and jobs for family members, medical treatment, land deals, and trips to the Super Bowl, Disneyland, and Las Vegas, the local Olympic Committee had gone far into illegal territory to massage votes. They weren't the first Olympic venue committee to have done so, but they were the first to be outed by the press. Investigations led to the expulsion of ten members of the IOC, sanctions for another ten, and deep reform.

Earl went back to his personal projects. He admits that neither the grand hotel nor the grand ski resort make economic sense, for profits will come only years after the enormous up-front investments. As one businessman friend put it, these projects "don't pencil." Earl himself admits they are "labors of love." Starting broke, he had gone out into the world and at Little America had fed the dreams of ordinary people on ordinary cross-country road trips; the very name of the place celebrated individual grit and heroism. After years of empire building in the surrounding states, he had come home to Utah with his fortune, to erect his physical declaration of wealth—the five-diamond Grand America hotel—within blocks of where he had started.

THE CLIMAX CAME FOR EARL HOLDING on February 10, 2002, when 30,000 spectators and volunteers cheered the racers as they boomed down his mountain in the men's downhill at Snowbasin. Flags from Olympic nations snapped crisply in the wind and sun. Austrian bands oom-pah-pahed, and alpenhorns rang out over the clang of the fans' cowbells. Three hundred million people watched the delayed broadcast.

Some of these spectators spent the night in Earl's Grand America. Earl's

ON FEBRUARY 10, 2002, NEARLY FIVE OUT OF EVERY ONE HUNDRED PEOPLE ON EARTH WATCHED THE OLYMPIC MEN'S DOWNHILL BROADCAST FROM SNOWBASIN.

hotels were rented only to the "Olympic Family," and Grand America was the highest-end "family" hotel of them all.

With his Olympic involvement, and in his eagerness to show off Grand America, Earl emerged from his reclusiveness and began to give hotel tours to carefully chosen reporters.

Earl also began to appear more frequently at public events. Serving front and center as host at banquets at Grand America, each year Earl looked a little more tired, a little more elderly. But still he worked the tables, chatting with the powerful, introducing himself to the masses, haranguing the help about problems with the dessert buffet—always proud of his hotel.

When Earl suffered a stroke in late 2002, the press wasn't informed until weeks later, after his condition was listed as stable. A few days after that his staff reassured reporters that the seventy-seven-year-old man was physically impaired but still sharp and smart and tracking the details of his businesses by phone from his Salt Lake City hospital room. Rumors circulated that he was a vegetable, that he couldn't speak. I laid these to rest when a friend told me that he had a lively conversation with Earl at Snowbasin. Apparently Earl was working the crowds from his wheelchair through the spring of 2003—buoyant about his plans, unwilling to even admit the stroke, telling people he had "had an accident."

Since then he has continued to improve, humbled physically and of necessity doing less micromanaging but still making the big decisions himself. Earl had told a reporter in 1997 that he would retire "when I die. What else would I do if I didn't work?" He pledged allegiance to his work ethic again at a 2006 tribute to him organized by supporters in the business community of Sun Valley. Earl responded to his five hundred well-wishers with a promise to "continue to build nice new things here for you. As long as I'm alive and as long as Carol's alive and as long as my three kids are alive, this will never, ever be sold. We'll run it."

Everyone thanked the Holdings for preserving the feel of the community through sensitive development and for what "the patriarch of Sun Valley" had *not* done, for choosing *not* to build on every last square inch of property. The realtor Jed Gray thanked Earl "for being a ski resort operator instead of a land developer." In a video played at the tribute Vice President Dick Cheney said, "Earl's life is a testament to good citizenship." Governor Dirk Kempthorne ended the evening by declaring January 30, 2006, to be "Earl and Carol Holding Day" in Idaho. Later that year, when Earl turned eighty, the Mormon Tabernacle Choir serenaded him and 650 guests at the Grand America, and Senator Orrin Hatch inserted a tribute into the Congressional Record that spoke at length of Earl's "good works" and "tenacity."

IN THE WINTER OF 1999 I again drove the familiar road across Wyoming, this time reversing the direction of my childhood ventures into the freedom of summer. This time I journeyed through a snowstorm toward Denver, not away from it, to move my aging parents from our family home to a retirement apartment. Rather than simply head east from Salt Lake City up Interstate 80, I left Utah on a more circuitous route that would take me on a tour of the Holding empire.

I began in the heart of downtown at Earl's granite obelisk, his rising Alpha-structure: the Grand America, where cranes perched high. Across the street lay two power centers of Salt Lake City, the imposing old City Hall and the new Utah State Courts building built on land that Earl had sold to the city. Next door at Little America, freshly redesigned placemats, promoting the hotel that would take Earl from "Little" to "Grand," declared that the new hotel would set "a standard of luxury for the new millennium . . . on a graceful scale never before seen in the Rocky Mountains."

From Salt Lake City I drove north. The highway sluiced along the narrow terrace between the Great Salt Lake and the foothills protected by national forest, through booming stucco suburbs that spin out minivans and preschoolers at astonishing rates. The first passage eastward through the Wasatch Mountains came at Weber Canyon, just before reaching Ogden. I took it, following the signs into the canyon and upstream along the river, entering the mountain front, the truck jumpy, caught in the teeth of the wind howling down from Wyoming.

Remaining on the highway, I skirted Mount Ogden along its southern base, admiring the peak from a distance but not stopping to observe the new lift cables strung taut up into the bowls—right up the Olympic downhill course. Earl's playground of technology and commerce. Earl's legacy. Snowbasin.

From here the interstate carried me east, through the mountains and into Wyoming as the weather grew nastier and darkness loomed. Standing in ironic clash with the yawning open space, new Little America billboards came along every few miles, as brash a mark of ownership on the treeless roadside as ever. Between the billboards crossroads mini-marts were the only commercial establishments. So many of these sported Sinclair neon that I began to suspect that Earl Holding owned *everything* along this stretch of Interstate America.

I remembered my childhood journeys here, before the interstate, when my parents and I felt like *we* owned the West. Our investment had nothing to do with money, for these were the public lands of the West owned by us all—the Great Divide, the Canyon Country, the Shining Mountains. Every vacation we had taken just enough money for essentials and lit out for new territory. The open road led to the Golden West, to national parks, to beauty, to delight.

Our only real estate, *real* ownership, was our house in the suburbs of Denver, the house my parents were only now leaving, a compact yellow rambler built in 1950—the year I was born—as Denver expanded west toward the lift of the Front Range. Our lot had seemed vast to me; when I crossed our third of an acre to the neighbor's horse pasture behind us I felt like I had made a real journey.

Now as I watched those Sinclair signs along the Interstate that proclaimed Earl's ownership, I wondered if this was what scholars pictured when they swept their hands through the air and nattered on about "hegemony." The word has to do with aggression and expansionism aimed at world domination. But its root is "leader." I thought about how difficult it was for me to regard Earl—a businessman and landowner of international stature and clearly on some level a "leader"—as anything other than objectionable. His drive to possess—no matter how "sensitive" and "high-quality" what he did after each new acquisition—made me fundamentally uncomfortable. In my childhood the successful businessmen I knew best were, apart from my gentle grandfathers, *all* objectionable—narrow, condescending, mean-spirited men.

They had dismissed me as an ethereal eccentric, a benign oddball. Even as a child I had disliked them. But society rewarded them with wealth and status.

These men were striving to embody the archetype that my wife's Uncle Melvin had in mind when he turned to me at a family dinner not long ago and described someone in reverential tones as "a good businessman." Melvin, a businessman himself—and a much kinder human being than my childhood antagonists—said this with the hush and seriousness one might use to describe real greatness. Hearing the timbre and weight of Melvin's voice bestowing the honorific "good businessman," I understood just how wide the gulf in values was between Earl and me.

The American value of free-rein enterprise now carried on by Earl has guided everyone from the mountain men, whom I envy for their chance to explore Indian America, to the corporations that followed, whose self-centered boomer mentality I decry. I know the mountain men were boomers, too—and I reluctantly admit that tycoons can be audacious and accomplished. Yes, of course, I'm inconsistent.

Melvin's invocation rang in my ears as I pulled off the highway and returned to sit in the original dining room at Little America for the first time in years. There was a new, gleaming, too-brilliant building next door, with fast food and high-tech gas pumps. New "Grand America" placemats had replaced the "Legend of Little America."

But the old motel and its lobby and restaurant remained as I remembered them, unrenovated. Inoffensive recordings of classical music played for me and the Wyoming ranch families out for Saturday night supper on this frigid February night. I sat in the same high-backed chairs I had perched on at five, at ten, and slouched in at sixteen. It was disorienting to be here in this museum diorama of my childhood, writing in my journal about memories thirty and forty years old.

It was ironic, too, that the very reason for my trip lay waiting in Denver, where I would encounter that childhood in sifting through the closets and shelves of my family home. In those boxes lay forgotten Little America key chains and Viewmaster reels, snapshots of my mother and father standing on the curb here, younger than I am now. I would gather these up, along with my rock and postcard collections and my newspaper clippings from the '60s, and drive back to Salt Lake City with my childhood in boxes in the back of my truck.

————————

The storm sifted snow across the parking lot to drift against the windbreak of Earl's blue spruce. Fuchsia neon reflected from a molded green Sinclair dinosaur grazing on the front lawn. Darkness settled; the ground blizzard grew more daunting. Back on the road I felt threatened by the semis barreling over the black ice and through the wind-driven blind of snow, a roaring force at odds with the tenderness of my memories. I drove east, into my future, back to my childhood—navigating the wire of asphalt strung through the night from Little America to home.

MOUNT OGDEN FROM THE SUMMIT OF ALLEN PEAK, SNOWBASIN, UTAH, 1999.

MOUNTAIN OF DREAMS

The West's real crisis is one of inertia, of will, and
of myth.

MARC REISNER, *CADILLAC DESERT,* 1993

THE WASATCH MOUNTAINS STAND AS A BOUNDARY between major continental
truths. Mountain and desert. Urban and rural. Tamed and wild.

Wasatch, *Wahsatch,* a lovely word, hard to translate from the languages
spoken by the Ute and Western Shoshone people who lived there. Some
people say it means something bland and acceptable, the "low place in a high
mountain," the place where the canyon of the Weber River slices through
Mount Ogden. Or that the name memorializes the Shoshone Chief Wahsatch. Others connect the word with a story that captures the flip side of
the mountains, the raw peaks rather than the wildflowered meadows. Winds
can roar over the Wasatch, reaching one hundred twenty miles per hour.
Snow stacks in drifts, storm after storm, up to five hundred inches each
winter. Once Ute men hunting in the mountains near Park City were overwhelmed by one of these big blizzards. When they found the one among
them who had been lost, their friend was dead, his penis frozen stiff.

Wuhu' Seai. Wasatch. "Frozen Penis."

The Utah Travel Council does not include this translation in their tourist
literature.

Mount Ogden traces a classic, sheltering, scalloped ridgeline. Not as jagged as the Grand Tetons or the Sierra Nevada. Not as overwhelming as Rainier or Denali. Not old and rounded like the Appalachians. Instead this mountain is perfectly shaped for hovering protectively over the people who live below. Mount Ogden is a life-giving watershed, a perfect ski mountain in winter, climbable and approachable in summer, generating affection and loyalty. The mountain is the stage for Earl's bargain; its history constitutes the backstory for all that happens here.

Nearly 80 percent of Utah's 2.5 million people live along the base of the Wasatch, one hundred miles of people, nearly doubling in population every thirty years, an urban island of ninety-eight towns growing toward each other along a narrow strip of irrigated desert land no more than ten miles wide squeezed between the Wasatch Mountains and those orphans of the Pleistocene, Utah Lake and the Great Salt Lake.

Despite the image of earnest Mormon farmers arriving in a wilderness outpost by handcart not so long ago, Utah is America's sixth most urbanized state. It is also our youngest and most fertile state, a smoldering population bomb, with 25 percent more births per woman than the national average. These days starter castles and tracts of characterless suburbs germinate from freshly poured foundations, shooting skyward faster than ripening grain in the fields across the road.

The range of peaks and the communities at their feet participate in a uniquely western geography, where public land and designated wilderness can lie literally just over the backyard fence. The juxtaposition of sagebrush and forest, water and rock, basin and range, valley and peak in such a short distance is exhilarating and intimate. People fall in love with this land.

The spine that makes up the Wasatch Range swings from one mountain to the next in graceful curves, a loose aggregation of separate mountain blocks, each sliced off in facets by faults and isolated as massifs by canyons and rivers. The clusters of peaks stand as small choruses—soloists, trios, sometimes a half dozen peaks rounding behind a valley.

The Mount Ogden massif stands with a broad base cut cleanly on two sides, north and south, by cold sweet rivers, the Ogden and the Weber. Its ridgeline of airy summits, strung on a single strand between the two canyons, unites a seventy-square-mile gathering of peaks. To the west the block of mountains falls away to the Great Salt Lake and its desert, plummeting

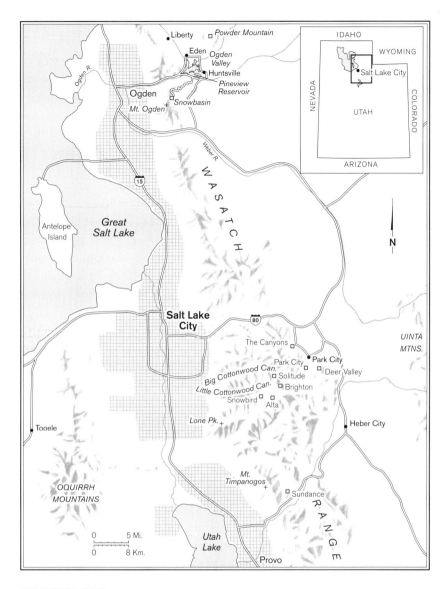

THE WASATCH FRONT.

5,000 feet in just three miles to the city of Ogden and on across the nearly flat prehistoric lakebed to the salty inland sea twelve miles further.

Ogden Valley, on the backside of the mountain, preserves a quintessential western landscape. In this miniature Jackson Hole, thirty square miles of checkerboard pastures scatter in an embracing circle, landmarked by picturesque barns and the tree-lined village grids of Huntsville and Eden and Liberty, the Quonset-hut chapel and silo of the Huntsville Trappist Monastery, the blue handprint of Pineview Reservoir.

These basics don't begin to do justice to the sensual experience of living in this landscape. The mountain's boundary is a sharp line, a metaphorical fence line you can pass over with a single footstep. Once you have taken that stride, you enter a zone of unpredictability. You leave a place you believe to be safe—the familiar cocoons of car, house, office—and give yourself to the potency of the mountain, the dangers of wild country. You add new words to your vocabulary: carnivore, thrill, fear, attack. You allow for the surprise of a cougar, the threat of a moose approached too close. Unlikely, but possible. Real.

I look up to Mount Ogden and think of the creative spirit that the Ute Indian people call *Sinawaf,* the One-Above, the He-She. The mountain has the same duality of gender as the creator who made these landmarks in the Ute and Shoshone homeland. In winter it stands as an abrupt wall, a rising masculine ice-blue peak. In autumn its ridges are soft-textured, angles and shadows made from orange oak and red maple, as if a linen handkerchief had been lightly dropped, to crumple and cling to the contours of the earth.

―――――

North America once was Indian America. Indigenous people lived from the land—managed it, burned it, and harvested it. Families and clans had specific gathering and hunting rights over landscapes, but the People knew with total conviction that no humans could own the Earth. The explorers who, beginning in the late 1700s, started turning up in the interior West did not understand this. They believed they could claim dominion over land simply by planting a European or American flag on a bluff overlooking a Pacific harbor or in the alkaline earth along desert rivers.

Into this world of Ute and Western Shoshone came the English and Scandinavian Mormon converts on a mission from their god. When the Mormon pioneers arrived in 1847 their leader, Brigham Young, stayed true to his New England heritage, which taught that forests and wildlife remained the inheritance of all. He declared, "There shall be no private ownership of streams that come out of the canyons, nor [of] the timber that grows on the hills. These belong to the people—all the people."

But his vision applied to only the white people. Within twenty years the Great Basin and Rocky Mountain native peoples had been displaced from northern Utah, their lands taken, their springs appropriated, their religion dismissed.

As Utah filled in with Mormons and non-Mormons, Brigham Young's ideas about communal ownership of resources began to carry less weight. Mormon culture chose instead to emphasize another of Young's teachings, the sanctity of industrious hard work. Secular entrepreneurial energy replaced sacred stewardship. This fit right in with the boom and buildup frenzies taking over throughout the West, where all growth and exploitation became synonymous with progress.

By 1889 more than one million sheep and 350,000 cattle grazed Salt Lake Valley and the nearby Wasatch Range. A decade later the number of sheep had tripled to 3 million. In turn the native ecosystems fell into disconnected pieces, each bereft of its supporting web of interconnections.

THE EDEN OF THE MYTHIC WEST abruptly became the shattered West, a land in need of restoration. Long before sagebrush rebels protested federal land management, citizens of the West pleaded for intervention from Washington. President Theodore Roosevelt and his forester Gifford Pinchot reacted by strengthening the embryonic national forest system.

The idea for a Cache National Forest began with citizen activists and county commissioners in the northern Utah town of Logan, who early in 1902 passed unanimous resolutions asking for governmental aid to protect and maintain their watersheds and withdraw them from settlement in "public reservations." Gifford Pinchot responded immediately with field studies, and when President Roosevelt came through Salt Lake City in May 1903 he spoke at the Mormon Tabernacle and signed the bill creating what would eventually become Wasatch-Cache National Forest.

Roosevelt said: "Do not let the mountain forests be devastated by the men who overgraze them, destroy them for the sake of three years' use and then go somewhere else, and leave so much diminished the heritage of those who remain permanently on the land." By 1910 eleven national forests had been created in Utah alone. The Church of Jesus Christ of Latter-day Saints, defying considerable public opposition, supported the designation of national forests to protect local watersheds. And yet overgrazing continued, especially beyond the forest boundaries, and erosion led to torrential flooding from the canyons into Wasatch cities.

High on the eastern flanks of Mount Ogden, the bowl now called Snowbasin enters this story of the West as "Wheeler Basin" at the beginning of the twentieth century. We can still hear stories from the people who lived through these early years, though we won't be able to do so for much longer. In 1999 I talked to surviving members of two of the families who once owned the lovely upper bowl of Wheeler Creek, seventy-seven-year-old Wiley Fowers and ninety-two-year-old Mark Johanson. Mark's brother Leo came home from World War I and homesteaded in the Basin. The Johansons later sold about five hundred acres to the Fowers at $8 per acre—within a single section of land that included Wheeler Spring, the source of Wheeler Creek.

At the age of twelve Wiley Fowers rode a black Shetland pony more than thirty miles with his family's cattle—across the desert, up along the rivers, and through the Wasatch Range—winding his way up into Wheeler Basin high on Mount Ogden. He began from Hooper, west of Ogden on the shore of the Great Salt Lake, where he was born and where he still lives and runs cows.

In the '20s and '30s, when young Wiley and his brothers spent their summers in Wheeler Basin with their cows, the resources of Mount Ogden were critically wounded. Overgrazing had so gullied the land that sheets of soil were washing away. Landslides slumped into the streams. Thunderstorms triggered horrific flash floods. Bernard DeVoto, born and raised in Ogden and the preeminent conservationist writer between Theodore Roosevelt and Rachel Carson, watched one flood in Wheeler Canyon in 1925. When he died in 1955 he was working on a chapter for his last, unfinished book *The Western Paradox* about the infection of the Wasatch by what he called the "fatal disease" of overgrazing. DeVoto described the moment when, "in Wheeler Basin, intolerably abused land had given up and let go":

> In the summer of 1925 my wife and I rented a cabin in Wheeler Canyon. . . . A couple of miles west of Ogden Valley, it comes down to Ogden Canyon from a small, high amphitheater at the eastern foot of Mount Ogden that was called Wheeler Basin in my boyhood, though it is now Snow Basin. I knew the whole area intimately and I had known Wheeler Creek as a clear and lovely mountain stream. It was different now. . . . Our cabin was on the steep eastern side of Wheeler Canyon, perhaps forty feet above the

creek. In August a cloudburst brought a flash flood down the canyon. . . . I remember it as following the short and furious storm by about three-quarters of an hour and lasting no more than twenty minutes. It could not have been more than eight feet high for it did not take away the hanging bridge to our canyon. But it did take away everything downstream from us that was lower than its crest. It dumped a lot of miscellaneous debris and filled a flume at the mouth of the canyon with sand, but though the greatest damage was visible it was understood only by the scientists: the bed of Wheeler Creek was gouged below the level of equilibrium that had been maintained since the Ice Age.

The lessons DeVoto learned in the Wasatch about aridity and fragility and the need for a national commons shaped his wise understanding of the West and was part of the vision he passed on to his friend Wallace Stegner. A direct line extends from the early history of Snowbasin to the sermons of DeVoto and Stegner that have inspired the environmental movement for the last fifty years.

The people of the Wasatch Front grew distressed about the loss of both topsoil and equilibrium, and they began to worry about the future of their watersheds. In the summer of 1929 unchlorinated water from Wheeler Creek contaminated the city water mains, and typhoid fever broke out in Ogden. The *Ogden Standard-Examiner* went on a rant about "this tragedy visited on the city" by a water department that was sending "messengers of death" into the mouths of babes. The State of Utah condemned Ogden's water supply. By the time things calmed down at the end of July, four people had died of the fever—and they were not all weak or elderly. Asa Chase Jr., the last victim of Wheeler Creek water, died on July 20 at the age of twenty-seven; his obituary appeared just nine months after his marriage announcement.

IN CRISIS, CONSERVATION AND ACTIVISM began to flower among citizens of the little city. Downtown Ogden businessmen began a campaign to transfer the Wheeler Creek watershed to Wasatch-Cache National Forest, for restoration and protection, in perpetuity. The city, county, Chamber of Commerce, and Rotary Club raised enough money to purchase 840 acres, which they leased to the National Forest for one dollar per year until the Forest Service budgeted funds to pay for the land. When homesteaders wouldn't agree to the city's terms, Ogden condemned and forced the sale of their lands. As a result, reclaiming Wheeler Basin left two conflicting legacies in the generations that followed. The families forced from their land still feel embittered. Those whose forebears saved the land still feel proud.

Snowbasin didn't come into the public domain for free. The American people paid for it—and they paid with cash. The Fowers and Johansons paid for it with their family land. Even in this celebrated moment of high civic mindedness, land was lost as well as gained, friendships were destroyed, and fear and anger were sown along with gratitude. The outcome depended on a jury condemnation trial. Nobody came away clean.

Five feet five, with the arthritic bowlegs of a lifetime horseman, twinkly-eyed Wiley Fowers can still get riled over the loss of the family land sixty-five years ago. Still indignant about city "harassment" and Forest Service charges that his family's cows had been polluting Wheeler Creek, he says, "You can't let those things worm on you; there's too many things to do in a day—too many post holes, too many sick cows. You can remember things, though."

Mark Johanson remembers things, too. "You live to be ninety-two," he says, "everything's changed. All the people you grew up with have died. People comes along and makes new names so I don't know where I'm at now." Mark was the last of eight children. His father had come across the plains with a Mormon handcart company. Mark is just one long lifetime away from his father's eyewitness accounts of Brigham Young, Jim Bridger, and the westward migration that now lies a century and a half back. "We lived off the land. We didn't ask anybody for anything, just kept a rifle in our scabbard. I was wild and woolly. It was wild, a frontier." When his family had summered in the Basin, "we done what we had to do. Maybe we overgrazed, I don't know."

Johanson reminds me of a Sandhill Crane—gaunt, a small head perched on a gangly body, sharp-eyed. I ask him how he feels about the changes at the Basin. "They can do anything they want now. It's the things you do at the time you're living. If it changes from the time you're born to the time you die, that's progress. Whether it's good or bad, it's movement."

––––––––––

Local pride glows in the old newspaper accounts of the reclamation of the ravaged watershed. The citizens who saved the Basin seventy years ago believed that the U.S. Forest Service should preserve and manage these lands and that public ownership was better than private ownership—that the government would act in the best interests of the people.

Franklin Roosevelt had rescued the country from the Depression with federal work programs, and federal conservation agencies had begun saving the land from the overgrazing and plowing that created the Dust Bowl. In the '30s many grateful Americans saw the government as powerful and benevolent.

The Wasatch restorers moved on quickly to create community ski areas on their new public lands. Ogden's citizens realized that the upper reaches of Wheeler and Strawberry creeks held the snow and curved away from the mountain at exactly the right pitch to create the mosaic of ridges, steep faces, and open glades that alpine skiers love. It took longer to learn that the slump and flow of active landslides and earthflows that had created this terrain—so interesting for hikers and skiers—also made it a challenging and potentially dangerous place to build roads and houses.

Wheeler Basin became "Snow Basin" when Geneve Woods, wife of an Ogden forester, won the Chamber of Commerce contest to name the newly developing winter sports area, her entry chosen over a thousand others. Decades later the owners decided that Snow Basin sounded old-fashioned. And so Snow Basin became Snowbasin.

The foothills and canyons of Mount Ogden came right to the edge of a town where the railroad and a small college diversified the traditionally Mormon community. In a barely postfrontier culture, parents felt comfortable giving their not yet wholly urban or suburban children free rein. When Depression-era classes ended at Ogden High School on winter afternoons, the teenagers spilled out and lugged their eight-foot pine skis to the 29th Street hill a few blocks away, where they jumped until dark. Bob Beck was one of those hot young skiers when the ski pioneer Alf Engen asked him along on a climb into the upper basin of Wheeler Creek in the winter of 1936.

As advisor to the Forest Service, Alf was looking for potential ski areas on national forest land. He had just masterminded the creation of Utah's first ski area, Alta. In 1938 he laid out Ogden's new ski area in the Basin and then spent two years supervising Civilian Conservation Corps boys, with a $200,000 budget, clearing runs and building a road into the Basin, planting seedlings, and beginning to restore the watershed.

By 1945 what Basin land the city of Ogden did not give to Wasatch-Cache National Forest outright, it sold at low cost. With congressional funding, the Forest Service purchased an additional 3,445 acres. The total federal investment lay somewhere between $20,000 and $40,000. Ultimately local citizens donated 1,850 acres to the people of the United States—the same land used today as the Snowbasin base area and most of the Olympic downhill course.

Ogden's citizens chose one overriding dream for the mountain, creating a *destination* and a source of joy for those who love to ski. The history of the "skisport" in North America carries Mount Ogden from these early days through decades of operating a local ski area on public land directly toward that moment when citizens again hoped to intervene in the mountain's future—and in Earl Holding's plans for the mountain.

THAT HISTORY OF SKIING BEGINS with a handful of Scandinavian miners trying out skis in the mining camps of Utah's Wasatch Mountains in the nineteenth century. Norwegian immigrants brought their jumping and cross-country skis to the Midwest. It took decades before skiing became popular as a national recreational sport.

The first United States alpine championship ski race, a downhill, took place in 1933, one year after the first Winter Olympics in North America at Lake Placid, New York. As more and more people tried to emulate the alpine skiers schussing and carving down the mountains, manufacturers started selling skis that would turn. In the mid-'30s anyone with passion and a length of rope looped around the drive of a Model-T engine could start a little tow on their favorite hill. A few of these end-of-the-road projects survived to become today's historic ski areas.

The world's first chairlift opened for business at Sun Valley, Idaho, in December 1936, where Averell Harriman and his Union Pacific Railroad had built a ski resort from scratch, creating a year-round draw for travelers in this remote western valley. In doing so they remolded the valley's image and, for the first time, marketed a high-status winter sports experience to a national audience of beginning and intermediate skiers eager to pay dashing Austrians for instruction in the new downhill turning technique. Alta opened its first chairlift—the first in Utah—in 1939, one year after the first New England chairlift began operations at Belknap Recreation Area in New Hampshire.

The last of these American pioneer skiers are still with us, though their ranks are fast thinning. Their stories thrill us, their humble beginnings warm our hearts. But nostalgia is tricky. The good old days are always a generation back—no matter which generation is yours. The past is a dream: some of us revel in it, some of us manipulate it. Either way, the truth slips away, to be firmly replaced by myth.

Snowbasin was there from the very beginning. The Norwegians who brought winter sports to America built a 150-foot jump in Ogden Canyon in 1934, cashing in on the new industry of skiing as a spectator sport. Within a few years they were running their skis downhill as well as cross country, learning to make turns on steep slopes as alpine skiing came to Utah.

After World War II the city of Ogden completed Snowbasin's Wildcat Chairlift, which had been begun before the war; they used horses to haul wooden towers up the city's hundred-foot right-of-way through the national forest, and Bob Beck helped Alf and Corey Engen dedicate the lift. He laughs still about "trying to keep up with those two clowns" while they skied down as a trio on that January day in 1946 with bundles of roses in their arms, scattering scarlet petals along the way. In these early years at least one of the three Engen brothers—Alf, Sverre, and Corey, immigrants from Norway who were making their way in the New World with Old World skiing skills—participated in every big scene at Snowbasin.

The national alpine championships first came to Snowbasin in 1947, during Corey Engen's five-year tenure as manager. As the century progressed, skiing would help breach the isolation of Utah society. More and more outsiders came, drawn by the bottomless powder snow, expanding resorts, the lure of adventure, and, eventually, the greatest draw of all, the grandest event in winter sports, the Winter Olympics.

ON AN OCTOBER DAY IN 1999 the Mount Ogden community convened to loop through this history and retell the legend of one of the mountain's heroes. Four hundred people gathered in burnished alpine light at the top of the new high-speed John Paul Express ski lift at Snowbasin to dedicate a ridge-top memorial to John Paul Jones. In telling the story of John Paul, we told the history of ownership on the mountain and sketched the parade of dreamers who had taken their turns as lead actors and actresses in this drama. In each of our personal outlines of the story we revealed our conflicting views of the mountain.

Sixty years before, John Paul Jones was one of the Ogden boys who cut elegant turns when he skied the mountain that hung suspended like a sublime stage set behind his hometown. When World War II shattered his quiet world, the midcentury moment of need swept him with the ski troops

TAPS ECHOES THROUGH MOUNT OGDEN BOWL AT THE 1999 JOHN PAUL
DEDICATION.

of the 10th Mountain Division from the American Rockies to the Italian
Apennines. As the 10th stormed Mount Belvedere in 1945, John Paul moved
into the line of fire wearing a helmet branded with a medic's red cross. A
German sharpshooter saw that cross as a bulls-eye. The twenty-year-old
with the round face and Jimmy Cagney smile fell—one more casualty in
the bloody battle to retake Italy.

After World War II, back home on Mount Ogden, his friends and his nieces continued to ski the bowls and faces of the backcountry beyond the lifts at Snowbasin, remembering John Paul's grace and his love for the mountain, mourning his death. About 1,947 members of the Snowbasin Ski Club made their lost friend immortal, linking his spirit to one favorite ridge. Nearly three thousand vertical feet from the spine of the mountain down to its base, this ridge hid private caches of powder snow that float up and over the shoulders of skiers making their turns down the lunatic steeps. This became the John Paul Jones Ridge.

And like a Shoshone Indian legend, the boy became a mountain.

I didn't grow up with this history or this legend. But I had become an apprentice member of the Mount Ogden community when I skied the mountain's ridges. I could imagine the array of constituencies surrounding me in the crowd gathered for the dedication of the John Paul memorial. For some of us the new developments at Snowbasin are a culmination, the proper expression of human authority over threatening wilderness. Development is simply business as usual—business as opposed to destiny, and requiring no further comment. For others—and these individuals are mostly absent from this gathering, the wild mountain has been lost to the evil forces of commercial gain.

Bob Beck believes that John Paul would have joined him in approving the development of the mountain: "He would have loved it." He and other old-timers had dreamed of big changes and spent years banding together in ski clubs to generate the support for programs and improvements. Now that the changes are here, they remember with tenderness the quiet days when the mountain was theirs alone. They are at once wistful and excited about the new Snowbasin.

The John Paul dedication began with the strains of taps echoing off the north face of Mount Ogden. A young black chaplain from the nearby Hill Air Force Base proclaimed, "Shoulder to shoulder, America is the anthem and cradle of democracy. Shoulder to shoulder, from her majestic mountains, let freedom ring." He filled Mount Ogden Bowl with the soul-jolt cadences of Martin Luther King Jr. Yet when we stood here shoulder to shoulder on land owned by all, were we indeed in this together?

I knew that many of the honorable elders gathered on the John Paul Ridge felt that land should be developed for the profit of industrious entrepreneurs, that they believed that their forebears had come to Utah to make the desert blossom like a rose. They defined heroism in terms of action rather than restraint, and they believed that public land exists primarily to serve human desires.

Fundamental differences in values flared among us but remained unspoken. The mountain light exposed our vulnerabilities and opened us to compassion. In this tender state we could be moved by speakers no matter what their values, each speaker focusing nostalgia like a magnifying glass to singe our hearts.

A quartet of elders presented the colors—men in their seventies wearing 10th Mountain ties and Division patches on their blazers, each man with roots in the mountain. At the rim of the cirque, stage right in the group, stood soft-spoken skier Bob Beck—a Bronze Star winner.

The mountain division veterans planted flags on either side of the lectern and gimped back to their seats with calmness and dignity. They had been here at the beginning. When they pass, we will lose our direct link to John Paul and the Snowbasin of the Thirties—and to the opening act of the drama of Mount Ogden, the skier's mountain.

Those of us who learned to ski in the postwar years boomed down the hills at our local ski areas in New England, the Rockies, or the Sierra, establishing our fierce ownership run by run. We still felt connected to the pioneer skiers who hand-cut ski slopes and patched up misbehaving homemade lifts. For our children, those times and people are remote—historic or entirely unknown.

While the old-timers shifted in their seats, Bob Chambers rose to speak for the next cohort of skiers. Seven years younger than John Paul Jones and Bob Beck, Chambers had been born in Jackson, Wyoming, where his grandfather made skis for going back and forth to the barn and doing a bit of jumping. And then "Alf Engen came to Jackson Hole when I was only nine or ten years old and showed people how to turn skis. We thought it was the greatest thing that we'd ever seen."

Chambers moved to Ogden in 1941. He told us the story of his fascination with "John Paul Jones and Bob Beck swooping down making graceful stem christie turns. When I tried to imitate them, I would always go head over heels. On one of those occasions Paul, as we called him, came over to find out if I was okay. He helped me back onto my skis, and at that moment he became a friend and an idol."

Bullet-headed, bald, compact, and with a smile so wide it strains his cheeks, Chambers is an emphatic man, still a wild skier after nearly sixty years at Snowbasin. He summarized the accomplishments of the 10th Mountain Division, heroes of the last six months of bloody fighting in Italy.

War was hell, but it could also be an adventure for a young man. Upon their return the 10th Mountain vets did not sink into the depressing sameness of postwar American suburbia. Instead of catching the daily commuter train in their gray flannel suits, they preserved the spirit of their war years by spending the rest of their lives as entrepreneurs, skiers, and mountain men. Two thousand of the nearly 20,000 veterans of the 10th became ski instructors; others were involved in founding or directing ski schools at sixty-two American ski areas. Together, developing mountains and taking risks, these men shaped American skiing, and their passion fanned a recreational pursuit into an industry.

In 1935 American skiers numbered about ten thousand. By the time the World War II veterans returned, a new generation was ready to follow the ski troopers down the mountains, and for a time skiing was the people's sport.

AFTER THE WAR CAME THE '50s—and my childhood—a decade-long celebration of middle-class America. I was shaped by this era, taught to believe in the power of the United States to do good in the world. The bedrock ideals of my New Deal Democrat parents shaped my attitude toward public lands as much as they shaped my attitudes toward social justice.

In those postwar days Snowbasin was run by the Ogden Water Department as a city park. Crops of local children rode up in school buses for lessons. They'd latch their cable bindings down onto wooden skis and waggle their toes in lace-up square-toed leather boots, trying to stay warm. Teenagers, wearing Levis and sweatshirts, could work a morning at the Basin for the city—shoveling snow, punching tickets—to earn a ski pass for the afternoon.

Corey Engen, frustrated by the Ogden bureaucrats who ran the area with "no foresight for the future," left his Snowbasin manager's position in 1951. When I spoke with him fifty years later, he still found those long-gone city officials wanting: "Those were nice guys, but they didn't have any heart in skiing, they weren't ski-minded." After Corey left, the city of Ogden finally admitted that Snowbasin needed its independence. In 1957 Sam Huntington became the first individual who was allowed to purchase the ski area permit—for $5,000.

Huntington, a stern man and a tinkerer, had built the nation's first double chairlift at Berthoud Pass, Colorado, in 1947. At Snowbasin he continued to work with lifts until he was electrocuted by one in 1962. A trio of Ogden businessmen took over until 1978, when they sold the Snowbasin permit to Peter Seibert, the founder of Vail.

As skiing became a resort-based business in the '70s and '80s, and Park City and Snowbird began to dominate Utah skiing, Snowbasin remained unpretentious, an artifact of the past with glorious terrain but few amenities. Right up to the 1990s Snowbasin survived only as the quiet and obscure domain of a few thousand resident skiers who loved the place. Unlike most advertising copy, the public relations slogan for Snowbasin—"Utah's Best-Kept Secret"—was true.

ENTREPRENEURS HAVE TO BE BIG DREAMERS, but, for an ambitious businessman, Pete Seibert was remarkably down-to-earth. Gregarious and open, with a lopsided smile, he had a streak of vulnerability that charmed nearly everyone during his tenure as Snowbasin's owner. Even the antiresort environmentalists liked him.

The 1999 John Paul dedication day brought him back to Snowbasin for the first time in years. He honored John Paul without romanticism, and he was matter-of-fact about his own service in Italy with the 10th Mountain Division. When I had looked him up at Vail the year before and asked him how the experience had affected his career, his answer had none of the public romance of the ski troops. He said, simply, "It interrupted it totally!"

Pete talked about how close he came to death: "It made me aware of opportunities. It made me very aware that if I wanted to get anything done, the monkey was on my back." After serving as a squad leader at nineteen and a platoon sergeant at twenty Pete came home from Italy minus a kneecap and with a reconstructed left arm and right leg. About the only thing to survive intact was the dream he had cherished straight through from his childhood in Bartlett, New Hampshire—to build a resort "like St. Anton, with lifts coming right out of the village."

Seibert created his own rehab program after the doctors had worked on him for eighteen months: he moved to Aspen to race—he raced for the U.S.

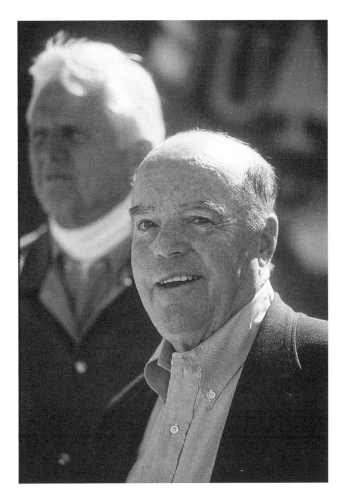

PETE SEIBERT (FRONT) AND EARL HOLDING, JOHN PAUL DEDICATION, SNOWBASIN, 1999.

ski team in 1950—direct the ski patrol, and help other 10th Mountain vets elevate the Colorado resort into Sun Valley's league. He moved to Switzerland to attend the premier hotelkeeper's school, L'École Hôtelier de la Suisse in Lausanne, and returned to Colorado to manage Loveland Basin. Through all these years he continued his search for the perfect mountain.

In 1957 he found it. Earl Eaton, one of his employees at Loveland, asked him to take a look at a mountain along U.S. Highway 6 west of Vail Pass.

Eaton had matched the terrain he knew from growing up in the Eagle Valley with the sense of skiing he had picked up cutting runs with Seibert. Pete climbed Eaton's ridges, and saw slopes that were scenically sumptuous but not too challenging for intermediate skiers. With the eye of a lifelong skier he could see how to develop those exquisite bowls. With the vision of a businessman he could see a new audience for these slopes. As one old friend said of him, Pete had "an idea a minute."

Earl Eaton ("the finder," in Pete's words) and Pete Seibert ("the founder") negotiated a special-use permit with the Forest Service in 1961. With financial partners they started quietly raising money at $10,000 a share and bought ranchland at the bottom of the mountain (much of it for $125 an acre—land that is now worth up to $4 million per acre). Vail Associates was born.

At Vail, Pete and his partners invented the ski community, a one-developer, integrated resort that focused not just on the wealthy but also on suburban middle-class families, as well as on real estate. For this achievement *SKI Magazine* in 1999 proclaimed Pete Seibert to be the third most influential skier of all time.

Vail took Pete Seibert on a tumultuous ride. During the first season, on January 10, 1963, only twelve lift tickets were sold at Vail; by the third season, three thousand skiers dependably arrived each day to ski the mountain. Growth came too fast; Holiday Inns and multistoried condos soon marred Pete's faux-alpine village, initially inspired by Zermatt, Switzerland. A fatal gondola accident hit the operation hard in 1976. After he was forced out of the Vail hierarchy, Pete and a partner resurfaced at Snowbasin, where they convinced thirty-five other investors to join them in buying the Utah ski area permit for about $2 million, twice what Pete had expected. "We really didn't buy anything," he admits. "We bought an opportunity."

Pete planned the new resort's base on the Strawberry Basin side and began to acquire private land, following the four-season condo–golf–winter–wonderland model he had refined at Vail. A little lower in elevation than the cluster of ski areas in the central Wasatch, and without the magical confluence of canyon and storm fueled by Great Salt Lake moisture, which brings five hundred inches of snowfall to Alta each year, there isn't enough snow on Mount Ogden to support the kind of major resort Pete envisioned unless he added intensive snowmaking, especially on the southern flanks of the mountain in Strawberry Bowl. But in Pete's eyes, despite its vertical drop of 3,400 feet—sufficient for an Olympic downhill—Snowbasin had the same friendly appeal to intermediate skiers as Vail. Much of

Mount Ogden is yielding and rounded beneath the craggy ridgeline, with snow conditions that change subtly from hollow to aspen grove to conifer slope in a continuum of diversity that backcountry skiers lovingly call microterrain.

None of these physical details mattered once Snowbasin began losing money at downhill-racer speed—$250,000 a year. Despite Weber County voters' approval of a $3-million bond to improve the lifts, despite his efforts to attract entrepreneurs to invest in his dream, despite his deep belief in skiing and in his employees, despite going after the big races even while he slid into bankruptcy, Pete hit a wall of recession in the '80s and failed.

Seibert needed a buyer. "I took $600 of my last $800 in the bank for the entry fee and went up and played in a golf tournament in Sun Valley. I knew I'd have an opportunity to get next to Earl Holding. I played golf, took some time out, and met Earl." It took a ruse, and luck, to meet Earl. It still does.

One man who has dealt with Earl Holding says, with respect: "When you do business with him, he will be looking out for his interests—count on it. You had better look out for yours—count on it. He will know what he's doing—count on it. You had better know what you are doing—count on it.

"Don't go bumbling around or you're going to take a beating."

———

When his turn came to address the John Paul dedication crowd, Pete Seibert repeated his favorite Earl Holding stories. When he first showed Earl the mountain, Earl kicked every tower of the five lifts to see if it was solid. "He kept asking, 'What elevation are we at now?' and 'Why is the wind blowing?' He is an engineer, you know."

Pete reiterated his firm belief that Snowbasin (with some help from snowmaking) is "the best potential ski area in Utah. It has the mountains, the slopes, the steeps, but it also has Strawberry Bowl—wonderful, wonderful skiing for the intermediates." And with a wry grin he reminded Earl Holding—listening and laughing from the front row—of the elevation where we were all gathered: about 9,000 feet.

After Pete sold Snowbasin to Earl Holding in 1984 Pete's creditors received just seventeen cents on the dollar. "There was nothing, really, to negotiate," Pete said. "We took the terms that Earl offered." When Pete sold Snowbasin, his dream became Earl's dream.

Pete Seibert died in 2002, after a short battle with cancer. Forever the dreamer, he asked his family to mix his ashes with cloud-seeding chemicals, pack them in a small rocket, and, when the weather was right, fire the concoction into the sky over Vail, where Pete's remains would be able to seed the clouds and blanket his mountain with fresh powder.

EARL HOLDING SPOKE LAST. He came to the microphone, his well-tended white hair and brown leather bomber jacket over white turtleneck and denim shirt giving him an urbanity none of the other speakers at the John Paul dedication could claim. He was gracious. He spoke of how "touching" the day was, how moving the story of John Paul. He listed his family members who had served in World War II. He paid tribute to Pete Seibert's wartime wounds: "He's a hero just like John Paul was a hero."

He told the story of Pete's phone calls over the course of two years, the failing operator asking the successful one to look at Snowbasin. "I told him I didn't want to even come and look at it for fear I'd buy it! One ski resort was enough! When I did come I brought my youngest daughter with me. We hiked up this mountain and across the ridge and down through Strawberry with chaparral clear up to my armpits."

Earl clearly loved to tell these stories. He teased Pete about how fast the old veteran had moved, with Earl struggling to keep up. At the end of that first walk, as they turned back toward the day lodge, Earl remembered that "my little daughter was on one side of me and Pete was on the other. She pulled at my sleeve and said, 'Dad?' Very quietly she said, 'Dad, you ought to buy this place.' I turned, and I looked down at her, and I said, 'Why?'" Earl plays this line hard, in a slightly exasperated tone, talking about his youngest daughter, Kathleen, as if she had been considerably younger and more naïve than the twenty-three-year-old geologist she actually was at the time.

"She said, 'Because it's so unspoiled and so beautiful, it will be a magnificent ski area.'"

Earl remembered that Pete talked about the names of the runs: Chicken, Chicken Springs, John Paul. He thought the first two were terrible, silly (though they appear on the USGS topographic map of the area), and he remembered a "Chicken Lips," too, though there isn't one. He told us that he planned from the start to change them to something more suitable for his resort.

I listened to his fierceness about names and thought about how names give Earl control. He defines ownership comprehensively. When today's Snowbasin visitors arrive they ski Blue Grouse, not Chicken Springs. In a generation no one will remember that locals skied out the base on "Chicken" or that they used to call the climb to the knoll where we sit the "Stairway to Heaven," and that this knoll gave access to the powder shots on FTG—"Fucking Too Good."

"But there's one name here that will never get changed," Earl told us. "This John Paul area will be here forever. And I am so proud to have that name. It means something." He paused, still irritated with those chickens: "It's not just a bird."

―――――

It's no wonder that local boosters believe in Earl's dream, Bob Chambers wrote in a letter to the Ogden newspaper in 1995: "Without further improvements and development, which will require an enormous amount of money, I don't believe that Snowbasin can exist as a ski resort, except on a very limited basis. . . . This opportunity to see Snowbasin developed with environmental expertise, enough money and by an organization that has a great track record, will probably never happen again. It appears that it is now or never."

The same sense of high-stakes, do-or-die emotions swirled through the gathering at the top of the John Paul Ridge that day: a mix of courage and regret, wistfulness, respect, and fierce protectiveness about freedom. We had stepped out of the flow of time to attend to the stories of John Paul. Now we were preparing to move, gradually, from the world of legend back into our mundane lives. I listened with interest, wondering what Earl would leave us with.

In his parting line Earl did not speak of maintaining the skiing legacy of John Paul Jones or his love for the sport. He did not speak of preserving the mountain's spirit. To the assembled lovers of skiing, the proud veterans, the family and friends forming the nucleus of the mountain's community, he promised, instead, that "we will do everything we can to make this place famous."

I wanted dreams. I wanted inspiration. I wanted hope. I wanted to leave with a celebration of our relationship with the American landscape resounding in my ears. Instead, the day ended with Earl, the good businessman, pledging to do a good job marketing the mountain—reminding us that the world is for sale.

THE AUTHOR AS A CHILD WITH HIS PARENTS, DON AND ISABELLE TRIMBLE, RIMROCK LAKE, WASHINGTON, 1953. PHOTOGRAPH BY AUTHOR'S GRANDFATHER, DONALD TRIMBLE.

THE PROPHETS
OF PLACE

What is important is anyone's coming awake and discovering a place, finding in full orbit a spinning globe one
can lean over, catch, and jump on. What is important is
the moment of opening a life and feeling it touch—with
an electric hiss and cry—this speckled mineral sphere,
our present world.

ANNIE DILLARD, *AN AMERICAN CHILDHOOD,* 1987

DREAMS LIE UNDER THE HARDPAN surface of the desert West, hidden beneath an
alkali-white crust. Stories underlie meadows; visions sleep in mountains;
every place name carries lives within it. And from these dreams and places
emerge the stories of generations of my family.

My father was born in Westhope, North Dakota. *West* and *hope*—the
destinies and desires of thousands of dreamers caught up by the frontier
distilled in two words. The town had existed for just thirteen years when
"Doc Charley" Durnin delivered tiny, premature Donald Eldon Trimble
and kept him alive by incubating him in a shoebox placed in the office
oven. March 6, 1916. Baby Don's parents, my grandparents, were authentic pioneer offspring. I heard their stories as a child, and they brought the
opening of the West close.

My grandmother Ruby Seiffert was one of the first white children—as
the family stories always put it—born in that part of North Dakota in 1892.
The Seifferts, Alsatian and Scotch immigrants, had made their way west
through Canada, from Ontario to Manitoba, finally crossing south over the
line to North Dakota in the 1880s.

One of the family homesteads lay along the curl of Antler Creek within sight of the international boundary, a little stream that ambled between the two countries through box elder, elm, and ash thickets—past a rock farmhouse, a plank bridge, a springhouse smelling of butter and cream. Another branch of the Seiffert family chose a spot along Antler Creek in 1883 when they spooked a remnant herd of buffalo. The guard bull roused his herd when he spotted their carriage from his lookout post on a hint of a hill—and on that rise they built their house.

My grandfather's Trimble forebears followed the American frontier westward from Alleghany County, Maryland, in pre-Revolutionary days—to Ohio, Iowa, and North Dakota. Branches of that clan reach back to the early Europeans' voyages to New England.

My great-grandfather Grant Trimble, the star of many of the family stories, was a terrific character: the flawed patriarch. He came west when he drove horses from Iowa to North Dakota, made a profit, and decided to stay. He platted and built the town of Richburg, North Dakota, in 1898, and an old family photograph shows his center of operations, a storefront for "Trimble's Dry Goods Department" and "Trimble's State Bank." Little-America-style promotional signboards completely covered the building: "The Greatest Sale of Modern Times." "The Wonder of the Age." "They Kan't Ketch Up." "Fat Bargains." "A Happy Shopping Place."

When the railroad bypassed him five years later he platted his brother's farm, which happened to lie next to the railhead, and competed for sales by offering land at a fraction of the price of the railroad's lots. The Great Northern succumbed to his bluff, lowered their prices, and gave him a major portion of the lots in the new town. Great-grandfather Trimble gleefully put Richburg on wagons, building by building, and moved his frontier minidevelopment to the new railhead town of Westhope a mile and a half away. His oldest son, my grandfather Donald Enoch Trimble, was the first graduate of Westhope High School. (There were only two graduates that spring day in 1909, Trimble and Warner, and commencement was alphabetical.)

In Wallace Stegner's pithy words, the families who came west at this time were "boomers" or "stickers." The boomers followed their dreams, booming and busting but always refusing to knuckle under to the reality of the dry West, always refusing to stay put and "stick." Grant Trimble was a boomer.

This was the homestead era as well, and the Trimbles and the Seifferts claimed land for their own. Public land was simply unhomesteaded land,

and that's where the men went duck hunting in the marshes, where young Don Trimble and Ruby Seiffert courted by hooking up the sidecar to my Grandpa's Indian motorcycle and bumping over the Turtle Mountains to Lake Metigoshe for picnics.

For a time, Grant Trimble avoided the bust; he even served as a state senator. The bust came in 1912, when he lost all his money in the wheat futures market. While cleaning out his office Grant found the deed to an apple orchard in Washington that he'd won in one of his business deals and forgotten. It was all he had left. And so the Trimbles moved to Toppenish, a small town in the Yakima Valley.

Unlike the tragic arcs of the boomers dramatized in Wallace Stegner's books, Grant Trimble put down roots in Toppenish. Giving up his wilder dreams, he transformed the Trimbles into settlers—"stickers"—for the remainder of the twentieth century.

IN MY CHILDHOOD MY PATERNAL GRANDPARENTS lived at the far west of our family space in the Yakima Valley in Washington. Here, in Toppenish, where my father had grown up, my father's parents and my grandfather's two brothers and three sisters all lived within a few blocks of each other.

The Trimbles had brought their stories with them when they moved from North Dakota. They were townspeople now, but they stayed close, interdependent, with the special affinity of those with a shared past—in their case the boom times back in Dakota. They would spread their Adirondack chairs in a backyard circle and sip iced tea, reliving life on the farms and surrounding prairie as an adventure, reliving the golden memories of their youth.

Those Toppenish backyards contained some of my first wild places. The great evergreen tree that sheltered my grandfather's fishing boat, where I would hide in sharp-needled shade. A cement-lined fishpond. A dusty alley with hollyhocks and bumblebees. These are my elemental, fundamental memories, from a time almost beyond memory. I can tell just how primal because when I recall those explorations, diving deep into that ancient lizard brain where awareness begins with scent, I smell that dust and those pine needles as much as see them.

The Trimbles' experience of moving with the frontier was classically western. They may not have trapped beaver with the mountain men, but my great-uncles' stories of hunting and fishing in North Dakota, the photographs of the family farm that freeze moments of my father's earliest childhood, all tied me to The West, as home and myth, and to the nineteenth-century colonization of the frontier and the great dividing of the continent into private and public realms.

———

From Toppenish the Trimbles looked up to the western horizon every day to see if their mountains were visible—the sublime glacier-covered half rounds of Mount Adams and Mount Rainier. These were ever-present, hovering forces in their lives. My father climbed these mountains as a boy with the Boy Scouts and the Mountaineers Climbing Club.

He took road trips with his pals, saving his money for gas so that he could see the saguaros in the Sonoran Desert, the Grand Canyon, the Great Southwest. When his family visited North Dakota, they detoured to Glacier National Park and to Yellowstone. He loved mountains, he loved the outdoors, and he studied geology in college so that he could work outside—putting himself through school with stints as a hard-rock miner.

After World War II deprived him of his home landscape during a three-year exile in the South Pacific theater, my father was delighted to be back on the road in the West. He had heard that the United States Geological Survey (USGS) was hiring in Denver. At thirty, footloose and in need of a job, this sounded good to him. He moved, within two years married the office clerk-typist—my mother—and spent more than thirty years as a USGS field geologist.

DAD AND HIS FELLOW GEOLOGISTS and their wives were my primary childhood circle. These scientists did field work in summer in wild country all over the West, then returned home to Denver in winter to work out the meaning of their notes and maps, publishing their theories as monographs. Their work verged on exploration less than fifty years after John Wesley Powell had worked in some of the same places.

When I read Wallace Stegner's biography of John Wesley Powell, *Beyond the Hundredth Meridian,* I realized that Powell and his protégés Clarence Dutton and Grove Karl Gilbert were icons for my father and his friends. And that, in turn, my father's cohort of government scientists were my models, the men I would choose to emulate.

The landscape where Powell and Dutton and Gilbert made their mark was the Colorado Plateau, that great maze of canyons carved by the Colorado River. My father introduced me to these places on family trips. Later

I worked in the canyon country as a park ranger. Today my retreat—my Eden—rises on a sandstone mesa with views across public land to a national park in the heart of the plateau. My imagination travels far but always comes home to these canyons.

———

The anti-intellectual stereotype of masculinity in the West veers in another direction entirely—that of the cowboy who turned up in western movies and television series of the '50s, a man of the land but one who is driven to possess, own, and dominate—quick to take up arms to defend his property. Americans fancy this stereotype. We imagine these mythic heroes as our leaders—and we keep electing to the presidency men who play to that myth.

My father and his friends, by contrast, were men who drank and swore but treasured clear thinking and well-spoken ideas. They socialized as couples, women and men together. With plenty of World War II footage on the black-and-white television screen of our living room, I knew what they had done in the war a few short years before. Now "going out with the boys," for them, meant getting together with their sack lunches at the office to talk politics, argue theories, and banter. They saved their extra energy for climbing mountains and anonymous ridges, intent on deciphering the story of the landscape. Mostly irreligious, geologic time was their scripture.

Their fieldwork mixed the physical and the cerebral. They drove Jeeps and forded rivers and sweat-stained their hatbands. They mused in grand scale, comfortable with the millions and billions of geologic time, but they spent their days in physical contact with the earth, picking up rocks warmed by the sun, collecting rough horn coral fossils and knife-sharp chunks of obsidian, kneeling to measure grain size and the angles of rocks jutting from the surface of the planet. Mapping and photographing and drawing in their journals, these men made art while doing science.

———

In my childhood, I chose my father's lineage for my connections. Geology was the bedrock underlying patriarchy. Science was our religion, western history and natural history our tribal lore, the public domain of the West our Holy Land. Like my father, I took as my prophets the pioneers and mountain men, the explorer-scientists and writers journeying and journaling across the continent, and paid due respect to Lewis and Clark and to my grandfather's pioneer energy.

A subliminal message ran through this history: that government was good. From Lewis and Clark themselves to Powell and the nineteenth-century surveys, Aldo Leopold, and Bob Marshall's invention of the modern concept of wilderness while working for the Forest Service—the stories that nourished me featured federal bureaucrats as heroes. I grew up with the assumption that civil servants did visionary work.

The visionaries' disciples were the men of my father's generation, not long back from the war, returned alive to family, to good work, and to the canyons and deserts and rivers and mountains of the West. These were the places that gave them their stories. These were the places that make us who we are.

PART II: THE GOOD BUSINESSMAN

SKIER BELOW THE NEEDLES, SNOWBASIN, UTAH, 1997.

THE LAST RESORT

Land to a developer is not a biological system. Ultimately, land is not even landscape, the roll of hills, the pattern of trees along a ridge, a sweep of meadow.... Land, to the developer, is a speculative matter, a question of the balanced bottom line, an investment.

JOHN HANSON MITCHELL, *TRESPASSING: AN INQUIRY INTO THE PRIVATE OWNERSHIP OF LAND,* 1998

OUR FRIENDS ROB AND DANIEL, father and teen-aged son, had been dreaming of skiing the West for years. Finally, one winter, they came from New England for the long-awaited visit with our family in Salt Lake City. We sent them up to the glories of Alta, Brighton, Solitude—to the local ski areas in Big and Little Cottonwood canyons, where we believed they would experience the heart and soul of western skiing.

To our surprise, they came down from the mountain unsettled rather than jubilant; they were disturbed by the lack of signage, the open expanse of the slopes, the ungroomed edges in the trees. This was an entirely different ski ethic from that of destination resorts; here there was only a loose set of rules, to be loosely heeded. Rob summed up this easygoing western ethic: "Here is the mountain, here are the lifts. Govern yourself accordingly."

The next day we suggested the gentler backside of the Wasatch, directing our friends over the crest to Park City and Deer Valley, where they would find perfectly groomed snow furrowed in familiar little corduroy ridges. Here they would find resorts that took care of them and endorsed their need for comfort and comforting. They returned ecstatic. And relieved.

Old-fashioned ski areas require an investment in trade for adventure—if adventure is what you want. Such places ask that you learn the lay of the land, make the terrain your own, keep your wits about you. You need to be comfortable with the thrill of newness: you must be willing to risk the foreign for the sake of learning and the pride of self-reliance. It's as close as you can get to backcountry skiing at a developed resort. Most vacationing skiers want that development, and so these less sophisticated ski areas are a dying breed.

I started skiing the winter the Beatles first sang on *The Ed Sullivan Show*. Returning to Denver from our lessons at the tiny Lake Eldora Ski Area, we filled the bus with an incomparable potion mixed from diesel exhaust, the giddy highs of first-time skiers, the hormonal fog of adolescents dreaming of getting their hands on each other, and the tension wrung from anticipating the Beatles on the *Really Big Show*. Skiing has seemed sexy to me ever since those first feverish trips in junior high. I still revel in the curve-hugging nylon clothing, the speed, the rhythm, the sharp clarity of cold and the dazzle of sunlight off fresh snow, the well-being of spent muscles.

These lightly developed mountains where I first learned to ski were not resorts. They were our community playgrounds—day-use areas for Colorado weekenders. Winter Park was owned by the Denver Parks and Recreation Department and serviced by the Rio Grande ski train. Loveland Basin and Arapahoe Basin and Berthoud Pass—all operating by permit on U.S. Forest Service land, attracted exclusively local crowds, with the nearest motels in the old mining camps a few miles below on U.S. Highway 6 or 40.

Skiing was my personal entry point into the landscape. Here I was an insider, with special knowledge gained from skiing long days with my buddies on slopes known only to us locals. We were creating a West of our own, thanks to the freedom bestowed by the automobile and by still unscripted slates on which we could create our stories.

Skiing has remained part of my life. I met my wife—who had moved west to ski bum at Alta—on a ski date. As grade-schoolers our two children grew to love Alta, where they too imagined they were exploring the mountain for the first time. They understand the difference between the backcountry John Paul Ridge you earned by hiking from the old Porcupine Chairlift for a half hour and the developed John Paul you now access by being whisked up Snowbasin's new high-tech lift. The hike created a sense of achievement and an intimacy with the mountain that no zippy new lift can match.

The antiexpansionist fans of the old Snowbasin could ski without worrying about the irony of "consuming" nature because so little money was being spent or made in the transaction. Old-fashioned ski areas used fewer resources—no electricity or water for snowmaking, minimal connection to the national and global economy, less of everything. To use the political columnist Thomas Friedman's metaphors of globalization, the old Snowbasin is the "olive tree," the new one, the "Lexus."

THE NATIONAL SKI AREAS ASSOCIATION held its 2000 convention in Orlando, to see what resort operators could learn from theme parks. Vail and Aspen, Park City and Jackson Hole, Sun Valley and Big Sky, Tremblant and Whistler, Mammoth Mountain and the cluster of Lake Tahoe areas—all have become four-season resorts, typically corporate-owned, with capital to make skiing a big business. Each strives to be the "number-one resort community in North America."

In *Downhill Slide,* his polemic against the New Ski Village, Hal Clifford describes this programmed experience, a cobbled-together amalgam of "the most pleasant, least threatening aspects of the upscale mall, the revitalized urban downtown, and the suburban McMansion . . . a corporately envisioned, architecturally executed form of social engineering that gives visitors no obvious reason to venture out to where . . . they might risk an actual, authentic encounter with someone who truly lives here—an organic, unscripted, noncommercial experience."

Some of us enjoy the frisson of patrolling into the unknown. Some of us are desperate to avoid it. Some of us find the New Ski Village pleasing, a place where everything is predictable and under control—what one ski company executive describes as "a collective expectation of a staged experience." Some of us find this a depressing surrender to America the Franchised. "Resorts" strive to create the ideal commodity, meeting every imagined desire with a program of amenities. "Ski areas" leave visitors to their endlessly complicated selves, each free to forge an individual relationship with the wild mountain. Ski areas are old-fashioned, eccentric, distinctive, community-based—each a poster child for singularity. Alta Ski Area is still small enough for the staff to call us one recent fall to say that they had found a pair of child's goggles with our son's name and phone number written inside. Did we want them returned? Could they mail them to us?

We all live conflicted, caught between competing demands. We want to be authentic, and we want to be successful. We want to be both independent and needed. Free and yet loved. Smart but down home. Expert but easeful.

I too want all of these for myself. I strive to live lightly on the planet, and yet I have purchased my dream acreage, built a retreat home, and diminished our open space in the rural West. I still prefer slow chairlifts that let me pause and look around, reconnect me with weather and context in between runs, and don't raise a gondola's fogged windows between me and the wild mountains. And yet, when development opens new mountains for skiing, I'll ride all the high-tech lifts and try all the runs.

Life is a giant, teetering, fun house of trade-offs.

And yet I believe that interchangeable leisure experiences do not satisfy our yearning for romance and simplicity, for community and the American spirit, and for enough wildness to nourish our ancient biological connections with the land. Consolidation and corporatization displace imagination. We have turned the Earth into a drive-in that fillets wild places into bite-sized nuggets of recreation.

Mutual antagonism makes reconciliation difficult, yet we cannot dismiss our ties to the other side of the moral mountain. We cannot forget that values are attached to people shaping mind and heart and soul. At their most intense the two land-use philosophies—maximum control versus maximum wildland—mirror the twin faces of our culture. We see a fault line rather than a continuum, prolonging the destructive duality of human-less versus human-controlled nature.

This is tricky territory. It's easy to sentimentalize. The lean and passionate outrage of our youth can evolve into big-bellied ambivalence. What we need is a good, cathartic middle-aged crisis that would force us to take stock of our lifetime's accumulation of assumptions and insist that we appraise with a clear eye where we stand.

ONE VERSION OF EARL HOLDING'S DRIVE to recreate Snowbasin in his own image is Shakespearean. In this version a controlling villain is arrayed against a muster of worthy but powerless characters, and the story features scoundrels and heroes and surprising turns. Earl builds and manicures with certainty that his doing so is virtuous. To his opponents his ambition is powerful and consuming and pitiless—his actions lack all ambivalence, subtlety, or irony. I feel righteous about chronicling this drama and giving voice to the angry men and women who refuse ever to buy gas from a station displaying the green Sinclair dinosaur logo.

But there are other versions.

Clint Ensign, who represents Earl's interests in Washington, D.C., told me that he's sick at heart about the criticism leveled at Earl and Carol Holding, who have been his bosses for more than twenty years. He feels that they are "wonderful, down-to-earth people who love the land, who love the West."

And of course in this insider's corporate version of the Snowbasin story, Earl himself believes that he is doing good. When asked in 2000 how he would like others to see him, Earl said, "I think I have great integrity, am hard working, reasonably intelligent, caring . . . that covers it."

Both versions begin with the same scene. When Earl took over from Pete Seibert, Snowbasin was a ski area, not a resort. Four chairlifts bumped leisurely up the mountain, while the wind sang through their rough metal edges and the loose pulleys on their tower mechanisms rang like carillons. An additional beginner's chair serviced the old School Hill bunny slope. A simple lodge housed cafeteria, ski school, rentals, and ski shop in less than 20,000 square feet. At the low end of snowfall for Utah ski areas and with no snowmaking system, Snowbasin often opened late and closed early.

Unless you could talk your way into a bunk at the tiny Hill Haus, the Hill Air Force Base weekend A-frame tucked in the trees behind the day lodge, there was no overnight accommodation closer than the slim pickings in Huntsville ten miles below, or the city of Ogden twenty winding miles away. Back then Snowbasin was losing money steadily—first Pete's money, then Earl's money.

The old Snowbasin didn't suit Earl's style. He did not want the old-timer's Alta or the low-key, studied elegance of Robert Redford's "anti-resort," Sundance. For Earl, simple ski areas were underachievers and thus commodities in need of investment, engineering, and modernization. Earl had already defined his model at Little America and Sun Valley: He wanted four seasons of full beds and humming technology. He wanted to rotate the tables. He wanted golf courses and gourmet restaurants and massive log-and-rock lodges. He wanted real estate.

What he owned—the bare-bones Snowbasin facilities and the permit to operate them, on public land—was insufficient, he knew, as a major four-season moneymaker.

Pete Seibert had been unable to keep up his payments on the more than 7,000 acres of private land on the east end of the Mount Ogden massif that included the gentle intermediate ski terrain of Strawberry Bowl. Earl immediately paid off this loan, and he eventually expanded his holdings adjacent to the forest to 10,000 acres. Local rumors suggest that he remains eager to buy more and that he continues to pressure neighboring landowners to sell.

Early on Earl decided that his new resort village must be at the base of the existing ski area, on what had been national forest, and public land, for fifty years. He chose the Wheeler Creek Basin—the heart of the old Snowbasin—for his lodge and prime real estate. Earl's choice mirrored the national trend. As Hal Clifford sees it, resorts were not just becoming "magnificent temples to skiing" but amenities to drive land sales; in this model skiing is the loss leader to bring customers from the lift to the realty office.

When I spoke with him in Vail, Pete Seibert told me that he had planned to situate the resort base below Strawberry Bowl, where the Forest Master Plan had approved such development. Earl, on the other hand, wanted his lodges on the original Snowbasin side, where his customers could look up at the jagged crest of the Mount Ogden massif. Pete believed that it wasn't necessary to destroy the beauty that drew the skiers in order to build the ideal ski area. But "Earl," he said, "wants it like Sun Valley, where he owns everything."

Earl Holding admits to being obsessed with owning land. When he purchased a coveted parcel next to one of his Wyoming ranches, his secretary asked him, "Aren't you pleased?" Earl replied, "I won't be satisfied until I own all the land next to mine." His employees gave him a brass plaque engraved with this comment—to memorialize their amusement, affection, and awe. No limits, no boundaries.

TO BUILD IN THE ORIGINAL BASE AREA of Snowbasin, Earl would need to own public land. He would need to persuade the representative of the American people, the Forest Service, to carve away the core of Wheeler Basin and give it to him for development.

The communities surrounding the mountain still nurtured a strong sense of pride from their success in the 1930s in saving the mountain from devastation. The agreement between the people of the United States and the Forest Service was a legal, permanent, sacred trust. But forces for growth were aligning at Snowbasin. Here was a mountain in the Rockies with great snow and a world-class vertical drop, terrain that could be developed and subdivided, and an owner with hundreds of millions of dollars to spend on creating one last megaresort. Snowbasin was headed for industrial skiing.

In 1998 Earl told the *Wall Street Journal* that before he bought Snowbasin in 1984 a Forest Service official had promised that the agency would look favorably on a land trade. He recalled that this official pledged that Snowbasin was the agency's first choice for expansion, "their favorite place to really see developed." Earl couldn't remember the official's name.

The USFS trades public lands all the time to consolidate "the green" on forest maps. Because they have extremely limited authority to buy land without going to Congress for approval and funding, the two big multiple-use public lands agencies, the Forest Service and the Bureau of Land Management (BLM), trade thousands of acres each year, giving up less crucial public land to acquire land in need of conservation. In a typical year the Forest Service privatizes nearly 80,000 acres in exchange for about 125,000 acres of new public lands.

Many noncontroversial trades happen at low bureaucratic levels. On larger trades, third-party mediators like the Nature Conservancy, Trust for Public Land, and the lesser known American Land Conservancy often set the agenda because they can afford to buy land. Too often the landowner who wants to trade drives the exchange, knowing from the get-go which issues are key, and knowing what the Forest Service wants.

Developers often blackmail the Forest Service by threatening construction on islands of private land inside public lands to force the agency to move such "inholdings" to the top of the trade list. Perhaps the best-known example of this ploy occurred when a Colorado developer began building an enormous ridgetop lodge in the West Elk Wilderness in 1992. In response to the public outcry that followed, the Forest Service felt compelled to exchange 105 acres near Telluride for the developer's 240-acre inholding. He thereupon promptly sold his newly acquired Telluride land for a multimillion-dollar profit.

Although the guiding principle is "value-for-value," each year the public loses millions of dollars because of deliberately low appraisals. When Forest supervisors grow too friendly with resort executives, their alliances may shift away from the traditional partnership with local communities. And when politicians get involved, land exchanges tend to metamorphose from administrative to legislative. As Janine Blaeloch, director of the watchdog Western Lands Project, has said, "You will often find traces of campaign finances in the shadows of federal land exchanges. Once a land deal goes to Congress, it's almost impossible to stop."

A 2000 federal review of land trades suggested that all BLM and Forest Service land trades be discontinued because of a consistent imbalance in land valuation that yielded a run of trades favoring the private landowner over the public trust.

———

Just over half of the skier days in America each year are logged at resorts operating on public land in sixty-two national forests in eighteen states. Many profitable ski areas operate on Forest Service land with no more than one hundred acres of private land at their bases for lodges and hotels. Alta, Utah, is one exemplar of a ski area where snowfall and terrain create ecstasy for the skier, but where resort amenities are minimal.

Here, operating by permit within Wasatch-Cache National Forest, the Alta Ski Lifts Company owns only the lifts. Private land developed from old mining claims is divided between the lodges and private homes of the community of "Altaholics," who are for the most part fiercely protective of the unpretentious atmosphere. Like most resorts Alta, too, has upgraded lifts, mostly by replacing old lifts in the same location. Snowbird, just down-canyon from Alta, is more upscale—with massive lodges and condos on just forty-five acres of private land embedded within the national forest.

At his Sundance Ski Area a bit further south in the Wasatch Range, Robert Redford owns 5,000 acres on the flanks of Mount Timpanogos, where he chose to make "the land . . . the principal thing to be observed." He describes most other ski resorts as having "a soullessness about them" and actively works to discourage the "monster-home" syndrome in his mountain community. The Sundance ski runs cover 450 of Redford's acres, and the base area, with its lodge, offices, and homes, takes up about 100 acres. His nemesis, longtime U.S. Representative Jim Hansen, who was until 2002 the powerful natural resources subcommittee and committee chairman from Utah's first district, introduced a bill in the U.S. Congress in 1996 in which he facetiously proposed establishing a designated wilderness on the remainder of Redford's private landholdings above Sundance.

With this bill Hansen meant to taunt the Sundance Kid and challenge Redford's support of the new Grand Staircase–Escalante National Monument in southern Utah. In reality Redford loved the idea. The Redford family has now set aside nearly 3,000 acres of their land in North Fork Canyon as the Sundance Preserve, protecting the land from development in perpetuity by means of a conservation easement held by Utah Open Lands. As in every conversation about open space, the chasm between differing land ethics yawns wide here, with those on each side finding quite different meanings in the Sundance Preserve's mission statement: "The promise of a particular place."

EARL ASKED FOR IT ALL. After acquiring the Snowbasin ski area permit in 1984, Earl requested that the Forest Service trade 2,600 acres of public land in the Basin to his resort corporation. He was asking for four square miles, about one-fifth the area of Manhattan. For comparison: of the hundreds of national parks and monuments, battlefields, and historic sites managed by the National Park Service (NPS), more than half are smaller than Earl's requested parcel.

This was his first move. One didn't need to be a radical to see the requested trade as one-sided and driven more by the desire for profit than by concern for public benefit. Wasatch-Cache Forest Supervisor Art Carroll politely but clearly told Earl, "As managers of these National Forest lands, we feel it would not be prudent on our part, nor within the scope of our authority to support the exchange of National Forest lands for commercial real estate development."

In 1986 Supervisor Carroll asked Earl to list all Snowbasin facilities that could not be sited conveniently on his private land and would be inappropriate on public land. Carroll hoped to limit the land exchange required for these structures to less than 200 acres.

A year later the Sun Valley division of Earl's corporation submitted plans for a full-blown four-season resort that could support thousands of people living year-round in Snowbasin. Earl now formally asked for 1,320 acres of public land and identified a few gems he proposed to purchase and trade for the Basin, including a prized hunting area east of Huntsville on Lightning Ridge; a boat ramp on Pineview Reservoir in Ogden Valley that Earl knew the Forest Service desired; and parcels along Mount Ogden foothills on the city side of the mountain that would guarantee public access to the forest.

The agency responded in June 1989 by initiating a full Environmental Impact Statement (EIS)—standard procedure for analyzing credible alternatives. The new forest supervisor, Dale Bosworth, assigned a team of three specialists to prepare the EIS: a recreation and lands forester; a hydrologist; and Joan Degiorgio, a forest planner with a law degree.

Mount Ogden was part of the geography of Degiorgio's childhood, as it was for so many people involved in the Snowbasin story. She had grown up on a farm near Ogden in an Italian-Catholic family that kept in touch with relatives in a village in the Dolomites. She thinks about the past. And, as a public lands planner, she thinks about the future. Degiorgio sees the full spectrum of arguments, from the perspectives of intellect and the law to on-the-ground learning. As we strive to integrate all these approaches, she notes, "in the interim, before we are all enlightened, what do we do? Planning land use is about being smart, making choices. How do you *not* be a planner?"

In 1990 Supervisor Bosworth had lured Joan Degiorgio away from her job with the State of Utah. Naively, she admits, she had hoped to join a decision-making agency focused not on politics but on resources. Instead Bosworth gave her the Snowbasin Environmental Impact Statement project, rife with politics.

To his credit, Bosworth left Degiorgio and her colleagues to analyze, write, and recommend a decision based on resources. She saw the document they created as a model for an "issue-driven" EIS. She still takes great satisfaction in her team's success in "bringing up the important questions." Their EIS did not address the value of the public land or discuss land the Forest Service might receive in trade but looked only at the need for a trade. The team also noted problematic physical issues such as huge areas of earthflows and unstable ground, threats to water quality and wetlands, and serious avalanche danger.

They also considered the "internal landscape" of attitudes and beliefs, acknowledging conflicts between two contradictory value systems. Some people saw "nothing particularly sacrosanct" about Snowbasin as long as the Forest Service acquired lands of equal value and continued to safeguard the watershed. For others "a special trust relationship" existed: "Given the manner in which the Forest Service acquired the lands—primarily through local efforts to protect the watershed—transferring these lands back into private ownership would . . . constitute a violation of the public trust." In the final Forest Service document the team summarized the position of those opposing resort development. These citizens "hold dearly the freedom and availability of these public lands to enjoy." They believe that "if the Forest Service had no legal obligation to retain these lands in public ownership certainly there was a moral one."

As for Snowbasin's role in the Olympics, the Salt Lake Organizing Committee—which by this time, in 1990, had been campaigning for the Games for years—told the EIS team that the selection of Snowbasin for the Olympic downhill and super-G events was in no way "contingent upon any land swap or resort development." This was long ago, before Salt Lake City was chosen as host for the 2002 Olympics and Earl cranked up pressure on the federal agency. This was in that innocent era when Wasatch-Cache Supervisor Dale Bosworth—a career forester who would be named chief of the Forest Service in 2001—sincerely believed that his agency could, without undue political meddling, ask its staff to master the issues and make a recommendation that reflected the best interests of the people.

IN FEBRUARY 1990 DALE BOSWORTH SIGNED the final environmental impact statement recommending a 220-acre trade—less than a tenth of Earl's original request. The document explained that this reduced acreage would eliminate earthflows and wetlands from the exchange while still allowing for construction of all proposed lifts. Bosworth believed that this transfer would give Earl enough land for a day lodge, an overnight lodge, a "corporate training center," twenty-one acres of parking, and sixty acres of single-family detached lots. Additional Olympic facilities and infrastructure for recreational uses could be built by permit on land that remained in public ownership. When Earl wanted to add condos, homes, and other development, he already owned ten thousand acres of private land just one and a half miles away.

Bosworth believed that his recommendation "allows the core development necessary to attract a destination ski market and to provide quality skiing both for residents and visitor skiers" while at the same time respecting a one-hundred-year-old "mandate to conserve mountain watersheds." Bosworth stuck to his guns: "I believe the importance of the *public* nature of the lands in question cannot be understated . . . this offers the maximum amount of land I can, in good conscience, exchange out of the National Forest System" (italics in original).

Pretty blunt. Randy Welsh, who was Ogden District Ranger for Wasatch-Cache National Forest at the time, agreed that the 220 acres were "more than adequate" for a resort. As he said, Park City and Snowbird "do fine with 50 to 100 acres." John Hoagland, later the Forest Service 2002 Olympic planner, also worked on the land trade. He articulated the positions held by the Forest and Earl: "Our analysis was spatial; Earl's business plan reflects his resources and objectives, which are different from ours. It's like Disneyland vs. Disney World."

I had to think about that comparison. But the words themselves carry the metaphor: a parcel of land versus an entire world.

At this point in the story the earnest foresters were in control and feeling good about allowing Snowbasin to develop while giving away the minimum of public land, our national treasure. Dale Bosworth had said yes to development but no to the full extent of Earl's dream. Thirteen years later, while serving as chief of the U.S. Forest Service, Bosworth told me that he still believed his decision had been "the right thing" for the mountain, for the people.

To his dismay, Bosworth's recommendation pleased no one. Two days after he signed the 220-acre decision, business and civic agencies of the three counties near Snowbasin met in Ogden in "emergency session" with representatives from the Utah congressional delegation. They feared that

Earl would pull out of Snowbasin if the Forest didn't meet his terms and that their communities would then lose all the business his resort might bring. Ogden Chamber of Commerce officials, in particular, were desperate for the economic benefits they were sure would come from Earl's mega-Snowbasin.

Earl had no need to stage-manage public response. His interests coincided so completely with this local web of power that he could rely on its members to speak for him without scripting. In the press, outrage over the "small" acreage recommendation came from the Weber County commissioners and other elected officials, not from Chris Peterson, Earl's son-in-law and surrogate.

In the end, everyone appealed the 220-acre Bosworth decision to the next level of power, to the regional forester, Stan Tixier. Local politicians and business groups asked that Earl be given exactly what he asked for, to do with as he wished. Environmentalists—the Sierra Club, Audubon Society, and Salt Lake City–based Save Our Canyons—appealed for the opposite reasons, wanting no trade whatsoever. It took Snowbasin a month to join the formal request for an appeal. Chris Peterson told the press that Snowbasin appreciated "the support the community has given us, but we're going to need a lot more support."

On the morning of March 13, 1990, Utah Senator Orrin Hatch spoke to Ogden community leaders who were meeting to form a task force to work toward the fulfillment of Earl Holding's dreams. Hatch put his arm chummily around Regional Forester Tixier and said, "Stan, are you going to help us out with this?" He turned to the audience: "I've never asked Stan to help us yet that he hasn't done it." And to Tixier: "I hope that puts you on the spot, Stan." A photo from this infamous meeting shows a superconfident Hatch, dressed in a casual sweater rather than his usual neck-throttling shirt and tie, his arm draped around an embarrassed Tixier.

Hatch, prone to speak inappropriately off the cuff, called Bosworth's 220-acre recommendation a "dumb-ass, boneheaded decision. I think anyone who doesn't support Holding's proposal is a Neanderthal." He told the audience that if they heard of an elected official who approved of Bosworth's decision, "I want to know. I'll kill them." Hatch seems really to believe in these polarizing positions. In 1998 he helped produce a pamphlet that includes "preoccupation with environmental issues" among the warning signs that children might be abusing drugs.

Tixier responded to Hatch with quiet facts about the 220 acres : "I think a lot of people who are criticizing the decision have not read it. It does favor a four-season resort. . . . The majority of the calls and letters the Forest Service has received have approved of the decision." But nobody seemed to hear him.

RANGY AND WEATHER-LINED, Stan Tixier is not a timid man. He takes his coffee with Tabasco. Raised in Albuquerque, he spent every childhood summer working on a Colorado cattle ranch, then spent seventeen years with the Forest Service in Arizona, where he worked his way from range conservationist to forest supervisor. He spent the last ten years of his career as Intermountain Regional Forester and retired in 1991 to raise horses in Ogden Valley, write cowboy poetry, and publish *Green Underwear,* a novel with a forester protagonist.

He told me that in this often-reported meeting in 1990 Hatch was "just performing. There was no follow through. I wasn't in his pocket by any means." Hatch himself says today that he was "clearly joking." Tixier was more outraged by then Utah Senator Jake Garn's behavior. He says that Garn called Tixier's office when he was out and "proceeded to chew out my secretary for the 'stupid' decision Dale Bosworth had made. She was almost in tears when I returned." Garn denies that this exchange ever happened.

When the appeal reached him, Stan Tixier hired a mediator. In meetings that often lasted until midnight Chris Peterson spoke for Sinclair; Susan Giannettino, who had replaced Dale Bosworth as Wasatch-Cache supervisor, spoke for the Forest Service; and several Ogden conservationists spoke for the environmental community. Years later Giannettino told me that her staff had found no information that supported exchanging "significant" acreage to "make this ski area work." She also could find no precedent "for the Forest Service disposing of lands of that quality or of that value."

Chris Peterson spoke strongly for Earl. In Giannettino's words: "They absolutely had to have 1,300 acres." When Chris started offering "incentives and strategies and mitigation measures"—though not backing down on the total requested acreage—Susan Giannettino observed the Ogden environmentalists beginning to buckle to Earl's prestige and persistence, "to give in and to try to get what they could." In her view the activists were not representing the national interest or a broad perspective on public lands. And no one outside of Utah was yet paying attention. She could not stand to let Chris Peterson and the local conservationists strike a deal, instead taking on the "natural resource stewardship role" of the Forest Service.

STAN TIXIER, 1999.

Jock Glidden, the longtime leader of the Ogden Sierra Club, remembers "those exciting days" somewhat differently than Giannettino does. He
says, "We wouldn't budge." After many nights of meetings all sides agreed
with the discouraged mediator: they were not going to come to an agreement. The phenomenon of "stakeholders" collaborating in the search for
sustainable solutions was just starting in the West back in 1990. It was too
soon for Snowbasin. Earl Holding would have found it difficult to accept
such a collegial setting, but if at this point participants in a truly collabo-

rative group with national perspectives could have labored their way through the issues to a visionary compromise, they would have prevented years of controversy and heartache.

———

In July, convinced that the Bosworth decision could not withstand further public pressure, Stan Tixier formally set aside the recommendation for a 220-acre trade. His written decision, eleven pages of call and response, addressed the issues raised by all the appellants. In contrast to the impassioned language used by the plaintiffs, Tixier, representing the Forest Service, analyzed the controversy surrounding the trade calmly, point by point.

The Forest Service EIS process had sputtered to a halt without a workable result; the owner of Snowbasin remained adamant about his needs. And so Stan Tixier scheduled a time to meet privately with Earl Holding. He felt that "during mediation, the environmentalists came to accept that there would be an exchange. I acknowledged the Forest Service was in agreement that an exchange was appropriate. The question was 'how much do you need?'"

FOR TWO HOURS, AT LITTLE AMERICA in Salt Lake City, Stan and Earl talked across a conference table about the need "to get the darn thing settled and move on." Recalling this moment, Stan pushed aside his now tepid but still hot cup of coffee and Tabasco and leaned toward me across the knotty pine of his kitchen table: "They didn't need but about 150 to 200 acres to build their hotels and lodges. As I was going into the negotiations, I was thinking 400 acres. He was thinking 1,200."

Stan was looking for compromise that both parties could accept, so he made an offer: "We would do it with less than 700 acres. Earl agreed." This compromise resembled one of the alternatives sketched out in the EIS. "I thought that was a generous amount. That was my decision. It was appealed by the usual suspects. The Chief of the Forest Service upheld my decision. I retired, feeling the matter was settled, and Gray Reynolds came and replaced me."

Joan Degiorgio wrote the record of decision, emphasizing that the 695-acre compromise withheld many wetlands and earthflows from the trade and retained federal jurisdiction and protection over lands most in need of professional management. With each step away from the original EIS, however, Degiorgio had grown increasingly uncomfortable with her assignments; she found herself writing "like an actress," searching for language from well outside her own circle of beliefs. She finally asked herself, "Do I want to spend my energy and talents supporting these kinds of decisions?" Four months later she left the Forest Service.

———

Stan Tixier more than tripled the National Forest acreage that the representatives of the people of the United States pledged to transfer to Earl. Though Stan felt he had to take action, to unfreeze the stalled administrative process he inadvertently supported Earl's claim that development required the "quality terrain and dependability of snow" only to be found in the higher-elevation north slope of the Basin. The formal decision, released in September 1990, restricted Earl's management of wetland and earthflow areas and firmly stated that "The Forest Service will not allow any further exchange of lands adjacent to Snowbasin either to SVC [Earl's Sun Valley Corporation] or other parties."

Two-thirds of this new acreage was developable, but it lay in three different development zones. Sun Valley hated trying to fit their vision into this footprint, but finally told the Forest Service, "We can do it."

EARL WANTED TO VALUE SNOWBASIN as rangeland, at $200 to $300 per acre. The Forest Service was determined to value the land at its real value—as a finished resort. Earl never quite got around to finishing a new Snowbasin Master Plan to match the scaled-back 695 acres. He stalled—strategically. Without Snowbasin's Master Plan, the Forest Service could not identify exact boundaries for trade and could not begin the appraisal process.

As early as January 1991 Chris Peterson, speaking for Earl, started equivocating in the press; Chris now insisted that Earl had accepted Stan Tixier's 695-acre compromise "on the condition that a speedy and expedient resolution" of the appraisals and land exchange be reached. He claimed ominously, "that doesn't seem to be happening." Earl and Chris recapitulated the familiar litany: the resort wouldn't work with a base at Strawberry, where the season was too short, snowfall too low, and second-home owners wouldn't be able to ski right to the lifts on the Wheeler Basin side. They let no one forget their ultimate threat: if Snowbasin wasn't allowed to keep pace with the times, if their big land trade was not forthcoming, they would have to close the ski area entirely.

If the *old* Snowbasin closed, the Wheeler Creek Basin would simply melt back into the national forest and remain public land and community watershed. After a land trade, and if at some point an intensively developed Snowbasin Resort became a liability, Earl could always sell it, to anyone, for any legal commercial use.

Stan Tixier may have felt that he had resolved the Snowbasin issue, but Earl wasn't satisfied. No deal was final. He began looking for alternatives.

———

Earl Holding spent the first years of the 1990s maneuvering to advance his land exchange. The Salt Lake Olympic Committee continued to campaign for the Games. Their interests began to mesh when the committee decided to promote Snowbasin as the site of the 1995 U.S. National Alpine Championship races. The Olympic Committee had Earl's attention, and they gave him a seat on their board. While celebrity racers like Tommy Moe and Picabo Street promoted Snowbasin's potential for world class racecourses—increasing the visibility of Utah as an Olympic venue—Earl fanned the subtext: the need to develop his ski area.

To facilitate these imminent national championship races, the Forest Service agreed to shift its focus. Why not go ahead and finish the lifts and worry later about the details of mapping out the 695-acre land exchange? After all, as experts from both the Forest Service and the Olympics Committee testified repeatedly, no land trade was necessary for an Olympic downhill run at Snowbasin.

And so the Olympic course designer Bernhard Russi went to work in earnest on his plans for the John Paul Ridge. Snowbasin applied for a construction permit in January 1994. Ogden boosters offered free car washes and ice cream to anyone who would write a letter in support of the proposed construction. The Forest Service responded in June, approving the new lift and ski run in a draft environmental assessment. Plenty of critics took aim at these developments, most passionately a small group of partisans who called themselves the Citizens Committee to Save Our Canyons.

FOUNDED IN 1972, SAVE OUR CANYONS soon became the front line of resistance to unlimited development in the Wasatch. Alexis Kelner, a bearded scientific illustrator, photographer, writer, and designer who publishes backcountry ski guides to the Wasatch, cofounded Save Our Canyons in his living room. Kelner is as bright, forceful, and eccentric as Earl Holding, but he's driven by an entirely different set of values. He proudly takes credit for fourteen years of work to create the nearby Lone Peak Wilderness, the flagship preserve of the Endangered American Wilderness Act of 1978, landmark legislation that recognized the importance of wilderness adjacent to cities.

Kelner and his wife vacation in a 1953 U.S. Army ambulance that he has been restoring for years. He told me that he favors campsites where alien abductions have been reported, in the hopes that he might be among the chosen. The Kelners' Salt Lake City home—located barely a quarter mile from Earl's—is an ongoing project and has the feel of a dark, disused mountain hut under renovation. The day we met we talked surrounded by tools, wood, boxes, and plastic-covered furniture. I suspect that the room has looked like this for a long while.

Kelner described the Winter Olympics as "a juggernaut that rolls over everything—totally out of local control."

Save Our Canyons's other founder, Gale Dick, a retired physics professor at the University of Utah, is just as colorful and opinionated in his language as Kelner though a tad more conventional in his life. He remembers his galvanizing moment, thirty years ago, when he drove up Big Cottonwood Canyon and realized that a proposed widening of the road would lead to urban development in the mountains, that there was "something at stake and a lot to be lost."

He laid out his ongoing concerns: "The Forest Service is a very weak agency that will always interpret its own management plan in the way most favorable to consumptive use. They almost seem *part* of the ski industry." Gale Dick can sound almost conciliatory. He doesn't regard Earl and his cohorts as actively wicked. He concedes that they are involved in a business, but he believes that there has to be a countervailing force.

At the heart of the conflict is a little-known fact. Growth in the ski industry stayed flat for twenty years; only after 2001 did skier and snowboarder numbers in Utah begin to grow again. Given that there is at best a constant number of skiers, all U.S. areas compete for the same pool, and they do this by investing in new facilities and enlarging their boundaries. Since most ski areas operate by permit on National Forest land, their need to expand drags them repeatedly into direct confrontation with the environmental community fighting to curb development on public lands.

Gale Dick dreams of mountains *with* ski lifts but *without* a "totally rapacious" ski industry. Skiing should be just one of many legitimate uses of National Forests. As he says, "The public land simply doesn't belong to the ski industry." Certainly the public treasury doesn't gain much from ski areas on national forests. Two years after 1996 congressional "reforms," the rent

GALE DICK, 2007.

Snowbasin paid for its permit amounted to seventy-four cents for every one hundred dollars in sales.

———

When the 1972 Salt Lake City Olympic bid sparked Save Our Canyons into life, the organization had immediate and overwhelming public support. In a poll held in 1972 by the city's *Deseret News* a stunning 88 percent of readers said no to a Salt Lake Olympics, expressing concerns about pollution of the canyons and diversion of public money to an elite event. Seventeen years later, during a 1989 referendum in Utah to vote up or down on community support for the Games, Alexis Kelner participated in thirty-nine live debates to argue against what he called "Utah's Olympic Circus," "an ugly intrusion into the social landscape." Nevertheless, the referendum passed, Utah citizens voting 57 percent to 43 percent to use public funds (repayable after a profitable Olympics) to create potential Olympic venues.

The Save Our Canyons leaders came mostly from Salt Lake City, its thousand members a band of outdoor people, academics, lawyers, professionals, students, and writers devoted to Wasatch wilderness. Their issues were regional and national, centering on the use of public lands for commercial profit. One former Save Our Canyons Board member, Ann Wechsler, admitted to me, "I don't ever want the public to know how ragtag we really are!"

Ragtag they may be, but they are effective. Gale Dick believes that "you've got to have a love affair with the Wasatch Mountains to sustain you through the tedium of following the NEPA process for twenty hours a week for ten years. The resorts and the Forest Service could never enlist that kind of passionate volunteer effort."

Alexis Kelner and Gale Dick and their ragtag band took the stand that the Forest Service must write a full Environmental Impact Statement before allowing new ski lifts at Snowbasin. They believed that the Forest Service had failed to address avalanche hazards and paid insufficient attention to public input and potential environmental impacts. They kept returning to their touchstone: "We knew what the truth was. Why not keep saying it?"

Save Our Canyons vowed to fight Earl Holding on principle. The organization "fought tooth and toenail," as Earl put it in 2000. "They had us at an absolute standstill. We studied all the things we could possibly study over and over and over again. . . . We just went through the process, over and over again . . . it's been one of the great frustrations in my life."

WITH THE LAND EXCHANGE DORMANT and lift building in limbo, Snowbasin decided to go ahead and build ski runs. In the summer of 1995 the Forest Service granted Snowbasin's request for permits to clear new runs. Save Our Canyons called this one more depressing and deceptive end run around the public process of proper environmental assessment—"almost . . . a conspiracy." To formalize their opposition to the John Paul Ridge expansion, Save Our Canyons filed suit in U.S. District court against the Forest Service. Joro Walker, an attorney for Western Resource Advocates, volunteered to take on the case, driven by that same need to tell the truth loudly and repeatedly. She told her clients they had a 5 percent chance of winning. In a preliminary hearing in September 1995, after tough questions from U.S. District Judge J. Thomas Greene, the Forest Service ordered that Snowbasin's work on the new runs be halted until the suit was resolved.

Over the succeeding winter, Save Our Canyons traded memos and motions with the U.S. Department of Justice. Joro Walker was able to add documents to the administrative record describing avalanche danger on the John Paul Ridge as being well beyond the ordinary. As the court date approached, Walker tuned out the distractions of the daily news to concentrate and marshal her facts. A compact outdoorswoman with the long view and reserves of strength of a rock climber, she can see a good distance out along the route while still making the hard moves right in front of her.

On July 30, 1996, she presented the Save Our Canyons case. She argued that the Forest Service had ignored evidence of avalanche danger that posed a serious risk to the public's safety and that, moreover, the agency had failed to take a sufficiently hard look at the cumulative environmental impacts of all the proposed lifts. In closing she suggested that the Forest Service had not properly considered Earl's full plans for a destination resort before issuing lift-building permits.

To Walker's "awe," as she puts it, Judge Greene agreed. In an unusual, immediate decision he ruled for Save Our Canyons and ordered the Forest Service to redo the Environmental Assessment that had allowed lift construction and asked the agency to pay special attention to avalanche dangers, slope stability, wildlife, and future impact. In the interim all work was to come to a halt.

With her prior trial experience mostly in the frustrating arenas of civil rights law, Walker jokes about this being the first case she ever won—so cleanly, so clearly—"at least for a minute or two." "I had actually gotten across what I believed to be the truth," she told me. A philosopher before she was a lawyer, she is comfortable with words like *truth*. "I cared so much about the land," she went on, "not to say that this victory would have guaranteed its preservation. The Forest Service could redo the EIS and come back with the same conclusion. But this judge, this person with an incredible amount of power, cared enough to buck the trend." Power, she notes, is a commodity that environmentalists lack. "We have the *antithesis* of power: a connection to animals, land, beauty, nondevelopment, pristineness, nonextraction. These things don't speak power in the traditional terms of money and political connections."

Walker was euphoric after the hearing before Judge Greene. But she had only that brief moment to savor the triumph of truth in the courtroom before events required her to resume her role as a philosopher with an acute appreciation of irony.

Gale Dick sees this Snowbasin lawsuit as pivotal in the development of Save Our Canyons: "The Forest Service *has* to pay attention when you win a lawsuit." Dick is convinced that the National Environmental Policy Act (NEPA) is the one crucial tool that environmentalists have to affect decision making. The law directs agencies to write Environmental Impact Statements, evaluate alternatives, and address the impacts of development. The public has the opportunity to respond, comment, challenge, and, if need be, sue.

Save Our Canyons still patrols the Wasatch, racing from skirmish to skirmish, hoping to limit resort expansion. Gale Dick believes that "the fact that we had a successful suit at Snowbasin slightly affected the Master Plan at Alta. The fact that we pursued Alta and lost changed the Forest Service position on Snowbird. Our pursuit of Snowbird will affect the decision on Solitude. Results from your work are decades in coming, sometimes. It is *so* wearying. . . ."

———

Every time conservationists succeed in curbing development, the triumph is fleeting. The builders return, their plans reincarnated. Draining and subdividing the Everglades, drilling in the Arctic National Wildlife Refuge, damming the Colorado River, allowing off-road vehicles in the Mojave Desert, logging unsustainably, fragmenting roadless wilderness—the agenda for my generation of environmentalists has remained dishearteningly stable for decades.

Agencies issue environmental impact statements. Developers appeal. Citizens protest. NEPA has created a framework for public process, but the downside of this "procedural republic" is the slow grind to a frustrating, divisive, hostile, stressful island of impasse.

Snowbasin was no exception.

EARL HOLDING AT THE DEDICATION OF THE WOMEN'S DOWNHILL RACECOURSE, SNOWBASIN, UTAH, 1999.

THE RULES
OF THE GAME

The problem originates in the contest of clashing values
between society and capitalism.... In the economic
sphere, efficiency trumps community. Maximizing returns
comes before family or personal loyalty. What seems
priceless in one realm may be wasted freely or even
destroyed by the other. Human experience is sacred to
society, a marketable commodity in capitalism.

WILLIAM GREIDER, *THE SOUL OF CAPITALISM,* **2003**

EARL HOLDING WAS AFFLICTED by what he described as "a real nightmare" back
in September 1995. The federal court was demanding restraint, and Earl, the
man of action, was suffering. At just that moment, Utah Congressman Jim
Hansen happened to come to Sun Valley to speak to Earl and a gathering
of other oil executives. Earl has described driving back to the airport with
Hansen and commiserating over delays created by ill-tempered citizens:
"[Hansen] asked me how the trade was going. I told him it wasn't going
anywhere. And he said, 'I'd be glad to help with that. I believe in Snowbasin
being developed as a major ski area. . . .' And I said, 'I think we'll probably
get it through.' He said, 'Well, I just don't know . . . if you want me to
help, I'd be glad to.'"

Hansen had the power to help. When the Republicans had swept the
House in 1994 Hansen assumed the chairmanship of the House Resources
Subcommittee on National Parks, Forests and Lands. In 2000 Hansen
moved on to the chairmanship of the House Committee on Resources, making him The Wilderness Society's designated "number two national enemy," right after the controversial Secretary of Interior Gale Norton.

Though he had one of the most consistently antienvironment records in Congress, Hansen himself says, "I like to think that I have saved the environment from the environmentalists." But as he headed toward retirement in 2002 Hansen admitted to having mellowed in his twenty-two years in Congress. He insists that he has spent more time in the outback than most of his opponents. Though he generally ridicules efforts at wildland preservation, he considers himself a Teddy Roosevelt conservationist and likes to remind us that as bishop of his LDS ward he used to gather up the whole neighborhood for trips to nearby Great Salt Lake, instead of encouraging families to spend their weekly assigned evening at home studying scripture.

"I disagree with him about virtually every issue, but he has a certain sort of integrity," says Karen Shepherd, the former congresswoman from the Utah district next to Hansen's. "What you see is what you get. If he was mad, he was mad. If he was feeling cooperative, he was cooperative. Hansen is a good committee chair because he knows the rules of the game."

As a child, James V. Hansen joined his father on forays from Salt Lake City into ranching and mining country in the Utah deserts. At the age of twenty-eight he settled in Farmington, just north of Salt Lake City. When he couldn't persuade the semirural town of 1,600 to fix its water system, he ran for city council. Hansen spent the next twelve years on the Farmington council, then eight years in the Utah state legislature. Before his 1980 election to Congress he continued working as an insurance agent and as president of a land development company.

The geologist and educator Genevieve Atwood served with Jim Hansen in the Utah Legislature back in the 1970s. She was parliamentarian when he was speaker, and she found him fair and connected, willing to take on big guns like Geneva Steel over environmental issues. She says now, "I wish I had my old Jim Hansen back."

As a United States congressman Hansen made a habit of introducing brash (and unpassable) bills that attracted press attention. In just one year, 1995, he found himself in hot water after proposing an independent commission to ensure that no funding would go to "substandard" national parks. Next he lobbied for a bill that would have allowed forty ski areas to buy the national forest land on which they were operating with permits and to assume complete control over development. Undaunted by public outrage, he introduced a Utah BLM wilderness bill —quickly dubbed an "antiwilderness bill" by conservationists—that proposed opening undesignated lands for development while allowing gas pipelines, communications towers, and dams within congressionally designated wilderness. This bill so sweepingly endangered America's redrock wilderness that the national environmental community rallied to defeat it.

This wave of protest swept me to Washington—right into Jim Hansen's office.

TO SPEAK INTO THE EARS OF LEGISLATORS, to create a main line between our hearts and theirs, my friend and colleague Terry Tempest Williams and I appealed to our community of writers, collecting essays to counter Hansen's anti-wilderness bill. We created a chapbook of twenty passionate pleas for Utah wildlands and traveled to Washington, D.C., with *Testimony: Writers of the West Speak on Behalf of Utah Wilderness* in hand.

On a September day in 1995 Terry and I distributed copies of our book in the House and Senate office buildings, trying, as a matter of courtesy, to reach each member of the Utah delegation personally. Terry had church and family ties to Hansen. Courtly and cordial, he invited us in to his office for a few moments.

A huge painting of Lake Powell hung over the congressman's desk. He loved that painting of the reservoir—the one landscape in Utah most astonishingly modified by human engineering, where we drowned the wild heart of the Colorado Plateau to make a place for houseboaters to frolic and to store water for Las Vegas and southern California.

Jim Hansen adored Lake Powell. Lake Powell makes me cry.

He proudly showed off the painting, and I tried to be both polite and honest by noting that the artist had captured in the sandstone buttes *above* water a little of the spirit of Glen Canyon lying beneath the artificial lake. I don't think Congressman Hansen noticed my carefully chosen words. I'm also sure he never looked at *Testimony* longer than it took to dismiss it.

A call came in, and the congressman's secretary fed it through, apparently unaware that we were there. It was a Tooele County commissioner from back home, upset about those "envarmintalists" trying to block Hansen's bill. I could picture the commissioner, sitting in his office in what had once been a thoroughly rural outpost but was now a booming bedroom community for Salt Lake. His gaze out the courthouse windows would pass over the nerve-gas-filled bunkers of the Tooele Army Depot and beyond, toward the Wasatch Mountains to the east and into the space and silence of the Great Salt Lake Desert to the west. I could picture the man sitting there, caught between the Old West and the New West, unwilling to admit the full consequences of the vise in which he found himself.

Hansen, deeply uncomfortable, tried to deflect the caller, alert his secretary, and get off the line. Terry and I tried not to giggle at the irony of the scene.

The call could just as easily have been from Earl Holding.

ON THE DAY I JOURNEYED TO WASHINGTON with my public lands gospel—on the very day, September 27, 1995, that Terry and I stood in his office—Congressman Hansen acted on his offer to help Earl with his "nightmare" nemesis Save Our Canyons. Without a single cosponsor he introduced a House bill to grant Earl 1,320 acres of public land and set aside all requirements for administrative and judicial review for the development of Snowbasin. No more NEPA. No more meddling from Save Our Canyons—after this bill they would have no legal vehicle for appeal. No more nightmares for Earl.

Earl and his allies had come to the conclusion that they just weren't going to break through the grassroots opposition. The citizens of Utah simply knew too much about the mountain and its history, about the nature of the land, and about the real needs both of ski resorts and of the Olympics. So Earl and his people went to Congress, where they could sell their bill to politicians who wouldn't question what appeared to be a straightforward request to help Utah get the Olympic Games. Janine Blaeloch, at the Western Lands Project, has seen this scenario time and again: the sudden appearance of a high-stakes goal followed by demands for immediate passage of overblown "national security land exchanges."

Earl Holding sensibly engaged the Western Land Group in Denver to help write and manage the Snowbasin bill. The principals in this company had drafted the language in the Federal Land Exchange Facilitation Act of 1988, and the company's founder, Adam Poe, makes his living by assisting private clients with federal land exchanges. Soft-spoken and efficient, Poe sees himself as a realist. He believes that he is in "the business of improving the portfolio of the United States. I see no reason for the United States to own any land that's being used as a golf course, or a parking lot, or unusable lands topographically more aligned with private land."

Clint Ensign, Earl's lobbyist in Washington, told me that he met with both majority and minority staff as "the bill went through five or six iterations. Even in the Utah delegation they would highlight the self-published newspapers of the opposition and say to me, 'how do we deal with these issues?' We would have been happy to have a boundary for developable land that would have been less than 1,300 acres, but years of working with the

Forest Service had produced nothing like a workable solution. Nearly half those acres are unstable."

Even though I didn't vote in his district, I thought Jim Hansen would grant me an interview. He was, after all, an elected representative of the people. But he stonewalled the press, shielding himself from his opponents almost as successfully as Earl. He held no open houses or town meetings. He spoke only to friendly audiences: bow-hunters, off-road-vehicle groups, veterans, church gatherings, Rotary clubs. He never laid himself open to free discussion, and he turned down my request to talk with him.

Land exchange consultant Adam Poe laid out the Snowbasin issue from the perspective of the Utah congressional delegations: "Utah just got the Olympics. They want to get this construction through. They have a history of litigation and acrimony. The Olympics are a big deal, a national issue. And the best way to get through the appeals process is to run a bill."

So run it they did.

Stan Tixier was horrified. After negotiating the 695-acre trade with Earl he had retired from his regional forester's position in 1990 to sip Tabasco and coffee at his little Ogden Valley ranch in Eden. He had been waiting for details of the land exchange and was disappointed with the lack of news. And then in 1994 he suddenly began hearing about legislation that Snowbasin "needed" for the Olympics, which would bypass NEPA and double the acreage being traded. Tixier noted that this legislative coup came only after "Holding's backing party," as he bitterly sums up the Republicans, took control of Congress. The press now reported that the 695-acre compromise couldn't work because of the difficulties of administering wetlands and earthflows bordering the lands privatized in the proposed exchange.

The forest supervisor who had signed the original exchange decision, Dale Bosworth, never wavered from his belief that a 220-acre exchange was fair and right: "I'm very conservative in my viewpoint about trading out of national forest lands," he told me in 2003, when he had become Forest Service chief. "I don't ever want national forest lands to be for sale—even for other pieces of land that we really want."

But by the time Bosworth had returned to Utah to serve as intermountain regional forester from 1994 to 1997, his original decision had been set aside. The newly negotiated 695-acre compromise left islands of land that the Forest Service retained, like "holes in Swiss cheese," in Bosworth's phrase. This "didn't taste very good to anybody. The effects on the land were going to be the same as they would have been for the 1,300 acres, but it was just going to be harder to administer." Bosworth figured the people of the

United States might as well get the maximum number of quality acres in trade. His first choice—220 acres—was no longer an option. He decided that the 1,300-acre exchange was preferable to the 695-acre deal Tixier had made with Earl.

———

The text of Jim Hansen's Snowbasin bill rolled along unequivocally, with great clarity. No wonder that members of Congress from elsewhere in the country assumed that the statements must all be facts. Point 1: Snowbasin will host the Olympic speed events. Point 2: "major new skiing, visitor, and support facilities will have to be constructed . . . on land currently administered by the United States Forest Service." Point 3: "the base area facilities necessary to host visitors to the ski area and the Winter Olympics . . . should logically be located on private land." Quick and brazen, a take-no-prisoners opening.

Then the bill paused briefly to address issues that might be raised by naysayers: land exchanges were routine; lots of studies and EISs had already been done at Snowbasin; Sun Valley Company was ready and waiting with parcels to trade. And so remorselessly to point 7: "Completion of a land exchange and approval of a development plan for Olympic related facilities . . . is essential. . . . The Congress has reviewed the previous analyses and studies of the lands to be exchanged and developed . . . and has made its own review of these lands and issues . . . and on the basis of those reviews hereby finds and determines that a legislated land exchange and development plan approval is necessary to meet Olympic goals and timetables." And without further ado, without explanation or justification, the bill designated an exchange of 1,320 acres.

Hansen called the land swap noncontroversial, a "simple house-keeping measure" that was necessary for the Olympics. The day after introducing the bill he added Snowbasin to the agenda of a hearing on other matters; he invited only Snowbasin's general manager, the Salt Lake Olympic Committee chairman, and Gray Reynolds, the former regional forester in Ogden and now deputy chief, who was to testify for the Forest Service.

Orrin Hatch introduced a companion bill in the Senate and held a hearing in early November to which he invited the same witnesses, adding only one other person: Jake Garn, the Olympic booster, former Salt Lake City mayor, astronaut, and former Utah senator. An outraged and excluded Save Our Canyons could only submit a statement after the fact, asking Congress to limit the trade to between fifty and one hundred acres, no more than actually needed for Olympic facilities.

THERE WAS CONSIDERABLE FINGER POINTING. Hansen kept saying that the exchange was the Forest Service's idea. Hatch's aides passed responsibility to the Salt Lake Olympic Committee (SLOC), whose boss now announced that he needed the land for the Games. In his Senate floor statement supporting Hatch at the end of October 1995 the junior Utah senator, Bob Bennett, stated that "this legislation is fundamental to the success of the 2002 Winter Olympics." Senator Hatch was more candid. He told the *Washington Post* that he backed the bill "simply because of his long friendship with Mr. Holding and because it was a good deal for Utah."

A deeply disappointed Alexis Kelner of Save Our Canyons said, "Olympics supporters had promised there would be no land-grabbing shenanigans." Save Our Canyons reminded the politicians and public of the Salt Lake Olympic Committee policy statement of 1994, in which the committee acknowledged that "existing ski and recreation areas have substantially all of the facilities needed to host alpine and other events . . . and no new development . . . is required for Utah to host the Olympic Winter Games." The Olympic Committee respectfully requested that "all proponents of private projects in the mountains and canyons of the Wasatch Front, in their efforts to obtain governmental approval of such projects, refrain from asserting that such projects would assist the Committee in . . . hosting the Olympic Winter Games."

Congressman Hansen responded to Kelner and his fellow activists: "There's always a few people who get a bone caught in their throat . . . this is not showing special favor but doing something important for America."

In the first news story on the bill, on September 30, 1995, Forest Service Deputy Chief Gray Reynolds said that his agency supported the concept of the trade but could not comment on the legislation itself because it had not had time to review the new bill. From that moment on, the Forest Service quibbled about fine print and opposed the "sufficiency" language in the bill that exempted Snowbasin from oversight via the National Environmental Policy Act, the law orchestrating public involvement and legal challenge. But no Forest Service official of national rank again questioned the size of the swap.

The Forest Service staff in the field were caught off guard. On first hearing of Hansen's bill that week, the spokesman for the regional forester back in Ogden artlessly declared that the agency was perfectly happy with Stan Tixier's 695-acre exchange from 1990. Randy Welsh, who was Ogden district ranger in 1995, told me later that he had originally assumed that the Office of General Counsel in Washington prepared the legislation. He now can imagine that the legislation may have started with Adam Poe at the Western Land Group, who may have passed it to Gray. "We saw it and said, 'this is terrible legislation. It's so one-sided. There's nothing here for the public.' We proposed a bunch of changes, but they were all waylaid in the Forest Service Washington office and never made it to Congress. Snowbasin crafted the legislation with Hansen exactly the way they wanted it. We had *no* input." From the moment Hansen introduced his bill, the Forest Service staff people in Utah were out of the loop.

When Stan Tixier called Congressman Hansen's office and asked a staffer why the acreage had been increased, he was told, "Because the Forest Service suggested it. It wasn't our idea to increase the acreage. It wasn't Holding's idea. Gray Reynolds suggested it." Hansen has often repeated this statement, saying that he had no interest in Snowbasin until Reynolds came to him and said, "We need this for the Olympics." When Stan finished his conversation with the congressman's office, he gulped and said, "Okay."

This was the story available to the public. This was the story available in the press. It appalled nearly everybody concerned with public lands and civic ethics.

I had heard little about Gray Reynolds, but suddenly he began to figure in every anecdote. Environmentalists began to realize that once their appeals reached Reynolds, they went no further. In my efforts to pry open the doors to the smoke-filled rooms, I've found that Jim Hansen lives up to his reputation for straight shooting. He was prepared to help, as he told Earl on that day in Sun Valley. But Gray Reynolds was the driving force.

REYNOLDS LOOKS THE PART of an old-time forester, stereotypically gruff and stocky. The son and grandson of Forest Service men, his parents were from Ogden, but he grew up in Jackson, Wyoming. He first skied at Snowbasin when he was seven. Reynolds competed in the 1957 Snowbasin nationals, at a time when you had to hike to the top of the downhill and all the grooming was done with foot power, on skis. I've followed him off the top of the Olympic downhill on the John Paul Ridge; he still skis with the edgy confidence of a racer.

GRAY REYNOLDS, 1998.

Reynolds was well respected in the Forest Service and became regional forester in Ogden in 1991, just after Stan Tixier and Earl Holding agreed to the 695-acre trade. Soon afterward, in 1993, Forest Service Chief Jack Ward Thomas named him to be his deputy chief. Reynolds moved to Washington, fully expecting to be in line for the top job.

Gray Reynolds once lectured me about how activists misuse the National Environmental Policy Act. The way they use the law, he believed, twists its purpose: "Environmentalists are upset because they can't stop the land exchange. To them, NEPA isn't about information; it's about how to stop something."

I heard a rebuttal to his charge from the lawyer-philosopher Joro Walker while she paced the floor at Western Resource Advocates in a neighborhood Salt Lake City office building collegially shared by several environmental groups. Here piles of legal documents filed on behalf of the environmentalists who so annoy Gray Reynolds rest assertively on work spaces four feet off the ground because Walker likes to work standing up.

Reynolds was insistent. Why bother to protest when "the public *has* input, represented by the Congress of the United States? The *Congress* is a public process. The *President* when he signs something creates public bills." When I relayed this to Walker, she shook her head. "There is a deep philosophical problem here. The Forest Service prefers to trade away land if there's going to be a lot of development. So the public subsidizes competition between resorts. Do we really need more ski resorts? We just keep chipping away and chipping away and chipping away. . . . It's a shame that money and power always seem to be antithetical to preservation."

IN THE BUREAUCRATIC HIERARCHY, Gray Reynolds worked for Jack Ward Thomas, chief of the Forest Service. Thomas worked for Jim Lyons, Undersecretary of Agriculture for Natural Resources and the Environment. Clint Ensign, Earl's Washington lobbyist, directed his pleas for help to both Reynolds and Lyons.

Lyons told me that he had been meeting with Ensign before the introduction of the land exchange bill, trying to "expedite but not legislate" the exchange. When Lyons came to Utah on a fact-finding visit, Earl himself drove their four-wheel-drive vehicle to the top of Snowbasin, a bumpy drive that made Jim "considerably nervous." The undersecretary listened while Earl stood on the ridgeline and "painted a picture in words of how he saw the mountain transformed to an Olympic venue. His capacity to take a vision and convert it to reality—it's remarkable. He loves what he *does* with the mountain. Some people are just motivated by accomplishment." But the imperiousness of Earl and his people got to Lyons: "They were determined to do it their way from the get-go. And that's what troubled me."

Lyons objected to exempting Snowbasin development from the National Environmental Policy Act and remained convinced that the exchange could have proceeded through normal channels. President Clinton's Council on Environmental Quality backed him up. Nonetheless, Lyons believes that "through some clandestine arrangement" that did not include him "an agreement was struck" about the content of the legislation. Gray Reynolds began to move it forward.

He did so by insisting that Earl needed the extra acreage to create a "manageable boundary" with the forest. In his testimony to the Senate in April 1996 Reynolds argued that the Forest Service and Earl Holding could not identify a single "block" of developable land in the midst of all those mud flows and landslides in Tixier's 695 acres and that therefore Congress might as well give Earl the full acreage. "To make a long story short," he told the senators, "there is not a difference" between the smaller acreage of Tixier's and Holding's compromise and the full 1,320 acres. "They are the same."

Gray convinced Jack Ward Thomas, his boss, that the Forest Service needed to legislate Earl's exchange, and the two men went to Hansen. Hansen himself said to Jim Lyons, when the undersecretary visited the congressman, that "Gray Reynolds sat in that chair you are in and told me that they needed to legislate this or it would never get done."

———

The least political of any player in this drama, Jack Ward Thomas had fewer reasons to spin his recollections than anyone I spoke with. He remembers going up to Hansen's office with Reynolds along as his deputy to ask the congressman to legislate the exchange. He remembers having been asked to do this by Jim Lyons! But he so thoroughly believed in the rightness of that request that he can't say for sure whether it was Reynolds's idea or his own. "I suspect it was me—Mr. Pragmatic." But Lyons may have "been talking to Gray without talking to me. Lyons didn't necessarily follow channels. It could have been Gray who said, 'Legislate it.'"

Thomas is from Texas, where he started as a hook-and-bullet wildlife biologist; even after decades as a renowned research ecologist, university professor, and high-level manager, his language retains a tangy dose of Texas. He assumed that the Olympic Committee had the support of the administration. He assumed that "national prestige was on the line." He assumed that the exchange was "necessary for the Olympics." Given that baseline he knew that under standard process "if we run into any glitches we won't be ready in time."

He also believed that if you didn't cut a "good, clean, clear" deal, you'd be "dragged down with perpetual eternal half-assed connection with that ski area." He was ready to trade for land that would serve the goals of the Forest Service better and avoid the complications of managing wetlands entangled with the private land of the resort.

"I did what I thought was right," Thomas told me. "I carried out the instructions that I thought we received, which were crystal clear, and, I thought, well justified. If there is a booger in there somewhere, I don't know where it is."

———

On November 3, 1995, Earl submitted his long-awaited master plan, detailing mountaintop restaurants, thirteen lifts, and real estate on 1,300-plus acres. Gray Reynolds continued to testify that "the administration supports the objective" of the bill, which was "to expedite planning and development at the Snowbasin Ski Area in preparation for the 2002 Olympic Winter Games." With just over half of the Resources Subcommittee members present one day, and before they had heard anything from the opposition, Hansen passed the Snowbasin bill on a voice vote 22–0. In the Senate Orrin Hatch passed a matching Senate bill unanimously out of committee.

Hansen was poised to advance Earl's bill in the full House of Representatives; Hatch planned to follow suit in the Senate. Earl looked unstoppable.

IN THE MIDST OF THIS RALLYING OF POWER, the land exchange stalled, a target in a national battle over public lands.

Bill Bradley, serving out his last term as a New Jersey senator, was determined to pass legislation before he left to preserve Sterling Forest, a threatened watershed on the New Jersey–New York border. Bradley wanted federal matching money to create a state park. To precipitate action on the Sterling Forest, he put a hold on every natural resource bill, including the Snowbasin and Utah BLM Wilderness bills that Orrin Hatch was shepherding through the Senate.

Save Our Canyons sent their board member Ann Wechsler to Washington, D.C., at the end of February 1996 to take the facts about Snowbasin and the passion of the opposition directly to Congress. She knew her brief well, that no Olympics-related construction would require more than 10 percent of the proposed swap. That the proposal's extraordinary NEPA exemption set bad precedents for resorts. That the directive to appraisers to disregard Earl's ownership of thousands of acres of land at the base of the mountain would inevitably lead to undervaluing. And that the Utah delegation had prevented these facts from reaching Congress and had scheduled no public hearings in Utah.

Every congressional staff person Wechsler met told her that they found these to be important and perfectly reasonable points.

During the spring and summer of 1996, Congressman Hansen and Senator Bradley traded volleys across Capitol Hill. On the same July day in 1996 that Joro Walker argued Save Our Canyons' position before Judge Greene in federal court, Hansen passed the Snowbasin Land Exchange Act unanimously by voice vote in the United States House of Representatives.

But the parallel bill was stalled in the Senate. In the House, Hansen added the Snowbasin and Utah BLM wilderness bills to a gigantic omnibus bill that included Bill Bradley's Sterling Forest money—along with a host of other environmental proposals, mostly popular and uncontroversial, and pork for everyone. The Clinton administration pledged to support the Sterling Forest funding and a package to preserve San Francisco's Presidio but promised a veto if the omnibus bill were to include the Utah delegation's BLM wilderness bill; the administration also objected once more to the NEPA exemptions in the Snowbasin land exchange.

Attaching riders and combining bills is an old tactic, and with members facing election in the fall, the omnibus bill became a high-stakes arsenal to be stocked and restocked. In a whirl of deals and bluffs, issues were pulled, run separately, and returned to the growing behemoth of the omnibus legislation.

In the end, with Bradley's blessing, Hansen ran Snowbasin and Sterling Forest together as stand-alone legislation. The newly cast Snowbasin–Sterling Forest bill passed the House unanimously by voice vote on July 30. The Snowbasin part of this legislation was called the 2002 Winter Olympic Games Facilitation Act.

Tit for tat. "Power is spent like money, like we buy lunch, without shame," says former congresswoman Karen Shepherd. Because Bradley finally succeeded in killing Hansen's Utah wilderness bill, he relented on Snowbasin. But the Snowbasin–Sterling Forest package didn't make it to a Senate vote before the August recess. So it was back to the omnibus.

After members of Congress returned—and in an incredibly confusing series of parliamentary maneuvers that only an insider could understand or explain—the omnibus legislation moved along, swelling to 126 component measures. The Clinton administration listed a number of grounds for veto, including Snowbasin. Hansen responded by pulling dozens of measures, but he held on to Snowbasin. He made it clear that nothing would move unless Snowbasin were included. On Earl's land exchange he was implacable.

As Congress's fall adjournment inched closer with the omnibus legislation still pending, the Utah delegation successfully pressured the White House. Katie McGinty, chair of President Clinton's Council on Environmental Quality, told me that the Snowbasin legislation "was just shoved down our throats. There was not a substantive discussion. It was a 'swallow-it-or-we-were-going-to-be-blamed-for-Utah-losing-the-Olympics' kind of deal."

Dale Bosworth suggests another explanation for the Olympic boosters' single-mindedness: the specter of Denver's withdrawal from the 1976 Winter Olympics when Colorado voters had rejected the Games even after their boosters had won the bid. Bosworth suspected that underlying the wrangle was a "huge fear that if something like that happened again, we'd never, ever get the Winter Olympics in the United States again."

It's hard to understand Hansen's ferocity about the Snowbasin land exchange. He certainly gloried in a fight with environmentalists that he felt he could win. As for Earl and his willingness to suffer public denunciation for his ambitions, in Gale Dick's words, "he accepted the role of bad guy without flinching."

––––––––

The national media had made Earl into that bad guy. His proposed land trade started turning up in headlines in January 1996, accompanied by lists of his contributions to the campaigns of Jim Hansen and Orrin Hatch. The articles used phrases like "narrow special-interest issues," "special legislative benefits that are reserved for the most generous contributors," and "intense lobbying for their pet perks."

In the years leading up to the legislative fight over Snowbasin, Earl did what any wealthy businessman in twentieth-century America did. He gave tens of thousands of dollars to the campaigns of people who would support him politically. In 1993, when Orrin Hatch ran afoul of the Justice Department because of his involvement in the Bank of Credit & Commerce International scandal, the Holding family paid $30,000 toward the senator's legal bills. But, as former congresswoman Shepherd says, Hansen and Hatch didn't do favors for Earl for money. The businessman and the politicians simply live their lives entwined—politically, professionally, and culturally. "Earl Holding is one of the richest men in the country. He is one of the two or three most important people in Utah. He doesn't have to say much."

All the players fell enthusiastically into line. The Ogden City Council passed a resolution in support of the land exchange because they believed in the coming boom and hoped money would flow from Earl's investments to secondary development and to the city. Within the Forest Service, the battle rarely penetrated far past the office of Gray Reynolds, and never to personnel in the field in Utah. Regional Forester Dale Bosworth was briefed by the chief, Jack Thomas, and by his assistant, Reynolds, but Bosworth knew that everyone deferred to Reynolds because he was the Forest Service official in Washington who knew the most about Snowbasin and its issues. For the same reasons Reynolds was also the contact person for Earl Holding and Clint Ensign.

Bosworth laid out the case for Gray's credibility: "He had been regional forester with that 695-acre proposal, and he didn't believe that decision was very workable. Then he went back to Washington, D.C., as deputy chief. He's got an extensive background in the Forest Service as well as growing up with skiing, so he is one of the real experts in the Forest Service in downhill skiing. He had the belief that the mountain should be on the national forest, and the base should be managed by the private individual."

Gray Reynolds spoke for the Forest Service.

Over at the Salt Lake Olympic Committee the experts had said repeatedly that no land exchange was necessary for races to be run at Snowbasin. But Earl had promised that if he got his land swap he would build all the Olympic facilities at the venue. The racers would have their lifts and runs and snowmaking—on Earl's dime. In 1998 SLOC would contract with Earl to use these race facilities for just under $14 million, along with reserving his Salt Lake hotels for Olympic dignitaries. But Earl had committed to spending more than $73 million on developing Snowbasin (including lodges and restaurants unrelated to the races) long before the Olympic bid was certain. These figures were many times what it would have cost merely to prepare the courses for race day. The SLOC board chair told the *Wall Street Journal* that the land exchange was "very much in our interest because our budget is limited."

Earl Holding didn't buy off the power structure. He lived within that web of power in Utah—and much was assumed, unspoken, unchallenged. The powerful would help him win his land trade, and, in turn, he paid for the development of Snowbasin.

As the story played out in the national conservation community, Snowbasin acquired some of the code-word status carried by other American landscapes, from Hetch Hetchy—the Yosemite canyon dammed a century ago and mourned by John Muir—to Glen Canyon, the Colorado River canyon dammed in 1963, inundated by Lake Powell, and mourned by David Brower. The very word "Snowbasin" became a symbol of the struggle for the future of the American West.

Back home, the citizens of Ogden Valley refused to bow to Earl's power and Jim Hansen's bullying. They "knew the truth," a different truth than the one Hansen and Holding were operating on, and they vowed to keep on saying it until they won or lost.

MOUNT OGDEN AND SNOWBASIN FROM SUSAN MCKAY'S PASTURE, HUNTSVILLE, UTAH, 1998.

MUSEUM OF
IMPROPRIETIES

Only losers care about process.

JON MARGOLIS, *HIGH COUNTRY NEWS*, 2004

MARGOT SMELZER PERCHED on floral upholstery in her quietly elegant living room. She was fuming, dismayed by events on Mount Ogden, where power politics had overwhelmed the public process she reveres: "It isn't the fact that we're losing the most important place in our lives to spend our Sunday afternoons. It's just that I think what happened was wrong."

Huntsville, whose seven hundred citizens constitute Margot's "we," impersonates a New England village and is consequently a bit too bucolic and comfortable to measure up to the mythic West. This Utah hamlet perches on the shoreline created in the '30s, when the Ogden River spread out behind Pineview Dam.

In winter the reservoir forms a frosty white Rorschach, dotted with ice fishermen; in summer it sparkles—a mirror cut by swooshing water-skiers and roaring jet-skiers. Antique barns punctuate the hayfields surrounding the village and reservoir, and white-steepled St. Florence's Catholic Church stands at the base of the old Snowbasin Ski Area road. A romantic landscape of ridgeline and mountain forest hovers over an art historian's vision of a classical agrarian landscape below.

MARGOT SMELZER, OGDEN VALLEY ACTIVIST, AT HER HOME IN HUNTSVILLE, UTAH, 2007.

Margot Smelzer, sixtyish and delighted with her new knee replacements, lives with her husband in a lovingly restored white frame house nearly as old as the town. In her living room a crystal chandelier hangs above an Oriental rug; a set of *Encyclopedia Americana* lines the bookshelf. She has lived here across the street from the Huntsville Park for thirty years, returning to her childhood hometown to look up to the alpine skyline of Mount Ogden with pride.

Margot has an old-fashioned respect for the social graces. She always refers to Earl Holding and to Jim Hansen and Orrin Hatch by their honorifics. She doesn't find anything wrong with "Mr. Holding's" expanding Snowbasin, though "I know he could have made money on something tucked in. I don't think bigger is better." But when "Mr. Hansen" and "Mr. Hatch" took on Earl's quest to privatize public land they took the issue "right out of the hands of the people." Margot believes that's "immoral—that's all there is to it. I know life isn't fair, but when you have agencies giving public land to a land developer—I have never been so shocked as when the politicians got involved and shot it back to Washington." Margot, the still idealistic daughter of her old-time forester father says, "I thought the Forest Service was perfect. Now, I know they can be bought."

A neighbor stopped by to talk about weather and gardens. After he left Margot returned to her floral chair and her agitation about community ethics and personal honor: "You do what's best for the country, not for the individual. I understand a thousand times that you don't become a billionaire if you say, 'just give me this teeny bit and that's okay.' But why can't Mr. Holding make a few less million? Why does he have to have everything his way?

"He could have been Hitler or he could have been Mother Teresa. It didn't make any difference that he was *nice*. But good heavenly days, I just don't think it was *right*."

EVERY SMALL CHOICE CHANGES each person's course in the stream of life. Along the way we rub and slip around one another, eddying out and flipping backwards and darting into newly created openings—a crowd of toy boats racing downstream toward the future through the ripples of pebbles tossed randomly in our paths.

Sometimes it seems that powerful people like Earl Holding dig the determining trenches. All currents turn into their channels. It's so easy to rush along—go with the flow—saying we don't have time to fight. Only a jolt, an issue or a leader, can rouse us from lethargy to action.

Up in Ogden Valley, when Margot heard about the proposed "giveaway" of the Basin she held dear, she grew angrier and angrier. Though she hadn't realized it, she had been carrying the seeds of activism all her life.

Margot's father, Horace Hedges, was one of the Forest Service men who had reclaimed an overgrazed Snowbasin and tended to the health of the Wheeler Creek headwaters after the people of Ogden insisted that these lands move from private to public. She remembers planting trees up there with him when she was seven years old. "It was a celebration, because it was so terrible before. It had been stripped, and then became beautiful from all the planting. It was the pride of Ogden." Several thousand of those trees were planted as memorials to commemorate Ogden-area casualties in World War II, and the possibility that these trees would become private property concerned the families who still honor their lost men.

As a native of the arid West, Margot considers water sacred.: "This isn't just a mountain. It's a watershed." To prove her point that watershed protection must always come first on the mountain, she pulled out a letter written by the Wasatch National Forest supervisor in 1949 and read it aloud, growing ever more passionate and emphatic as she came to the end of the letter, a pledge by the Forest Service to keep "guarding the health of our citizens."

Though her father had died in 1959, Margot glowed when she spoke of him. "He was a natural caretaker—what the Forest Service should be. He taught me that you have to abide by laws. I felt I should go to these meetings in my father's memory, in his honor." She sighed: "I'm sure my father and I are environmentalists. But I don't belong to a club or go sit on a mountain." Her activism lay dormant, waiting for a quickening, for just the right moment to germinate. It took a charismatic leader who came to Ogden Valley in the spring of 1996 to inspire her to action.

This intemperate and intense young man named Bill Cain sparked both Margot's activism and a grassroots engagement in the community at large. Bill arrived in Ogden Valley with an unlikely resume for rural Utah—graduate student in computer engineering at the University of Utah, teacher of primitive survival arts, and facilitator of quasi-Native American Vision Quest retreats in the mountains. He had read about the plan to build a new lift at Snowbasin in 1994 and thought, "No one is going to challenge this in the entire state of Utah." He saw it as a "spiritual battle, good vs. evil. I felt I had to respond."

Bill Cain had been to Snowbasin only twice. But he believed that he had to challenge the expansion and slow it down until a coming forest master plan could deal with change more thoughtfully. If he didn't fight, didn't argue face to face with District Ranger Randy Welsh, he felt there would be no force for "common sense and balance and harmony" to counter the "evil" of "moving money, regardless of the consequences."

He delivered a fifteen-page critique of the lift proposal to the Forest Service in the summer of 1995. From that point on, the newspapers began quoting Bill Cain along with the other two principal opponents of Snowbasin expansion, the Ogden Sierra Club and Save Our Canyons. The traditional conservation organizations, though considered radical by their opponents, looked pretty staid by comparison with Bill.

Bill speaks emotionally of his childhood on two hundred acres in California: "It's impossible *not* to learn when you are in the woods, impossible not to know the pure peace, pure freedom, that you can only get through connection to the earth." About the development of Snowbasin he says,

"Calling this money-sucking black hole that seems to self-propagate *evil*—no less than a cancer upon the landscape—is not a judgment, it's just a statement of fact." And he talks about the "sad, sick waste" driven by Earl Holding.

As easy as it is to mock Cain's rhetoric and conspiracy theories, he is refreshingly candid and impressively willing to act on his passions. "I would get *so* angry at being lied to—to see people like Hansen, Hatch, and Bennett look people right in the eye and *lie*. People refuse to acknowledge what they see. It's a weird denial, like mass hypnosis. How can they keep re-electing these people?"

The members of the little organization in Ogden Valley he inspired in 1996, Save Our Snowbasin, still speak highly of him. They told me: "Bill was the catalyst." "He was a wild man, with more energy than five people." "I admire him so much. He's the one who lit the torch under me." "His wife must be the most patient woman in the world."

By the time Hansen and Hatch were moving the Snowbasin Land Exchange Act into conference committee in early May 1996, Bill was desperate to open the bill to public scrutiny. He enlisted three fellow students from a University of Utah biology class and stuffed every mailbox in Ogden Valley with a sheet announcing a public meeting at the Huntsville Library. That first meeting deteriorated into a standoff between Bill and Earl's spokesman, Chris Peterson. Bill offended the Holding contingent; some of them thought he must be on drugs. But this first bombastic meeting led to a second meeting one week later.

The flyer announcing this second meeting called for a "Save Our Snow Basin Coalition" and began, "Dear Friends and Neighbors: Don't let our community be overrun with Park City-type development. Let's preserve our rural life style and protect our community from developers, such as Earl Holding, who are only driven by greed and profit."

Many would have said, "The land exchange bill is already in conference committee in Washington, after passing in both Houses. It's too late." But citizens were aroused, and Cain's energy was contagious. He inspired idealism and commitment. And then he passed the mantle of leadership to several local women.

MARGOT SMELZER WAS AT THE CENTER of this circle of women. She had been willing to accept a 695-acre land exchange, to sit back and be a watchdog, because that compromise "was done through the public process." But the subsequent end-run to Congress appalled her, and she started going to her

BONNIE COOKSON BESIDE HER BELOVED OGDEN RIVER, 2007.

neighbors with petitions. She stood toe to toe with Chris Peterson in meetings. She called her friend Bonnie Cookson, who had recently retired from teaching sixth grade in Ogden Valley.

Margot saw Bonnie as a more public person than herself. Where Margot is a softie, Bonnie is more brusque—she had to control those sixth graders, after all. Bonnie agreed to introduce the speakers at the second meeting, vowing that since she had taught her students that "bad government happens when people do nothing" she had better take a stand on an issue that mattered to her. And this issue mattered a lot. She and her husband had raised their four children in a house along the rush of Ogden River, deep in the canyon below the mountain, "where we live just a little closer to God. There was always something wild in our yard: all the neat plastic toys don't quite equal what Mother Nature can provide."

Bonnie was beside herself with emotion when she spoke with me on a late summer's day in 1998, sitting in a window seat, sun pouring in over the shoulder of the mountain: "How did it happen? It's all awry, it's frightening. This is just such a tremendous loss—to give public land to a private individual. I can't believe adults would do that to future generations. If this had gone through legitimately, I'd have a broken heart. But it wouldn't have left this sense of betrayal."

––––––––

At that second meeting in the library, Bill Cain divided the gathering into groups representing each local community, and he asked each to come up with a plan, to elect two people to speak for them, to "take the action, send out the alarm." He was "almost swaggering around the room," he remembers, thrilled by the high level of energy. Once the locals were aroused, he withdrew.

The remaining twenty-five or so members of Save Our Snowbasin, mostly women, continued to meet—"this small, disheveled, unorganized group," in Bonnie Cookson's words. Looking back, Bonnie says that they didn't have "a good, firm root system" until the Democratic challenger to Jim Hansen spoke strongly against the Snowbasin swap and helped give the group a focus. At that point Save Our Snowbasin began to plan in tandem with the campaign to try to unseat the longtime incumbent.

In mid-June the group sponsored a rally in front of the Ogden Federal Building. One "determined little old lady in tennis shoes" wouldn't give her name to the reporter who covered the protest, but she dressed as the Grim Reaper, with a placard over her chest that said THE LAND SWAP MEANS DE-STRUCTION AND CONTAMINATION. PLEASE LEARN THE TRUTH. Save Our Snowbasin's stand took on gravitas when major national environmental organizations joined them in sending formal letters to Congress to oppose the land exchange.

––––––––

Balding, bearded, and scholarly, Jim Hasenyager, an Ogden attorney who has lived in Huntsville for twenty years, became the formal spokesman for Save Our Snowbasin. Before traveling to Washington, D.C., in September to discuss the mountain with members of Congress, he wrote a cogent six pages titled "The Truth about the Snowbasin Land Exchange Act, H.R. 2402." Here he suggested a practical alternative: why not construct one new lift high on the mountain, providing access to the downhill run for the Olympics—and allow the land exchange to follow normal administrative process? He concluded: "No man or woman, regardless of wealth or political influence, should be above the law."

Hasenyager told me that the reaction of the members of Congress was straightforward: "Wish we'd known this sooner." Ann Wechsler, of Save Our Canyons, had received a similar reaction that preceding February. Hasenyager shook his head ruefully; it looked like Jim Hansen may have been right and that indeed "it was too late" to stop the Snowbasin bill. It was clear, too, that the Clinton administration had other plans to counter the antiwildlands forces in Congress.

ON SEPTEMBER 18, 1996, PRESIDENT CLINTON took historic action that would complicate all Utah land management issues for years afterward. Standing on the rim of the Grand Canyon in Arizona and looking gingerly northward into hostile Republican territory in Utah, Clinton signed an executive order that created the Grand Staircase–Escalante National Monument on 1.7 million acres of Utah BLM land. This act triggered an outburst of wonderfully theatrical posturing by every Utah politician.

Clinton's executive order thrilled me, for I deeply believed in the preservation of these public lands. If the locals didn't understand their national significance, I was more than willing to go with a top-down assertion of power. My glee was tempered, though, as I noticed similarities in the language used by Ogden Valley farmers and southern Utah ranchers. I had sympathized with the Ogden Valley folks who protested Earl's application of power. I dismissed the southern Utah folks who protested Clinton's application of power. In one story I was with the powerless, in the other I was in league with the powerful. My inconsistency troubled me.

––––––––

The Snowbasin bill came up for its last bit of wrangling. In the course of back-room politicking, the administration withdrew its objections, telling the opponents of the Snowbasin land swap, with regret, that the president, having proclaimed the national monument, couldn't veto Earl's bill and "hurt" the Utah delegation twice in two weeks.

Members of Congress deferred to Hansen, the local representative and the committee chair. They deferred to Gray Reynolds as the voice of the affected agency. And, of course, they had all the facts only if their staffers communicated what they had learned from citizens protesting the bill.

At the last possible moment before the fall recess the Omnibus Parks and Public Lands Management Act of 1996 passed in the House late on Saturday, September 28, with a vote of 404 to 4; the bill passed unanimously in the Senate on October 3. The legislation encompassed 113 projects from 41 states; the Snowbasin Land Exchange Act was Section 304 of more than 1,000 sections in the bill. When President Clinton signed the act into law on November 12, 1996, Utah Senator Bob Bennett said, "It removes the last cloud over the Olympic Games in Utah," a statement heavy with irony given the scandals to come. By the day of the signing, Jim Hansen had been elected to his thirteenth term.

Earl Holding, with stalwart support from the Utah delegation and from Gray Reynolds, had succeeded in confounding all his opponents. Hansen and Hatch had been happy to support Earl; passing the Snowbasin bill not only advanced their interest in promoting development and business but also gave them a chance to thumb their noses at the environmentalists they detested.

Undersecretary Jim Lyons sounded much like Margot Smelzer when he summed up the Snowbasin legislation: "Money and power equals influence in Washington, D.C. Snowbasin is a good example. You had people of influence, people with resources, and people with motive, who were going to make things happen. Their way. And they did."

In speaking with Jim Lyons and Jack Ward Thomas, I had the strong sense that these two were honest men trying to do the right thing—to honor the law and stay true to the interests of the people. Thomas is a wildlife ecologist by profession, and Lyons is a policy expert, more political and more "eastern." But consider where each went after leaving government service: Thomas now teaches at the University of Montana—where, he observes, "pontification without responsibility is a hell of a deal"—and Lyons rejoined the faculty of the Yale School of Forestry after a stint as director of the Casey Trees Endowment Fund, a nonprofit with the mission to "regreen" Washington, D.C.

Joro Walker, Save Our Canyons's lawyer, laments the land exchange act as "an awful way to go about things. It preempts environmental laws. It preempts judicial review. No base facilities at all were built at Lillehammer for the 1994 Winter Games. You need a lodge maybe, bathrooms for sure. But condos? Golf courses?"

For twenty-five years Save Our Canyons believed that good would prevail most of the time. After all, the Forest Service owned 80 percent of the mountains. And meager water rights placed sharp limits on development. These two reassuring facts seemed considerably less incontrovertible when

Congress traded public land for single-family homes, the equivalent of allowing Earl to buy the mountain. Snowbasin embodied a sea change in environmental faith.

Earl Holding plays clever chess. He sacrifices few pieces and protects his king. It's easy to see Earl as the black king, the public as the white, and the Forest Service as a docile platoon of ineffectual but decent pawns. Except for Gray Reynolds.

In the Clinton administration Gray Reynolds had both the wrong politics and the wrong language. When I asked him what was at stake at Snowbasin, he said that what mattered most was "how well development meets the long-term needs of the American public, their ability to use the mountain." He went on to say that the national forests were "key to the rural development of this nation and to the wise use of natural resources. The agency provides a key partner to development."

For the greenest officials in the Clinton administration—Jim Lyons, Bruce Babbitt, and Al Gore—Reynolds's invocation of "use" and "development" occurred much too often. And "wise use" was code for commodity extraction. Lyons focused on this when he described his relationship with Reynolds: "He was very committed to commodity production, had a real timber focus—more traditional in outlook. We were good friends early in our professional interactions, and then came a great deal of friction."

During that time of friction, the administration asked Forest Service Chief Jack Ward Thomas to replace six senior staffers, among them Gray Reynolds. Thomas asked why, for he was not displeased with their work. When given no persuasive grounds for dismissal, Thomas refused to do it, and he informed the administration that if they acted despite his protest, he would resign. "They"—as Thomas always refers to the executive branch appointees above him—backed off.

———

Jack Ward Thomas retired, coincidentally, the week after the Snowbasin Land Exchange Act passed in October 1996; Mike Dombeck replaced him the following January. As chief, both men considered ecosystem management to be the foundation of Forest Service policy. Their approach didn't mesh with Reynolds's more extractive philosophy, and after Clinton's 1996 reelection, Gray was pushed out against his will. When Jack Thomas called to extend his sympathy, Reynolds was in tears.

Gray Reynolds retired from the Forest Service on February 28, 1997. One week later he accepted a new job as Snowbasin general manager.

THE MEMBERS OF SAVE OUR SNOWBASIN were devastated by the loss of the Basin and outraged by what they saw as Reynolds's defection to the enemy. They had become activists not because of the proposed developments but because of the stymied public process. Although each of these men and women had a personal relationship with the mountain, they spoke not as wilderness warriors in from weeks in the backcountry but more like colonial patriots, on fire with civic and moral outrage over the breaking of a sacred covenant between government and citizenry.

The modern environmental movement grew out of nineteenth-century romanticism and a growing awareness of the closing frontier. We had settled on our creation myths; by fighting for wilderness, we protected these sacred origins. And if wild country was sacred, then the agencies upholding the public trust had by God better do a good job of protecting our inheritance, our Eden. As environmental historian William Cronon writes, "The myth of Eden describes a perfect landscape, a place so benign and beautiful and good that the imperative to preserve or restore it could be questioned only by those who ally themselves with evil."

Gray Reynolds made such an alliance when he "gave away the land," in the words of one Ogden Valley grassroots activist. "He was totally bought out. It's like having the general of the army protecting you go to the other side. It's betrayal." Another local observer called him "the whore of Babylon."

Reynolds accords multiple use the importance of a religion, which is why he could jump from the green Forest Service flagship to Earl's luxury liner and remain unapologetic. Any accusations of *quid pro quo* rile the Sinclair men. They swear that there was no conflict of interest, that he is a man of principle and integrity, and that they were completely surprised when he left the Forest Service. Earl Holding told the press that he contacted Reynolds shortly after learning that he had left the Forest Service (it must have been a short time, indeed): "He's a bright, intelligent, well-educated man. He'll really fit our outfit extremely well." Clint Ensign, Earl's Washington point man, told me, "We fully expected that Gray would be the next Forest Service chief. There had never been a political appointment. We were completely surprised when he left the Forest Service." They had simply offered a good man a good fit.

Looking back, Jim Lyons was careful in his choice of words, calling Reynolds's change in employment simply "the ultimate irony" of the Snow-basin story. When Reynolds spoke about this controversy with me, he said: "I really don't care what the press thinks. I've been as ethical as possible." He went on to say that he believed the exchange was "in the best interest of the public."

Jack Ward Thomas defended Reynolds's choice. He may disagree with him on policy, but he values the man. "It looked bad, but there was nothing illegal about it. If you were Earl Holding, and you wanted to hire somebody to make that work—here's a guy that was an Olympic quality skier, knows skiing, used to be there in the area as regional forester, knew the drill, knew the Forest Service, a very personable guy who knew everybody in the community—so you pick up the phone and say, 'Hey, you want to come to work for me?' He didn't want to leave the Forest Service. And he damn sure hadn't cut any damn deal."

Susan Giannettino, who had worked with Reynolds as Wasatch-Cache Forest supervisor when he was regional forester, summed up his motivation more simply than anyone else. "I don't believe Gray felt he was being political. I believe Gray felt that he was doing what was appropriate for the Forest Service and, frankly, for Utah and the community and the Olympics." She emphasized the old racer's love of skiing, remembering going with him to visit the six ski areas whose lands she managed: Reynolds would "just disappear down the mountain going a hundred miles an hour on these incredibly long old-fashioned skis." She would keep snowplowing and eventually catch up.

In Giannettino's words, "he placed *very* high value on the importance of being a partner with the ski industry because of where he came from—his passion for downhill skiing. It doesn't surprise me that Gray would be more willing to listen to an argument that you really need all these acres to be able to support the appropriate development of a ski area than somebody like me or Stan Tixier or Dale Bosworth."

If "evil" can be found anywhere in this story, as Bill Cain insists it can, it's evil at its most banal. A remarkably simple principle drives this wide-ranging parable: Gray Reynolds made Earl Holding's land exchange happen because Reynolds loved to ski.

FUNDAMENTAL SYMBOLS SWIRL in the waters of Wheeler Creek as it flows from Mount Ogden through the Basin. The Mountain: pilgrims climb mountains and come back with fire in their eyes, holy books, and messages from

WHEELER CREEK, LIFELINE OF MOUNT OGDEN AND DEFINING FORCE OF THE
SNOWBASIN LANDSCAPE, 1998.

God. Water: purity, our lifeblood, our essence, the major part of who we
are. The Forest: symbol of the wild and forbidden, sheltering Trees of Life,
Trees of Knowledge.

At first, European colonists saw the New England forest as pagan, dangerous, and terrifying. As they cleared their way westward, they turned into
romantics, which spawned a sentimental literature of the woods epitomized

by James Fenimore Cooper's Natty Bumpo and disappearing Mohicans. When the colonists encountered the uncut woodlands of the West, they felt that God had given them a second chance.

It's a short leap from thinking of the Basin as a lovely natural place to thinking of it as holy. In this "vegetable theology" traced by Simon Schama in his *Landscape and Memory*, the forest "is the tabernacle of liberty, ventilated by the breeze of holy freedom and suffused with the golden radiance of providential benediction." Other biblical words occur in the lexicon of Snowbasin. *Covet. Trespass. Bear witness. Honor.*

Any number of people have told me that they felt a religious reverence when skiing on Mount Ogden at the old Snowbasin. Generations of locals had invested in a relationship with the mountain when they learned to ski here, created public lands from reclaimed private lands, and made pilgrimages to their communal mountain sanctuary.

Sharon Holmstrom, an English teacher at Snowcrest Middle School in Ogden Valley, admits to being unreligious. And yet she took on a serene glow when she revealed, almost in a whisper, what she feels while riding into Mount Ogden Bowl on the Porcupine Chairlift: "For me, God sits right up there on the ridge at the top of Porky and smiles at the skiers. On a day with a skiff of powder and sun shining through golden snow crystals, everyone grins: 'Just another lousy day in Paradise.' . . . The mountain itself is a character. Just the way it sits—it has its backside to the population center of the state—it's a private mountain that smiles in upon itself. We're in Paradise and the rest of the world doesn't know it. There's a real sense of ownership."

In one of his "Outdoors" commentaries in the *Ogden Standard-Examiner,* columnist Jim Wright captured Earl Holding's breathtaking authority in an ironic description of a game played by Snowbasin visitors. Wright called the game "Earl Rules," employing the verb function of *rule.* In his imaginary competition players take turns bantering back and forth:

"Wonder if Earl knows his beaver built a new pond on Wheeler Creek."
"You mean Earl's Creek?"
"Technically, guys, this is Earl's Pond on Earl's Fork of Earl's Creek."

Wright played with the idea of naming everything after Earl. His satire climaxed with the sentence "Surveys show that less than 25 percent of Northern Utahns actually believe Earl is God, so only one or two of us really thought those were Earl's clouds. Earl's mountain, sure, but not Earl's clouds." Wright protested that the game went over the top, even in jest, when players moved on to "In the beginning, Earl . . ."

———

Earl Holding had wanted the Basin, and the politicians and Forest Service enabled him to have it. It took twelve years. But Earl won. And the politicians won. Olympic administrators won. Business won. And now Earl also had Gray Reynolds.

The Forest Service still trusted Reynolds; older Forest Service veterans tell me that they believe him to be "a tremendously ethical man," one of those old-time foresters with green underwear and green socks. Another summed up his role as "a nice guy who did a bad thing." Reynolds's lifetime of contacts and goodwill at the highest levels eased Earl's path at every step.

Many citizens felt that they had lost. It's like the famous line from Supreme Court Justice Potter Stewart, who would not define obscenity but knew it when he saw it. Ordinary citizens believe that Earl crossed an ethical line here; even if what he did was legal, they know in their gut that it was wrong. Over and over, discussions of the Snowbasin legislation ended with the emotional lament "I just didn't think it was right!"

Genevieve Atwood, a fifth-generation Utahn, former Utah state legislator, and former Utah state geologist—a non-Mormon "Big-Tent Teddy Roosevelt Republican who likes Ralph Nader"—speaks about these issues with relish. Italics don't do justice to Genevieve's delivery. She is emphatic, exuberant, and collegial in her delivery: "The currency of government is *trust.* The currency of private enterprise is *money.*" She loves to talk, and almost sings her best lines. What happened here, from Atwood's perspective, "was a bullying. It makes me trust government less. Pressures were put on ordinary people, who have a normal distribution of courage. And not everybody is courageous."

The most succinct summary of this long, troubling narrative came from Gale Dick of Save Our Canyons: "Snowbasin is a museum of improprieties."

KENT MATTHEWS, SNOWBASIN MOUNTAIN MANAGER, SUPERVISING THE
TRACK HOE PIONEERING THE ROAD TO THE TOP OF THE JOHN PAUL SKI LIFT,
MOUNT OGDEN BOWL, 1997.

TRACK HOE

The destiny of man is to possess the whole earth; the destiny of the earth is to be subject to man. There can be no full conquest of the earth, and no real satisfaction to humanity, if large portions of the earth remain beyond his highest control.

JOHN WIDTSOE, *SUCCESS ON IRRIGATION PROJECTS,*
1928

I DROVE UP THE NEW JOHN PAUL road with Snowbasin mountain manager Kent Matthews in his corporate vehicle, a weathered Ford Bronco that should have quit running years ago. Near treeline, we parked and watched the road builders blade the last few turns of the route, creating the high-elevation access the lift builders would need.

I watched the track hoe operator position the teeth of his bucket before slicing irrevocably into pristine alpine turf. He was opening a swath to the top of the knoll where the upper terminal of the John Paul lift would stand. The smells of virgin earth and sun-warmed fir and diesel fumes mingled in the air. Matthews was delighted with the success of the efficient, powerful machines, thrilled that there was dirt for his roadbed under these rocks.

I knew Kent Matthews cared about the mountain. I understood that a new lift was necessary for the downhill race. I knew that I would love skiing this ridgeline. But I couldn't shake the feeling that I was witness to a crime.

BACKCOUNTRY SKIERS HAD BEEN SLIPPING away quietly to the John Paul Ridge for decades. No major cutting or grooming had taken place since the local race committee grubbed out a national championship downhill course for a single season in the 1950s. To reach the John Paul, a skier had to climb up through Mt. Ogden Bowl from Porcupine Lift. After a half-hour's stomping through snow, the John Paul felt like backcountry.

The transformation of the mountain began in the spring of 1997 following passage of the Snowbasin Olympic Facilitation Act and its exemption from NEPA. Kent Matthews directed the first cuts on the John Paul downhill course, starting with a fifty-foot clearing down its center. A track hoe and CAT bulldozer cut three new mountain roads to the 9,000-foot ridgelines. Matthews asked the operators to "do as little as possible but enough to make that road drivable." He was "tickled" at their success and insisted that the track hoes—45,000-pound backhoes on dozer treads— were "dainty" in their work. "It's all the earthwork and all the snowmaking that's going to hurt it, not the track hoes." Come fall he would revegetate every scar on the mountain with a first seeding. The Forest Service watched his every move.

He had marked course designer Bernhard Russi's vision on the ground from his skis, tying orange flagging tape onto the midsections of aspen saplings that poked through the snow. Kent needed to do this before summer arrived and the John Paul Ridge grew its fresh tangles of maple and ninebark and alder shoots in what he calls "the jungle zone." Kent has been building and revegetating and caring for these slopes since his childhood in nearby Huntsville, when he and his four brothers had worked for his father, Dale, Snowbasin's mountain manager before him. At sixteen, "young and crazy," Kent Matthews was clocked at seventy-three miles per hour on the 1957 downhill course off the summit of Allen Peak, the same headwall used as the men's Olympic start; that year the winners went five miles per hour faster.

Matthews spent more than thirty years working with the mountain, missing only three years when he couldn't bear to watch Pete Seibert drive the area into bankruptcy. Earl Holding—whom he describes as "one peach of a guy"—talked him into coming back. Now he bridles a bit when young forest rangers new to the area, and ski area managers who work in shirts and ties, tell him what to do from urban offices. He describes with pride the paths of Snowbasin's lift lines and trails, both old and new: "That's all mine."

Headed toward sixty, Matthews shows sun-leathered skin between the collar of his cowboy shirt and the rim of his tractor hat. He is a nonpracticing Mormon who swears a bit and jokes with the construction workers, speaking with the cadence of John Wayne when he does so. He works a topic, coming at it with phrases from several sides, much as he works with the quarter horses he breeds.

He doesn't come right out and fume at environmentalists who criticize ski area development, but an edge of defensiveness creeps into his voice when he addresses their concerns: "We all have a mentality of being gentle with the mountain. In 1979, when I did the Middle Bowl lift and trails in one summer, I was half sick, wondering if there was any way it would be restored. We worked hard to restore that. When someone tells me nothing has been done here, I smile. That puts a smile on my face."

BY THE END OF JUNE 1997 NINE GRIMY MEN AND WOMEN had made the first cut for the men's racecourse. Plagued by deerflies and mosquitoes, slicing into wasps' nests, keeping an eye out for aggressive moose, they lugged their chainsaws up the route designed by Bernhard Russi and flagged by Kent Matthews.

This was a drama I could take in. By the time I had chatted with two members of the crew, Vicki and Shawn, I had interviewed nearly a fourth of the work force. Each day these men and women completed tangible, straightforward tasks and moved the downhill course an increment closer to completion. But they weren't likely to receive complimentary tickets to the Olympic races. The work was too hard, crew turnover too frequent. They would collect their seven-dollar-an-hour paychecks and move on.

Whenever the trail crew stopped for lunch and crawled under a tarp stretched from their truck, shielding them from afternoon thundershowers, they looked down the 65 percent grade at the bottom of the course past freshly cut aspen stumps and lopped-off brush to the lapis of larkspur spangling a meadow. A dirt road skirting the base of Mount Ogden bisected the meadow and passed a lone white fir that marked row 1 of the stadium that would seat 15,000 spectators cheering themselves hoarse in 2002, less than five years away.

Ten thousand more spectators would line the course. An additional 300 million people would turn on their televisions to watch what these laborers had begun, and it would take 2,500 people to manage the event. Shawn and Vickie's workplace would become the stage for a hundred dreams in 2002, when the Winter Olympic downhill and super-G racers would thrill us with their ecstatic, barely controlled freefalls down the John Paul racecourses.

Bernhard Russi was the bridge between the workers clearing his course and the moment when Snowbasin would become a television location; his work linked the old Snowbasin, with its cadre of multigenerational partisans, and the new Snowbasin, the Olympic venue where racers take the mountain and move on. Russi remained sensitive to the tugs in both directions; he respected the mountain while fulfilling his mandate to prepare Mount Ogden for the race of its life.

BERNHARD RUSSI UNDERSTANDS HIGH DRAMA. The Swiss racing star was the smoothest and most technically adept downhiller of his generation. He won the 1972 Winter Olympic downhill in Sapporo, Japan, but lost four years later to Austria's Franz Klammer. At that 1976 Innsbruck race Klammer was racing in front of his entire worshipful country and simply had to win, doing so with a legendary beyond-the-edge performance that left silver-medalist Russi shaking his head in astonishment at what arguably became the most famous downhill run of all time.

These days Russi designs smooth and technical downhill courses. He told me that he gasped when he first saw Mount Ogden. It was a perfect mountain for the ultimate downhill line.

The men's course begins on the ridgeline of the Mount Ogden massif at 9,289 feet on Allen Peak and plunges down a 72 percent grade before easing into a long traverse before the first jump. "At the top they'll be going ninety miles an hour, faster than a Formula One racing car," says Russi. "It's triple or quadruple diamond. BLACK!" Olympic downhill skier Tommy Moe takes the automotive analogy a step further: "You're pretty much your own race car."

Russi combines boldness and restraint in his work. "The more we touch, the more we lose—not just in terms of ecology but in terms of racing." He still looks dashing. When he met with the Forest Service and Snowbasin and Olympic committee staff to discuss the course, he took control of the room. His lanky body unfolded and every person deferred to him. One Olympic staffer called him "the Michael Jordan of Switzerland."

The Forest Service managers had taped a map of his racecourse to the window of the old Snowbasin lodge. We looked from Russi's craggy face—his overbite just toothy enough to eliminate him from a starring role as a Swiss Yves Montand—to the marker lines on the map and, beyond, through the windows, to the green glades and groves of the Mount Ogden massif. Eager to reassure the foresters, Russi launched into narrative, with occasional small, charming fractures in his earnest English: "Building a downhill is more than mountain planning. We don't want to put the shape on the paper, we want to do it on the mountain. The flow of the whole downhill

BERNHARD RUSSI EXPLAINS HIS DESIGN FOR THE OLYMPIC RACE COURSE, 1997.

course is right. It's very natural. All you have to do is put the puzzle to-gether and follow the flow of the mountain, the bowls, the ridges, the tree islands, the timbers."

In late summer 1997 Russi spent three days on the mountain, walking up and down both the men's and women's courses, imagining where to set gates. Everywhere he decided to widen the course or make a change, he did so for reasons of safety, to make room for netting. All the while he kept tipping his head from side to side, as he calibrated the angles, recording them in his pocket notebook. He began to name sections of the course, the Diamond Bowl, the Gold Bowl, the Silver Bowl; a nasty side-hill traverse he christened *Hölle*, hell in German.

By Olympic race day in 2002 we had abandoned Russi's appellations and applied our own American myths to the place. And so the course came to be the "Grizzly Downhill," named after Old Ephraim, an enormous animal—one of the last grizzlies in northern Utah—who had been killed not far away in 1923. The sheepman who had matched wits with the bear for ten years said later that if he had to do it over again he would not have trapped Old Ephraim—the animal had been too magnificent. In the end the names on the downhill course came not from Bernhard Russi's imagination but from the lore of bears and mountain men: Ephraim's Face, Flintlock Jump, Hibernation Hole, Rendezvous Face. The women's Wildflower Course ran through Sego Start, Shooting Star Jump, Paintbrush Meadow, and Columbine Turn. Both courses preserved the name of the original ridge in the John Paul Traverse. A tree spared by the designer became "Russi's Lone Pine."

———

While the course was under construction Russi returned to Snowbasin every couple of months. He often spent time on the course alone, virtually sneaking into town to do his work. A few days after the controversial running of a Russi course at the Nagano Olympics in February 1998 (a downhill run first thought too easy, then, after Hermann Maier's spectacular fall had been replayed endlessly, judged to be recklessly dangerous), Russi spent a day on the John Paul Ridge; he walked up the mountain and worked his way down once, slowly.

I picture Russi alone with his mountain, skiing the freshly cut course for the first time, studying every turn, comparing each section to the Nagano course and applying what he had learned in Japan. At the end of the day he met briefly with the Forest Service. And then he went home, with no fanfare and no press. His intensity and perfectionism aren't that far from Earl Holding's.

An "easy" downhill run is fast and straight and therefore dangerous, especially to the racers who aren't world champions and ski last. A "technical" downhill is not as dangerous because it slows the racers if they don't ski the turns well. The Snowbasin course is both fast and relentlessly technical, with constantly varying terrain, high speeds, tight turns.

Russi ties these ironies together, searching for the right words in English. You want "good sport." You want good theater. But you want safety—so you must control the racers' speed. And you want to do as little earthwork on the mountain as possible. All these constraints lead in the same direction: to obstacles and jumps.

Russi sees these factors working together in a circle. He sees himself as a sculptor who starts with a general shape and molds the details of the course down the mountain, controlling the rhythm turn by turn, step by step.

The downhillers, especially, develop a relationship with the mountain. According to Carrie Sheinberg, who raced on the U.S. women's team for eight years and covered the 2002 Utah Olympics as a journalist: "They have an amazing connection to the terrain and come to an agreement of sorts with the mountain. Depending on their character that might be, 'I'm going to conquer you,' or it might be 'I'll take care of you, you take care of me.'"

The 2002 racers judged Russi's super-G men's course to be the hardest they had ever skied. Only thirty-four of the starting fifty-five men finished the race, foiled by Russi's Buffalo Jump at the top of Rendezvous Face and the super-G rule that limits racers to only one inspection from the side of the course and no training runs. Sheinberg told me that "what the racer sees almost never translates to television. You'll never know how incredibly icy that was, how incredibly steep. But on that last face in the super-G, the spectators actually could watch those mammoth men—giants, almost mythical figures—try with all their might and not be able to make that first gate below the jump."

WHEN I CAME TO THE MOUNTAIN in the summer of 1997, I came to the old Snowbasin. Back then there were just 27 employees in the summer, 105 in the winter. The new Snowbasin did not yet exist.

I could identify each vehicle in the cracked asphalt parking lot at the old day lodge. Kent Matthews's personal vehicle, an enormous lunk of a pickup he drove up the mountain from his 170-acre ranch thirty miles away in Morgan Valley, spent the day parked in front of Snowbasin's command center—offices still housed in a singlewide trailer painted brown and skirted with plywood. Next door two Forest Service vehicles stood in front of the snow ranger's office—a log cabin that had originally been used for restrooms. Two green-shirted foresters leaned against their green trucks and talked into their cell phones (the phones, thank god, were not green). Next to them two small ATV four-wheelers with helmets perched on their seats waited for the bouncing trip up the switchbacks of the Mountain Road. Near the construction crew's trailer nine trucks marked the edge of the lot, each emblazoned with "W. W. Clyde & Co., General Contractors, Springville, Utah."

And my red truck. In 1997 that was it.

But an eerie, high-pitched mechanical wail came from the mountain and slipped away. Chain saws, from the crew clearing the lower reaches of the John Paul Ridge. Radio communications boomed from the W. W. Clyde diesel fuel truck, tracking conversations between various equipment operators on the mountain. Every five or ten minutes a flurry of dialogue squawked out; an occasional metallic clunk punctuated the intervening silence as a mechanic worked on a tire twelve feet in diameter.

For safety on the sixty-five-degree run-out of the men's downhill course, the track hoes worked from a cable attached to a winch. One bulldozer worked the Rock Garden—a problematic boulder-filled slope on the Women's Downhill—filling the Basin with crank and clangor, squeaking and grinding, as the CAT appeared in a clearing, disappeared, then reappeared. When I couldn't see the machines, the sound seemed to emanate from the mountain itself.

This was a moment to weigh, the transition from old to new. I perched on the hood of my truck and wrote in my journal.

I knew the next four years here would be a three-ring circus. The mountain almost seemed to be turning into an appliance—a huge malleable lump to be shaped and argued over and skied upon, its wildness replaced by mechanical parts. And yet no matter how much we may desire simplicity and control, a mountain simply cannot become a machine. Our conceit of careful oversight turns illusory when avalanches roar down from the ridgeline, as they do every year, martyring sufficient numbers of skiers to give names to the summits.

A tourist couple pulled into the lot and wandered into the small lodge, which had been left open and unattended. There was nothing there for them; the cafeteria and ski shop were closed for the summer. The couple used the bathrooms, took a snapshot, and drove away. The Forest Service men put down their cell phones, hopped on their four-wheelers, and headed up the mountain.

I followed the rangers on foot and came across a dozer working the Mountain Road. As I approached a snarl of bushes shielding an aspen grove I heard an aggressive snort. As the brush crackled and branches snapped, I quickened my pace. From the road ahead the operator yelled at me over the clamor from his engine: "Did you see the size of the rack on that bull moose?"

Even with the clank and roar of the dozers, this was still a wild place.

As I watched the dance play out between the Forest Service, Snowbasin, the Olympic Committee, and the contractors, I reminded myself of the roles that were missing: the ensemble of plants and animals that live in the Basin, of course, and even the audience—the public. For this was a ballet without its longtime managing director, the Environmental Protection Agency, without the chance for the public to review any of the decisions or plans, and without recourse to NEPA law, which would have allowed citizens to ask the developer to slow down. With the passage of Gray Reynolds's and Jim Hansen's bill that previous fall, Earl Holding need answer only to the Forest Service staff. Only they could provide brakes; the agency had become a stand-in for public engagement.

The foresters sought to make lemonade from these lemons. Bernie Weingardt, Wasatch-Cache National Forest supervisor from 1995 to 2000, told me, "Without NEPA, now that the people *have* to trust us, Snowbasin could be a model to earn back the public's trust." Jim Lyons, undersecretary in charge of the Forest Service in Clinton's Department of Agriculture, gave Weingardt high marks for his "great deal of fortitude" in "handholding Earl" and keeping him on track environmentally when the legislation "could have allowed them to bulldoze whatever they wanted to bulldoze." Most of the daily crossfire of forest politics passes through the office of the forest supervisor, and Lyons credits Weingardt with "a great deal of integrity and a true conservation commitment."

———

I spent that first construction season walking the course with the forest rangers, photographing the track hoes, and listening to Bernhard Russi, Kent Matthews, the Forest Service, and Olympic staff negotiate. Gray Reynolds, when he attended these meetings, remained silent. By federal regulation he was forbidden to deal with the Forest Service during his first year as Snowbasin general manager. Dale Bosworth, still regional forester at the time, was impressed with how absolutely Gray observed this separation. There was no winking and talking behind his hand. He followed the rules. Bosworth believes that Snowbasin's development turned out better because Gray was there. "He knows the Forest Service. He knows ski areas, he knows the land. And he knew Earl Holding. He was able to make sure that things were done right—from a land ethic standpoint."

By the end of the summer, the courses existed. Even in the clatter and whine of machinery on these dirt scars, with flagging in four colors that confused everybody, and with slash piled high every fifty feet or so in regular patterns—dozens of tipi-shaped mounds the foresters christened "the Indian Village"—I could begin to picture the race.

During the winter of 1997–98 there were new fresh-cut runs on the John Paul Ridge but no lifts to serve them. Snowbasin looked much as it had for twenty years, and fierce and affectionate locals continued to patronize their sleepy ski area. The next summer the pace of change accelerated. With the winter ski season ended on April 5, 1998, lift building began on April 6. By the end of the month Kent Matthews began appearing in news photos standing by enormous holes that housed the concrete footings for the lifts. Though the holes were huge, they were perfectly groomed. As one contractor put it, "Earl lives for things being clean." By December Matthews was gleefully load testing the four new lifts and waxing sentimental about a dream come true: "I've been thinking about the route of some of these runs for years." With his prayers answered for sunny construction days, he now shifted to pleading for "a great, big snowstorm."

MR. HOLDING, AS MATTHEWS ALWAYS CALLED HIM, bought Kent a new truck in 1998. The old Bronco from the old Snowbasin was retired.

A new hierarchy emerged in 1998 after Gray Reynolds's one-year exclusion from interaction with his former federal employer, the Forest Service. When Earl's son-in-law, Chris Peterson, attended a meeting, he spoke for Snowbasin, and Gray and Kent were quiet. If Chris wasn't there, Gray became the public voice of Snowbasin. Kent became quieter and quieter. As his exasperation grew over press coverage critical of Earl's land exchange and accelerated development, he also grew leery of talking with me. But Kent was a loyal soldier. He spoke highly of the changes to Snowbasin, mind-boggled by the scale: "I get up every morning and try to do my best to contribute something positive to what's happening here. This is about we, not I."

In 1998 the new lifts went in. Two gondolas, a high-speed quad, and a tram, all constructed by Doppelmayr, the premier lift-construction company Earl had chosen. Twenty-two miles of trench began to reach toward the summits, to be filled with snowmaking lines and 132 miles of conduit carrying 264 miles of fiber optics and power cables. As I listened to the engineers plan the reshaping of the mountain—adding a hundred feet here, taking away a hundred feet there, digging trenches for pipe and cable—their nonchalance about such invasive work made me think of thoracic surgery. Cracking open the mountain's chest, rewiring its internal anatomy.

I can see Mount Ogden as twin expressions of the Force in an as-yet-unfilmed episode of *Star Wars*—a Darth Vader of a mountain, but with its twisted and mechanized side balanced by the wild and unquenchable positive Force still emanating from forests and peaks. Lifetime Snowbasin skiers have described to me feeling trapped in the "cognitive dissonance" between these two visions. As hot young skiers fond of the John Paul backcountry, they yearned for a chairlift that would make it easier to ski the powder. They could never have imagined the scale of what Earl did here. And they don't quite know what to make of it. They expect to quit skiing at Snow-

basin once it turns "snooty and expensive and weird." One local skier bran-
dished a Snowbasin trail map, jabbing at the heading "Our Mountain": "I
feel that Earl is directly snubbing me. It *used* to be ours. Now it's Earl's."

Earl himself told the public, "We just need to make sure we do something nice that our company can be proud of."

I spent a June day in 1998 with the Doppelmayr men who were building the
new lifts. Jeff Kelso, foreman of tower installations, strode around with a
radio strapped to his chest like a second heart, impatient for the snowpack
to melt and make his work easier. "Everybody thinks we just plant little T-
bars and they grow up to be quad chairs and gondolas," he joked. He knew
better—thirty-one towers better just for the John Paul Express.

Randy Glieke was the project boss for Doppelmayr. A master of organization, he radiated calm as his crew of seventy people prepared to stretch
120,000 pounds of cable under 180,000 pounds of tension and pour 350,000
pounds of concrete in the Middle Bowl Gondola terminal alone. Flying
and bolting lift towers was one of his favorite moments: "One day you
have a bare mountainside, the next day you have a whole mountainside of
towers."

Randy and Jeff, both of whom had global experience, judged Mount
Ogden to be "a *real* mountain." Difficult access, rocky enough, challenging
enough. Randy: "That John Paul is a *real* lift. The skiing you access off
that kind of vertical is as good as you get anywhere in the world."

To examine the site of tower 16 high on the Middle Bowl Express we
walked two hundred yards away from the Mountain Road and rock-hopped
through talus and then across a snowfield. The tower anchor site was free
of snow, rock surrounded by dirt plowed by pocket gophers and sprouting
with waxy yellow glacier lilies. Randy and Jeff bantered. They looked at
the bedrock exposed by the laborers and concluded that they needed to pin
the box to the rock, to the mountain itself, rather than blast out the rock
and pour concrete into the hole. With this decision, Randy pulled out his
cell phone.

While Randy made his calls, strolling in circles near treeline, his management directives beaming off across the continent, Jeff was on the radio
to crews elsewhere on the mountain. Mentally mapping the events of these
few minutes, I imagined a chart of most of the western hemisphere, showing
origins and destinations of telecommunication, fabrication, and precipita-

tion. As they worked the airwaves and I waited for them, a front moved in, and the temperature dropped fifteen degrees. Snow began to fall in tiny froths of dustlike crystals. Unprepared for the storm, I started to shiver. But I realized I was shivering only partly from the cold. I was also being snowed under by technology.

The mountain was changing faster than I could keep pace. No one in the ski industry could remember a resort undertaking so much in such a short time. At this speed how could the Forest Service, masters of "mitigation monitoring," possibly supervise effectively?

IN THE FOLLOWING SUMMER OF 1999 FORTY TRACK HOES crisscrossed the slopes. W. W. Clyde had $50 million worth of equipment on the mountain.

A hive of workers designed a pump to fill a one-million-gallon tank from three freshly drilled wells sunk deep into the aquifer underlying Mount Ogden. They installed snowmaking equipment for nearly 325 acres of ski runs, laying two twelve-inch pipes—one for air, one for water—running up and down miles of trenches. To Earl's disappointment, the water was so mineralized it was nearly brown, so the artificial snow wasn't as sparkling white as he would have liked. Races would run on this manufactured snow, the downhill courses shaped by twenty-seven Snow Cats, seventeen winch machines, and an army of 1,500 volunteers who foot-pack the courses, in spots injecting water sixty-eight inches down to preserve the hardened surface and to keep it icy, grippy, and fast.

To add an inch of artificial snow to natural snowpack on a single acre of terrain costs about $1,000. Electrical bills to run this system can easily top one million dollars a year. Hal Clifford points out in *Downhill Slide* that this extravagance also brings with it the pollution from coal-burning power plants that generate the necessary electricity, "turning coal into snow."

High on Allen Peak, at the very top of the men's downhill, Forest Service botanists discovered a tiny alpine plant growing in crevices of the summit block, a unique species of mustard called Burke's draba. Course construction destroyed between three and five hundred plants of a known population of five thousand but spared the remaining plants by leaving the last two-hundred-odd feet of snowmaking pipe above ground. The forest ecologists FedExed displaced mustards to the Denver Botanic Garden—where seeds were collected for permanent ultracold storage and the Snowbasin drabas added to the arboretum gardens—but construction extinguished at least 10 percent of the wild population.

Each year Earl's contractors raced to finish the ever-multiplying number of projects on the mountain on schedule, before winter and in time for the Olympics. I stopped making any effort to keep daily or weekly track and simply checked in at the end of the summer. I had seen little of Kent Matthews for months. Word had it that he had been demoted. Chip Sibbernsen, the Forest Service liaison to the project, showed me around on an end-of-the-1999-construction-season "media tour." I was astonished, resigned, and numbed by the amount of building.

Chip pointed out the 543 snowmaking guns sticking up from the snow. Miniature weather stations rose at every fifth gun, relaying humidity and temperature to the huge central compressor, which was housed in a building whose façade looked much like one of Earl's ski lodges. Here computer controls allowed an operator to fine-tune, like a symphony conductor, the mix of compressed air and water (3,000 gallons per minute) that created artificial snow. The new Snowbasin skier, instead of being the wild powder hound adventurer of old, would be the luxury resort skier who is led from sign to groomed slope to base lodge, who follows the snowmaking guns down the mountain, barrel to barrel, dot to dot. Snow will be a commodity, Earl's product to sell at Sun Valley and Snowbasin, just as he sells oil at his refineries and gas stations.

IN 2000 TRANSFORMATION REACHED the Mount Ogden summit itself. The old single forty-foot radio tower had been inconspicuous. Now a new road provided access to three new towers (rising to one hundred feet) and a 1,200-square-foot building topped by a helipad. Three million federal dollars funneled to the city of Ogden had paid for the facility—more NEPA-exempt Olympic infrastructure delivered without public discussion or environmental assessment.

To the disgust of the Ogden Sierra Club, construction workers had dumped white waste rock over the side of the mountain, destroying yet another population of the rare draba, and they had made the summit look more like an industrial zone than a mountaintop. When I climbed through autumn-red maple and golden oaks from Taylor Canyon through Malans Basin to eat my lunch perched on the summit helipad, I admired a view that stretched from Wyoming to Nevada, but I was disheartened by the intermittent whirring of the communications machinery. A mountain summit usually strikes its chords from wind and silence. The peak of Mount Ogden now made noises like my refrigerator and furnace kicking on and off.

A huge "H" marked the concrete pad—presumably to guide approaching helicopters in bad weather. I couldn't help but think, though, that it was Earl's mark. A heraldic crest on the mountaintop entrance to the redoubt of a crazy recluse, like the ornate retreat at the summit of the Alps stormed by James Bond in *On Her Majesty's Secret Service.*

I looked down to where Earl's Needles Lodge would stand, where we will watch lightning from cushioned leather seats, cozy and safe among the crags of the ridgeline. Warmed by massive rock fireplaces, we will sip wine beneath enormous chandeliers ringed with gold dragons. Urgency will disappear. Earl will have shielded us from the mountain's threat.

It's all an illusion, though. Danger lurks under every civilized exterior. As restorative as a mountain can be, it is a wild place where the powers of the earth supersede our puny efforts at human control. From the spine of this mountain avalanches rumble down in winter. The earth itself—the Green Pond Slide and the Bear Wallow Slide—flows through the center of Earl Holding's resort. Several hundred feet of the glacial ridge above the Bear Wallow Slide have already slid downhill, recognizable as earthflow by the lumpy terrain. At any time, in any season, the mountain can flex its muscles. We are always vulnerable.

Mountains are serene. Mountains are fierce. Do not take them for granted. Earl can insist on loyalty from every employee, but he can't expect it from the mountain.

NEW ENTRY ROAD TO SNOWBASIN UNDER CONSTRUCTION, MOUNT OGDEN, UTAH, 1999.

PNEUMONIA ROAD

The true extent of the victory will never be known—the
role of luck being unassessable, the effects of intervention
being ultimately incalculable, and the assertion that
people can stop a volcano being hubris enough to provoke
a new eruption.

JOHN MCPHEE, *THE CONTROL OF NATURE*, 1989

OGDEN. PETER SKENE OGDEN. Short, dark, good-humored, tough, French-
Canadian Québecois, explorer of the Middle Rockies and Great Basin in
the 1820s and 1830s.

In 1825 Ogden led a formidable band of fifty-eight Hudson's Bay Company trappers deeper into the continent than they had ever gone. They
ranged south far beyond the Snake River country to foothills below a rocky
crest where meadowland greened with spring and creeks teemed with
beaver. It was the dream country of a mountain man, a scene in a reverie I
can imagine: Beaver swims through earthpure water as cold as stars on a
January midnight. Streambank nods with tender columbine and fistfuls of
lupine. Beaver dives into den; trapper wades into water, soaking leather,
gasping with the shock, baiting his stick with the musk from the scent
glands at the base of the tails of female beavers, tying a float to his trap. Fantasies of rendezvous mask the cold, a vision of eager and affectionate Shoshone women, of packsaddle mounded high with furs.

Peter Skene Ogden and his mountain men followed the easiest horseman's passage into the valley when they crossed the hills between Ogden

Valley and Weber Canyon, a trail used by native people for centuries. The journal-keeping trapper Osborne Russell followed the same route in 1841 when he made a January elk-hunting trip alone into Ogden Valley from his winter camp near the Great Salt Lake.

From this history, the southern entry to Ogden Valley acquired the name Trappers Loop. At least the place did not become yet another landmark named for Peter Skene Ogden. Ogden is an inelegant word. Ogden's Hole. Ogden Valley. Ogden River. Ogden City. Mount Ogden.

In French it would be softer, as Peter himself must have pronounced it, *Oag-danh*. In English, the consonants take over, dislodging any lilt or elegance. The word carries none of the grace of the places. No hint of the aspen leaves trembling in breezes round with summer heat or edgy with autumn coolness. No musky incense from sagebrush after a rain. None of the bright intensity of high-elevation sun backlighting plumes of snow. No dance, no glitter from the spray off Wheeler Creek.

But sibilant or severe, these place names carry stories.

WHEN EARL HOLDING BOUGHT SNOWBASIN in 1984, one paved road linked the ski area and the little Ogden Valley towns to the outside world. The road wound around the north end of Mount Ogden through narrow Ogden Canyon to the city of Ogden. To the south, Trappers Loop and its eight miles of rolling hills separated Ogden Valley from the Interstate highway along the Weber River. Only a rough dirt road traversed Trappers Loop.

The eight miles of switchbacks from Ogden Valley to Snowbasin followed the path of least resistance, engineered when roads followed wagon tracks and Indian paths and deer trails. Where the road crossed the active Bear Wallow Landslide, the state highway department had to slather on a foot of asphalt every year to fill continually collapsing roller-coaster dips. Complete failure of the flowing hillside remained a perennial threat.

This Snowbasin road climbed to a breathtaking pass at the Forest Boundary, where the view compelled you to stop and park and look across the valley of Wheeler Creek, past the lumpy earthflows that gave the Basin its relief, and into the solar plexus of the massif, where the steep slopes of the ski mountain plummeted down from the peaks. The recumbent body of the mountain confronted you, and when you dropped away into Wheeler Creek and began to curve along the hilly slopes of the earthflows up toward the ski area parking lot, you sensed that you were climbing onto the massif itself, clambering onto its side.

For fifty years the approach to Snowbasin traced this roundabout passage

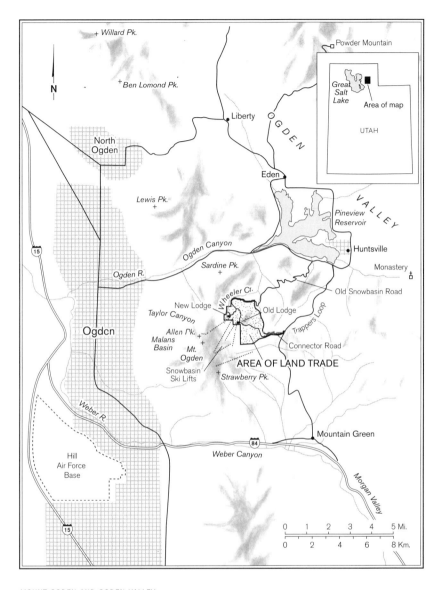

MOUNT OGDEN AND OGDEN VALLEY.

through Ogden Canyon, into the valley along the shores of Pineview Reservoir, and up the old switchbacks built by Alf Engen and his Civilian Conservation Corps crews in 1938.

Earl Holding wanted to make Snowbasin as tempting to destination skiers as Park City and Snowbird. He wanted to steal business from Colorado, which had nearly 13 million skier days every year—21 percent of the national pool of skiers and snowboarders—and add to Utah's annual total of 4 million. To straighten the winding journey and shorten the distance from Salt Lake City's airport to Snowbasin, as Earl wished to do, the obvious route lay over Trappers Loop.

———

Trappers Loop Highway was constructed without fanfare but raised plenty of eyebrows. In the late 1980s the Utah economy was depressed. Big road projects were the last thing on the mind of the state legislature. Nevertheless, within five years of Earl's purchase of the ski area, and with Earl's donation of a right of way through his own land to make it possible, the state of Utah had funded and completed Trappers Loop Highway.

Whatever the behind-the-scenes machinations that led to its construction, Trappers Loop was paid for by the state of Utah. With the new highway in place, Earl lacked only a three mile spur road to whisk skiers—on good highways all the way—directly from Salt Lake City to Snowbasin. In 1990, Earl told Regional Forester Stan Tixier that he would build and pay for this road connecting Trappers Loop with his ski area "right away."

EARL PUBLICLY, AND REPEATEDLY, confirmed his promise to build the connector road. But the 2002 Olympics made a convenient excuse for backing off; Earl began to demur. Through his governmental affairs liaison, Clint Ensign, Earl claimed to have negotiated away his promise in 1995. Ensign also catalogued Earl's investments in the ski area and Grand America Hotel and concluded that these adequately took care of Earl's obligations to Utah's Olympic bid. Earl couldn't "do it all," so he asked state and Olympic officials to relieve him of his road-building commitment.

In the fall of 1997 Utah Senator Bob Bennett stepped in to help. From his position on the Senate Appropriations Committee, he funneled $800,000 in federal money to the Forest Service to design and engineer the road connecting Snowbasin to Trappers Loop. Citizens, believing that Earl was getting a sweetheart deal and that the people were being snookered into building the "Holding Highway to Holdingville," cranked up the heat on the editorial pages. Scott Leckman, Bennett's Democratic opponent in the 1998 election, opposed tax money for the Snowbasin road and pointedly noted what no one else seemed to want to say: if the federal government didn't build it, Earl obviously could afford to pay for it himself.

Bruce Babbitt has described federal land-use policy, with sadness, as little more than "money-subsidized development"—with transportation as its spearhead. The Utah State Legislature passed a resolution in the spring of 1998 that barred the use of state money to construct Earl's road. Senator Bennett told the press that a $15-million appropriation of Forest Service money for the road would be his top Congressional funding priority in the summer of 1998 (evidently more important to him than education, health care, or foreign policy). By the time Congress adjourned in October, Bennett had his appropriation.

By diverting federal construction money through the Forest Service, Bennett was able to tie the new connector road to the land exchange legislation and exempt the construction project from oversight via NEPA and the Clean Water Act. Congress had once again intervened on Earl's behalf. And, again, the politician moving the legislation—in this case Senator Bob Bennett—insisted that the Forest Service had come to him and asked for the legislation. His justification, his answer to every challenge: *the Olympics are coming, the Olympics are coming!*

When Senator John McCain of Arizona rose on the Senate floor to decry these "Games-driven congressional giveaways," he asked, tongue in cheek, "Is this a great country or what? A millionaire developer wants a road built; the federal government supplies the cash to construct it. A billionaire ski-resort owner covets a choice piece of public land. No problem. The federal government arranges for him to have it. . . . How can you get yours, you ask? Easy. . . ." Just attach to your project—"virtually any project"—"the magic word, Olympics."

In 1998 Chip Sibbernsen was the Forest Service "venue manager" at Snowbasin, the frontline contact with Earl and his dreams. Sibbernsen took an assertive stand on protecting soil and water but limited what he called his "decision space." Earl's job was to propose projects; Chip's job was to react—responsibly. He told me that this was the "best thing I've worked on in twenty years: The clock is ticking in real time, and we have to overcome so many challenges and obstacles—each the issue of the day. It is a very energizing experience."

Sibbernsen looks as earnest as he is; he has wholesomely rosy cheeks, an open Danish face and a quick smile, a barrel chest, and blond hair sufficiently thick to look as if it needs no combing after a shower. He commutes to work sixty miles each way, driving home at night to his son's soccer games and his wife's home cooking in Logan. The most devious thing about him is his pair of PhotoGray glasses, which darken in sunlight.

Chip absolutely, sincerely, honestly felt that the Forest Service was doing a good job of representing the interests of the American public as Snowbasin expanded. He felt that Gray Reynolds did an outstanding job as his Snowbasin counterpart in meeting the very requirements that he had signed off on when he had been deputy chief of the Forest Service. Chip believed that without Gray the agency would not have had the access to Earl "that led to the quality job of reclamation, visuals, water quality protection, and infrastructure." Chip was eager to brag about revegetating the mountain. He wanted this new connecting road to be "an environmental showcase."

I WATCHED THE CONNECTOR ROAD blossom into cartographic reality in a series of meetings of the Snowbasin Access Road Partnering Team in the spring and early summer of 1998. Chip Sibbernsen had convened this group of environmentalists, Forest Service specialists, agency and local government representatives, engineers, and Snowbasin staff to plan the new road and make final recommendations to the district ranger. The meeting venue shifted from the Salt Lake City offices of the engineering firm designing the road to the vintage WPA building housing the Ogden Ranger District to the new Weber County Complex. The location mattered in subtle ways. The Forest Service staffers seemed to take up more space in their own building, which had a little of the dark mustiness of the forest floor about it, while the engineers' antiseptic glass and metal conference room gave extra-hard edges to their numbers and charts. Chris Peterson represented Earl most of the time; Kent Matthews and Gray Reynolds attended sporadically. Earl never appeared. The road engineers joked that Earl Holding might not exist at all.

Chris Peterson resembles a smoother, ruddier, fortyish Bill Bradley. Even in his conservative tie and starched shirt he looks as if he had recently stepped from a collegiate basketball uniform at a top-flight school like Harvard, where he indeed received his education. Chris shields his father-in-law. He holds his cards close. His wife, Anne, works in the family empire with her

FORESTER CHIP SIBBERNSEN SPOKE FOR MOUNT OGDEN AS EARL PROCEEDED WITH HIS DREAMS, 1998.

mother, Carol, but Chris never mentions his wife or his mother-in-law. He nearly always refers to Earl as Mr. Holding.

Ever quick with precise details, Chris asked the engineers: "Do the traffic models measure the distance from Salt Lake City to Snowbasin at fifty-one miles or thirty-nine miles?" Up the old road or the new shorter route? "The new road reduces travel time by 20.4 minutes." All of these differences would matter to skiers in Salt Lake City hotels deciding which resort to patronize on a bluebird day. With the completion of the new road connecting their resort to Trappers Loop, Earl and Chris could offer the wealthy patrons of Grand America and Snowbasin a package linked by what was essentially a controlled-access company highway.

Jock Glidden, the environmental conscience of Ogden, represented the Sierra Club on the Partnering Team. Freshly retired from the philosophy department at Weber State University, he was still bitter from his negotiations with the Forest Service at the beginning of the land exchange battle eight years earlier. He worried about how seriously the team would take his advice. But with the thought that "perhaps environmentalists have more power now, I'm ready to try again."

Lean, compact, and moustached, Jock loved to cross-country ski to Green Pond in Snowbasin. Some years before he had come across a knoll with a 360-degree view flagged with a sign that read "Earl's Castle"; presumably some of Earl's people had planted it. He yanked out the marker and tossed it in a gulch. Futile, but it sure made him feel better.

———————

Planning this road was high-stakes work. Each of the three possible road alignments crossed two active earthflows. Every alternative sliced into the mountainside above the Wheeler Creek watershed, opening up the potential for silt or pollution damage. Unless Bennett's exempting legislation passed, the U.S. Army Corps of Engineers would be required to sign off on the project if it looked like it would destroy more than one acre of wetlands.

This piece of the power puzzle was new to me. The Clean Water Act gives the Corps jurisdiction over the nation's water, from the deltas of the great rivers right up into the glacially scoured cirques of Mount Ogden. No road could happen here without Corps approval. If the road required any "dewatering" of the landslides, the engineers would have to redirect that water elsewhere and replace lost wetlands.

After Bennett's bill passed, however, the Corps stopped attending. Once Congress added the connector road to the list of Snowbasin projects exempted from NEPA and Clean Water Act oversight, the Corps felt that their time would be wasted; surely, too, they understood the convenient politics of backing off.

CHRIS PETERSON LOVED DATA, and he was always ready to fire up his laptop and display his three-dimensional maps of Mount Ogden with a score of overlays. He knew how many species of bats had been recorded at Snowbasin. His comments about moose and elk were based on personal experience: "For fourteen years I've made a point to cross-country ski out there day and night during different months in the winter." He worried that the Olympic Committee would clear too much forest and meadow for buildings and parking—the plan called for 2.2 million square feet, almost fifty acres of cleared ground—which would be used only during the fleeting two weeks of the Olympics: "But the world doesn't end in 2002. There's a future here. When the orange fences and bleachers and scaffolding go away, the people of Utah and the owner of this resort want this to be a beautiful place."

Peterson was describing his own future. As heir apparent, Peterson himself will be "the owner of this resort" in not too many years. More than once he noted that the upper and middle alignments, which allow a main artery into his real estate and easy access to development, would "make Earl a quick nickel" because they "build his backbone." The lower alignment, which stays on the outskirts of development and requires longer internal roads, would "provide a slower dime—harder for him but allowing for quieter, slower, more thoughtful development."

Earl wanted to site his own roads and wait for that "slow dime." He wanted to keep the access road away from his village, and he told Chris that "the upper alignment is a disaster for the resort." But Earl lost this round. Over Chris's protests, the Partnering Team chose the upper alignment. They were more concerned about keeping the road far from Wheeler Creek—which could suffer catastrophe if the Bear Wallow slide were to move and the road to collapse—than about shielding Earl's resort homes from traffic.

Between meetings I asked Genevieve Atwood to give me a lesson on landslides at Snowbasin. As Utah state geologist in the 1980s, she had studied thousands of landslides and had "fallen in love with these conveyor belts of carnage." She understands gravity. She sees so much unstable territory at Snowbasin that she warns any developer to "hang on to your wallet. Fifty percent of the terrain in the Basin is unstable." She went on to muse about the politics of development in such "extraordinary places." "Here the complexities of the people mirror the complexities of the land."

TWO DAYS AFTER SHIVERING in the June snow high on the mountain with the lift-building crews, I took a cold, rainy walk with the hardier members of the road design team down the newly chosen route of the connector road.

We had waited a few days until one man walked the route, a Global Positioning System scanner in his backpack, and flagged the center line of the new road every thirty yards with pink tape. Solar flares forced the delay. They interfered with satellite transmission to the GPS, and so we here on earth had to postpone our schedules because of inclement weather 150 million kilometers away.

We nearly canceled our exploratory walk-through because of the miserable weather on the mountain, but since we had gathered from all over the Wasatch Front, most of us decided to go ahead. The hike along the uncut route definitely qualified as bushwhacking; for four-and-a-half hours we struggled through maple and oak, with constant rain. A lush understory—of Solomon's seal, camas, larkspur, balsamroot, corn lilies—testified to the wettest June in years. Lovely. But when the rain stopped for ten minutes toward the end of the walk, my hands were too cold to work my camera. One of the biologists who had mapped wetlands here joked that if he had done his work today he would have reported, "Yeah, I found wetlands—one very big wetland three and a half miles long."

That day I wore an old rain jacket whose waterproofing could no longer shield me from a storm like this. At the end of the walk-through I was drenched, chilled, and soaked to the skin. Back in my truck I stripped and stiffly pulled on dry clothes in the blast from the heater. Within two days I had developed a deep cough. I felt weaker and weaker. The doctor diagnosed mycoplasmic pneumonia the following Saturday.

I was chagrined. Snowbasin had worn me out, to be sure, but this was a high price to pay. I was aware that technology on the mountain was racing ahead of my ability to track it. As construction shifted from downhill racecourse to resort infrastructure, I was losing interest in the details—and feeling guilty about that. Now that I had been knocked out of fieldwork, I had an excuse to sit back and try to come to grips with my ambivalence. As I regained my strength, I thought about change in new, broader ways.

In a *Washington Post* article about Earl Holding and his mountain, Utah Senator Orrin Hatch had defended Earl by comparing his plans for Snowbasin with what he had done at Sun Valley. Surely, here, too, Hatch said, Earl would again "develop an environmentally beautiful resort." That phrase placed "develop" and "beautiful" only two words apart, with "environment" between them; "resort" was a given, a fait accompli. Hatch clearly assumed that developing a resort was preferable both to leaving the land alone and to nurturing a low-tech ski area for locals and hard-core visitors. Bigger was better; faster was better; famous was better. Manmade was better as well as more "beautiful." Hatch had grown up in Pennsylvania, but both Hatch and Holding come from a Mormon culture that still believes in large families, breeding new pilgrims to work with industry, and faith to make the desert blossom and turn nature's wasteland into a human paradise.

American culture tells us we must develop. We must stay on deadline. We must make decisions—right now. This same unreal urgency convinced us to walk the connector road in the rain. If I'd been alone on the mountain, I would have retreated from the nasty weather. But we conjured the need to see the route, to see it today, and so I went along and had to live with the consequences.

———

Earl Holding was around to see power plants and dams and water projects blanket the West after World War II—the Big Buildup, as one of our wise men of the West, the writer Charles Wilkinson, calls it. Earl is an engineer; his first job out of college was with the U.S. Bureau of Reclamation at the height of dam-building delirium. As Earl said about Sun Valley, "All it takes is money, and we've got that. We will spend whatever we need to do a super job."

An unsettling and unspoken question underlies this eager pledge of Earl's. It's simple but strikes to the heart of the conflict at Snowbasin: a super job of *what?*

Every mountain, every wild place, harbors the tensions of opposing forces, and all religions and philosophies understand this fact. Harmony and balance don't arrive until storied heroes battle dragons for human souls. Good and evil. Yin and yang. We must acknowledge these dichotomies and then pass beyond them. Wisdom lies in the shifting frontiers. This mountain is the fulcrum for each pair of dualities; its summit is the pivot for the morality play of the land.

QUIETLY HEALING IN MY ATTIC OFFICE, I looked back over my journals. The pages were filled with notes from interviews with all manner of people. Their range revealed a network of relationships. Their roles began with those doing the most elemental work: the laborers who shaped the mountain, shovelful by shovelful, ski run by ski run. Like everywhere in the West, these workers know the land in its full intimacy, yet hardly ever do we acknowledge the learning gained by labor. Construction remains too close to what we dismiss as destruction.

I could picture the players standing in a circle, their words rising up at me from the pages of my journals, countering each other in ringing debate-team tones.

Among them mountain manager Kent Matthews taking his usual verbal back road to comment on his frustration with the no-growth group: "Stagnation shuts down a lot of things." He was ready to move Snowbasin into big-time development: "I'm excited to think I get to implement what this mountain needs. I'm excited as the dickens."

Earl with his version of what the mountain "needs" articulated by Chris Peterson: "We worked hard to create a vision of a resort that lies lightly on the land. We're always thinking about the hypothetical arrival experience of a tourist from Miami. For downhill skiers this is as close as they get to wildness."

Forest Service point man Chip Sibbernsen staying calm—maybe too calm—in the face of conflicting views: "You have a normal distribution of points of view." As with every issue the bulk of opinion, the top of the bell-shaped curve, fell near the point of maximum ambivalence. The superdevelopers and the most passionate antigrowth factions lived out there at the tails of the curve.

Save Our Canyons leader Gale Dick summing up the two sides in his way: "The environmentalists are doing their job. The ski business is doing its job. The only player capable of the necessary mediation is the Forest Service. And they can't—they are too much involved as co-developers with the ski industry. We've gone through thirty years of ski area master plans, and now it all starts all over again. It's a perpetual death dance that never ends. We are never going to *convince* ski areas to do what we want them to do. We're going to have to force them. They simply disagree with us. That's why we have to go to court."

––––––––

Earl learned about ski areas from Sun Valley, where he acquired a resort that carried with it nearly fifty years of history and growth. With Snowbasin he acquired a ski area he could shape from what he called "virtually raw ground" into an Earl Holding "masterpiece." At Snowbasin Earl was never going to be content with the small profits of an Alta-style operation. He sent Chris Peterson to a thousand meetings to represent his position, not to discuss or change it. Dialogue is our only hope for finding common ground, but Earl holds out for his position. His motive is not, I think, solely to increase his wealth, though he continues to grow his fortune. He is not corporate as much as he is obsessive and quirky, driven to create his own vision of the world.

At Snowbasin Earl insists on maximum control, and he wants Snowbasin to be consistent with the rest of his empire. The stone facing the new buildings comes from a quarry near Hailey, Idaho, to match Earl's Sun Valley buildings. For months Earl considered changing the name of the resort itself to Sun Valley, Utah; that would have been the ultimate statement of ownership, the final elevation of franchise over local tradition.

"Snowbasin" had never been a successful name for a business. Earl didn't want to be connected with something unsuccessful. But Utahns would not let go of the name because to them Snowbasin meant community and history. And Idaho hated the idea of a second Sun Valley. Eventually Earl compromised with SNOWBASIN, A SUN VALLEY RESORT and changed the logo from the former stylized Snowbasin pine tree to the smiling yellow Sun Valley sun.

AFTER TWO MONTHS AWAY, I RETURNED TO THE MOUNTAIN in the fall of 1998. During that interval the Snowbasin lifts had gone up, along with more roads and huge parking and staging areas. Bulldozers were smoothing the runs, track hoes working the summit ridge, and helicopters buzzed back and forth across the mountain, ferrying concrete and steel. I looked up through binoculars at the frenzy of construction and felt sick to my stomach. For the foreseeable future this was going to look more like a war zone than a peaceful place in the wild Wasatch Mountains.

———

The following spring, just two weeks after beginning construction on the connector road, the W. W. Clyde workers found a Cooper's Hawk nest smack in their path. The contractor and the Forest Service worked around the nest for the next six weeks of the 1999 summer building season, gingerly skirting the site with their earthmovers—and losing forty days while waiting for the three nestlings to fledge. The Forest Service cut the nest snag after the birds left and saved it for the natural history exhibit to be placed in Earl's lodge. The discovery of two Flammulated Owl nests at the Bear Wallow Slide postponed work along that section until September.

Jock Glidden came up once a week to monitor construction for the Sierra Club. He learned a lot about road building—a new knowledge base for a philosophy professor. The two crucial sections to track were a cut and a dam. The huge cut-and-fill where the road left Trappers Loop accounted for 40 percent of all the earth moving and one third of the total cost of the road. A rock buttress dam where the road crossed the Bear Wallow slide constituted a half-million-dollar ditch involving 30,000 cubic meters of rock thirty-five feet deep, and pipes to bring water through the dam and under the road before returning it to downstream wetlands.

Much as Jock hated the idea of public money creating this grand entryway to Earl's new resort, he couldn't disagree when Chip Sibbernsen said, "I don't mean to be facetious, but there have been no issues on the road." A vast system that called for check dams, silt fence, straw mulch, chipped wood, erosion control blanket, brush barriers, straw bale barriers, and sediment ponds held back the hillsides eroding from the construction zone toward Wheeler Creek, and together they stemmed the tide of "issues." The Forest Service stated flatly, "This road project hasn't discharged one teaspoon of sediment into a stream."

Still, one issue emerged during spring snowmelt after the road's first winter. In April 2001 a two-hundred-foot section of the month's-old road at the edge of the Bear Wallow Slide started slipping downhill, cracking wide the fresh pavement. Within three weeks the earth had dropped twenty inches. The road engineers were chagrined. They had expected slippage and maintenance but not this much, and not here. Later that summer another forty drainpipes were driven into the mountain to move water under the road; another $300,000 was spent—this time coming from state highway maintenance funds—and construction traffic resumed.

THE LINE OF PICKUPS WINDING UP THE MOUNTAIN every morning to report for work and fulfill Earl's dreams no longer included Kent Matthews. On Friday, November 3, 2000, after forty years of working with the mountain, Matthews put in his last day at Snowbasin.

The following Monday he became general manager of Powder Mountain, another underused jewel, just across Ogden Valley. My first conversations with Kent had been in the decrepit office trailer that served the old Snowbasin. His office at Powder Mountain was an empty condo; we talked around a coffee table in the loft bedroom, our feet cradled in a '60s-style shag rug. I think we both found the rickety trailer and this aging condo more comfortable than the log-cabin castle of the new Snowbasin mountain operations building.

It was now a year since he had left the Basin, and Kent refused to wallow in self-pity: "Bitterness doesn't work. There's a lot more to lose by being negative. You've got to be man enough to move on." Kent told me of having been gradually marginalized in the Snowbasin hierarchy. He had been promoted to area manager and then shunted into a new "base manager" position in December 1999. He had been hearing unsettling rumors about his future for a year, but Earl never talked to him directly. "They didn't fire me," he told me, "they played with me. They made it impossible to continue.

"I hoped I could find a way to remain there and be productive because I thought so much of the place—not because I thought so much of Earl. If you don't fit the mold, you don't have a chance. Virtually all the personnel has changed up there, including my two sons, who left before me. Both are more bitter than me."

Between Kent and his father, Dale, the tenure of the Matthewses at Snowbasin lasted fifty-four years. His sons might have extended that heritage. Kent knew the ski area better than anybody and ran it on a shoestring for years, but he is not political: "I never had a pipeline to Earl."

Kent had been the point person on the mountain, but he had no real authority. "Earl expected me to care for his investment properly, and yet all conversations between him and the Forest Service were done outside my presence. I never knew what their dream or goals were. Gray Reynolds was decent and good on a professional level, but he would *never* answer your questions. I was told pretty plainly by the Forest Service what I could and couldn't do. I felt like the striking plate for their frustrations because they couldn't take out their frustrations on Earl. It was that double-standard that presumably got me."

For fifteen years Earl Holding amazed Kent with his willingness to reach for the biggest goal imaginable. "How can we be critical? A lot of people who had superb intention, excellent financial backing, lacked the mental picture and goal to go as far." But he doesn't buy Earl's philosophy: "Use 'em and burn 'em out and dump 'em and move on! I would think your conscience could carry you farther by being nice—being human."

Kent hasn't gone back to visit Snowbasin. But he still believes the mountain deserves the recognition it's going to get from "rearing itself to a position of excellence within the industry. I know Snowbasin needed to change. You had to have the ski product before the real estate would be valuable. You can't drive a 2000 automobile that has the same feeling as a 1949 Chevy."

As a man who has manipulated and engineered a mountain since he was eighteen, Kent Matthews isn't a purist. He loves Mount Ogden, but to him "it's not holy ground. It's a piece of Mother Earth that God gave us all to work with, to manage."

Kent's attitude toward the mountain is traditional, mainstream, commodity-based. In this view the American landscape tended by those of us who have conquered it in the last five hundred years is a garden in need of planting and pruning, not a wilderness to be left on its own. Kent may not want to confront the Snowbasin staff, but when he drives to his new job he cruises Trappers Loop past the new resort and admires the development of the mountain he loves.

He keeps going, descending into Ogden Valley to the villages of Eden and Liberty, where he turns right, up toward Powder Mountain. He has left Snowbasin behind, but he can't leave behind the battle for the future of the American land.

BELOW MOUNT OGDEN AT THE MOUTH OF TAYLOR CANYON, WASATCH-CACHE NATIONAL FOREST, UTAH, 1998.

PUBLIC TRUST

Who owns the West? All of us, of course.

WILLIAM KITTREDGE, *WHO OWNS THE WEST?* 1996

EACH FALL JOAN DEGIORGIO BEGAN her first lecture on public lands at the University of Utah by aiming a small hand mirror at her class and reflecting the expectant faces of students back on themselves. She opened her course with this gesture and an explanation: "Public lands show us who we are. They are such a gift, and how we treat them tells us what we think is important. When we sell public lands, it tells us where our values are—whether we value timber over recreation, mineral development over wildlife corridors, and water development over riparian habitat."

The mirror has a clear plastic frame. It's transparent, cloudless, guileless. Her students can see through the edges to Degiorgio, and in the reflection— too far away to isolate single individuals—they can see the roomful of learners, a framed oval cross section of their community.

Degiorgio believes in the power of that mirror she holds up to her public lands class. "If you look even deeper in that mirror, it tells us the deep values." These are the values that motivated Save Our Snowbasin, aroused Margot Smelzer to action, and shape my relationship with the West. Public lands are our commons, our refuge.

As the Forest Service bird-dogged Earl Holding while he rebuilt the mountain, the land exchange itself disappeared into years of negotiation, appraisal, and real estate deals. The drama of construction and development was winding down (without public comment, of course) as the saga of changing ownership, from public to private, headed toward its final curtain. Every scene in both story lines fit comfortably in the twentieth-century history of public lands in America.

THE DENOUEMENT OF THESE INTERTWINED STORIES began when the Snowbasin Land Exchange Act became law on November 12, 1996. The legislation detailed what developments could now be built at Snowbasin—all with no legal recourse by citizens to the courts or the process but with constant supervision by Forest Service personnel. Within two months the Forest Service and Snowbasin produced a document that laid out their plans. In one of his last acts as deputy chief, Gray Reynolds signed off on this "addendum" to the legislation.

While construction began, the land exchange itself began to grind through protracted bluffs, deals, and endless minute details, all in secret. The law stated that within 120 days of signing the Forest Service would appraise the federal acres that were to go to Earl. The legislators set no deadline for appraising the more than 4,000 private acres of land to be traded. In an unusual move, the bill tied all appraisals to the value of land at the time of the bill's passage, 1996—thereby circumventing the need for continual reappraisal but also preventing either party from profiting from changing market value.

The original authorization of national forest land exchanges in 1922 established the overriding principle of "value-for-value," rather than "acre-for-acre." And so, if the beneficiary of a trade needs to purchase a thousand acres of land outside the forest to match the value of a single acre of federal land inside the forest, so be it.

The public pins great hopes for fairness on the appraisal process, but we are frequently disappointed. In the case of Snowbasin, the question was how to appraise the land overlooking Wheeler Creek that stands undeveloped now but will be worth a fortune once Earl pounds his "for sale" signs into the ground. Ideally, those numbers should reflect the fact that resort residential property hovers in the same elite value zone as residential real estate in San Francisco, New York, or Dallas. And those final appraisal values determine just how much land Earl must provide in trade.

Earl's legal team began clearing title to the private lands named in the bill. Adam Poe, at Denver's Western Land Group, facilitated Snowbasin's path through the bureaucracy after Chris Peterson came to him saying, "We have a lot of work to do, and we don't have a lot of time." Poe streamlined the process and paperwork. Peterson dealt with landowners. "We deal with conservation," Poe told me, "but we are a for-profit real estate broker." That admission opens the Western Land Group to plenty of criticism, for they use inside connections and experience to clinch land exchanges for their clients.

Earl's purchase of one prime 12,000-acre property fell through because, according to Poe, the sale was torpedoed by "endless family votes and squabbles." As Poe put it to me, "To get the highest priority choice, you have to wait for Aunt Martha to die. So you may go on to priority number two or six." Sinclair began to look at other private land in northern Utah adjacent to Wasatch-Cache National Forest. Given the magnitude of this search, the legislated deadline slipped away: once that happened, nothing held anyone to a timetable except good intentions—and the coming Olympics.

Meanwhile the Forest Service began responding to a stream of letters from Save Our Canyons board members and SOC attorney Joro Walker, asking for maps and documents and insisting that the Basin needed to be appraised fairly, with full weight given to its future value as a high-density development. Walker found herself dealing once more with Dale Bosworth, the forest supervisor who eight years earlier had signed Joan Degiorgio's EIS recommending a 220-acre land trade. Bosworth had returned to Utah for a four-year stint as intermountain regional forester. In June 1997 Walker wrote to Bosworth to articulate the conservationists' concerns, above all their belief that unless the new lands added to the forest truly equaled "the significant worth" of the 1,320 acres that Congress had granted to Earl, "the land swap will be an unlawful windfall for Sun Valley at the expense of the public good."

This was indeed the crux. At Deer Valley, the comparable high-end resort in Utah, large *unimproved* parcels were selling for $20,000 and $40,000 per acre. With infrastructure, Deer Valley building lots of less than one acre were going for $600,000. Conservationists believed that Snowbasin real estate was worth comparable amounts, and, as Save Our Canyons's Gale Dick put it, "They're going to have to trade Box Elder County [almost 6,000 square miles of northern Utah] to get the equivalent value."

Advocates of privatizing the public lands are comfortable with these prices. Free exchange moves resources to those who value them most, they say. The catch is in that word "value." If a biologist values Flammulated Owl territory with all her heart and soul but makes only $30,000 a year, she won't

NEW MOUNTAIN HOME BELOW STRAWBERRY PEAK, 2001.

be buying Earl's parcels of forest land in Snowbasin where this threatened species breeds, popping out fierce little balls of gray fluff that pass for owlets every spring. An intermediate recreational skier with several million dollars in the bank, however, can acquire that same owl habitat rather casually for a getaway home.

EARL'S PEOPLE AND THE FOREST SERVICE ANNOUNCED that the appraisal would start in the summer of 1997. They made the same announcement again in

January 1998. To avoid speculation on the lands in play, they did not release the appraiser's name.

Such secrecy drove Save Our Canyons crazy. Forest Service officials reassured them. Don't worry: the law dictates an appraisal based on the "highest and best use" of the land. Don't worry: the law instructs appraisers to disregard "improvements" at the resort but not the resort itself. Don't worry: any decent appraiser will consider the development to come. But the dissonance in language remained, for the law required that the Basin be appraised in its unimproved state. And Utah is one of the few states without mandatory price disclosure when lands are sold. With appraisal details being kept secret, conservationists had no recourse but to wait, write impassioned and well-argued letters, and vent to the press.

———

From the Ogden City side, the mountain meets the city abruptly in a boundary drawn with a knife blade. Ogden's streets climb eastward until they dead-end at the national forest; there, beyond a narrow band of Gambel-oak terraces, the mountain rears up nearly a mile into the sky. The scenic gateway to the Mount Ogden massif is a bold, stream-carved V in the mountain front that leads into a canyon rising steeply to the ridgeline. This is Taylor Canyon, the broadest entry into the mountains from the city as well as a favorite hiking area.

Taylor Canyon, the gem of the land exchange, had for years been at the center of every discussion of the trade. Well aware of this fact, Earl had acquired the canyon—from the edge of the city to within a thousand vertical feet of the summit—just before the previous owner could trade the parcel to the Forest Service. Earl knew a strategic bargaining chip when he saw one.

The legislation specifically named Taylor Canyon as land the public would acquire in trade for Snowbasin. The Forest Service clung to Taylor Canyon as an anchor of rightness in the quicksand of the exchange. If they had to acquiesce to Earl Holding's vision for the mountain, they were damn well going to add Taylor Canyon to the block of green on their map. The agency let Taylor Canyon stand in full public view because it was secure—Earl already owned it—and because it might keep speculators' attention away from other properties they hoped to acquire.

With the enthusiasm of a politician desperate to give his ailing local economy a jolt, the mayor of Ogden entered this mountain Monopoly game in midsummer 1998 by reviving an old notion: why not build a tram up Taylor Canyon to the top of Mount Ogden? Such an attraction could bring a flood of tourist dollars to Ogden from some of the 12 million people driving by on Interstate 15 each year, the mayor argued, and he proceeded to spend $200,000 for a feasibility analysis. In response, Chris Peterson let it be known that there was a 50 percent chance that Sinclair would take Taylor Canyon out of the trade.

The citizens went wild, cranking up the letters-to-the-editor machine that had been idling since the passage of the land exchange bill in Congress.

Meanwhile the *Ogden Standard-Examiner* announced that the Forest Service had finished surveying the 1,376 acres of public land in the Snowbasin swap. The "agreement to initiate" the land exchange was signed later that week, and the Forest Service finally named the appraiser. Interestingly, this appraiser worked for Adam Poe's Western Land Group, the Denver firm that had represented Sinclair in shaping the land exchange legislation. Expertise and power kept close company on Poe's staff, which included on its roster a lawyer who wrote the Federal Land Exchange Act while counsel to the House Natural Resource Committee.

For the next six months all further details disappeared behind the blank walls of the federal bureaucracy and Sinclair. The local public was left to ponder the mayor's dream, a Mount Ogden tram that threatened to remove Taylor Canyon from the land exchange and perhaps derail the swap altogether.

At a tramway hearing in the lovely art deco auditorium at Ogden High School in the fall of 1998, the citizens who loved the mountain trooped out to protest the Disneyfication of Taylor Canyon. An older woman who lived at the mouth of the canyon told the hearing that it "cramps my heart" to think that they will take away "our last canyon." Jock Glidden said, "We walk Taylor Canyon and we can enjoy the illusion of wilderness, the illusion that we are in a roadless area. Looking up to cables would destroy this." It may be an illusion of wildness, but it's an illusion that hikers can reach in a stride, incorporating wildness in their daily rhythms. At the hearing the speakers were clear: "As a community, we do not want this—for our mountain to be defaced."

No builder stepped forward. The tram issue faded away. Ogden's citizens waited for more word from the black box of the land exchange.

A FULL TWO YEARS AFTER THE LEGISLATED DEADLINE, the public heard that the land trade appraisers had completed their job. That was it—no further details came for another two months. Then, in March 1999, Ogden District Ranger Ruth Monahan divulged that to equal the value of 1,300 acres of national forest land at the base of the resort Snowbasin needed to come up with "significantly more" than the 4,171 acres of potential trade lands detailed in the legislation. She couldn't say what the values were; she claimed that information was so confidential that even she didn't know the numbers. Once more, all work disappeared from public view for months.

Adam Poe doesn't think that the appraisals were politically driven. For him the "beauty" of the exchange was the 1996 date of value. "As the exchange dragged on for years, we didn't need to continually reappraise the package." This meant, too, that Earl sometimes had to buy at the higher 1999 prices when his people negotiated purchase after purchase, trying to come up with acreage equal in value to the jewel they would get in the end.

Earl used Taylor Canyon as his heaviest hammer. Without warning, in October 1999, Earl filed easements for building a tram up Taylor Canyon himself. Earl wanted it all: to give Taylor Canyon to the people and to reserve his right to profit from the gift in perpetuity. But the Forest Service reacted strongly: "It's an encumbrance that the United States can't accept." Two days after filing the easements, Earl backed down.

Periodic reports of "we're close" turned up in the press over the winter of 1999–2000. Mounds of paperwork fueled the delays. Then in April 2000 came a flurry of news. Numbers began to leak out—the revelation of just how many acres Earl must trade for Snowbasin, more than 11,000. And then, just days before a scheduled signing ceremony, the Forest Service placed everything on hold yet again. A forgotten contract between Taylor Canyon's previous owner and a neighbor had suddenly surfaced to threaten future access to the mouth of Taylor Canyon.

Earl seized on this issue in a last play for retaining control over the canyon and its tramway route. Even after the agreements had been put to bed and were ready for signing, he nearly killed the land exchange. Ogden's new mayor, Matthew Godfrey, imagining those tramcars full of money, eagerly voiced his support for Earl. Each side accused the other of bad faith. All admitted that their working relationship was deteriorating.

With support from the Clinton White House, the Forest Service's forest supervisor and regional forester refused to give in. They insisted on acquiring Taylor Canyon in the exchange. They would not and could not accept the land with encumbrances. The Forest Service spokesman said, "It's not only unacceptable. It's illegal." The agency insisted that Sinclair clear the title. Everyone knew the crucial facts: Earl couldn't start building his Snow-basin base facilities until the trade was final. And only two summer seasons remained before the 2002 Olympics.

———

In the midst of this accelerating animosity, Olympic boss Mitt Romney sought to allay fears the public might have about how Snowbasin would be used for the games. To the delight of the environmental community, he blew the cover of the power structure of Utah when he said that the land trade, even if it went south, wouldn't cripple the Snowbasin downhill races. The Olympics were a go with or without Earl Holding's deal. The land for the race itself had been part of the Snowbasin ski area permit for years. The lifts had been built. Without Earl's grand lodge, SLOC would have to spend $200,000 for tents at the base area. But they had money set aside for just such contingencies.

Romney, who had been recruited the year before to save Utah from the Olympic bribery scandal, was too busy redeeming the Games to be thor-oughly plugged in to the local powers that be. He didn't know, or hadn't re-membered, to stick to the party line that the land exchange was necessary for the Olympics. Instead, he sounded like a spokesman for Save Our Canyons—whose leaders, of course, merrily played up his remarks.

Ironically, by the time the Olympics came to Snowbasin in 2002, the crowds shuttled to the mountain each day by bus to cheer the racers were restricted to the temporary stadium by strict post–September 11 security measures. To Earl and Carol Holding's distress, Olympic visitors never came anywhere near Snowbasin's lodges and ridge-top restaurants with their soaring cathedral ceilings and palatial marble- and brass-fitted rest-rooms. The tens of thousands of visitors saw only the base of the racecourse, a Snowbasin platted by miles of plastic sheeting over chainlink fence. They learned about the rest of the resort only from the video commentary deliv-ered to them in repeating loops while they waited in the bleachers for each race.

The experts and the environmentalists had been right all along: the land exchange had nothing to do with the Olympics.

ON MAY 23, 2000, THE PEOPLE of the United States and Earl Holding traded deeds—1,377 acres of Snowbasin for 11,757 acres scattered across the north-ern Wasatch Mountains. On May 24 the banner headline on page 1 of the

Salt Lake Tribune read: "Snowbasin Land Swap Finally Signed: Developer Earl Holding backs down, agrees to give up Taylor Canyon."

Taylor Canyon sidetracked the swap, but Taylor Canyon also saved it—by raising the stakes and giving the Forest Service the courage to stand firm. By insisting on the inclusion of the 847 acres in Taylor Canyon, the Forest Service had made Earl blink.

Both sides compromised. The Forest Service accepted Taylor Canyon with minor encumbrance, but Earl agreed to cover any future costs on the two acres at the mouth of the canyon where the neighbor's developments could affect public land. The appraised value of the Basin land was $4,134,000, about $3,000 per acre. The appraised value of the land Sinclair gave up in trade was $4,269,600, about $363 per acre. The Forest Service would pay Earl the difference of $135,600.

Since all the appraisals were pegged to the values in November 1996, the date of legislation, some of Earl's later purchases surely cost him more than their trade value. In the end he may have paid more than the $4-million valuation to come up with sufficient land. And, in the end, he still got the Basin for a song. This is a man who spent something like $250 million to build the Grand America Hotel in downtown Salt Lake City and develop Snowbasin without borrowing a dollar. Four million dollars represented perhaps one-tenth of 1 percent of his assets.

———

My journey into the heart of the bureaucracy leapt forward when I spoke with Lori Blickfeldt, a realty specialist in the Forest Service Intermountain Regional Office in Ogden who oversees the file of legal documents, reports, and titles for land exchanges. She told me, "I usually have a pride of ownership in these things. I don't even want to think about this one. I do think this was good for the public, but all in all, it was a bittersweet exchange."

She understands her role clearly. "Our business is to keep the map green; we aren't in the real estate business." Ranger districts see proposals daily for "a piece of the green." To respond appropriately, Blickfeldt judges each on its potential for "greater public benefit."

The Snowbasin exchange was anomalous for a number of reasons: its legislative nature, its bypass of administrative and judicial review, its high-stakes politics and press scrutiny, and, finally, Earl's relentless efforts to control every step. Earl's wheeling and dealing over each individual parcel reminds me of bargaining in a third-world market. Both sides expect the back and forth exchange to lead to the sharpest bargain. And yet the travelers bargaining for a piece of folk art or handwoven tapestry are rich beyond imagining when compared to the artisan.

Lori Blickfeldt said that "flabbergasted" was insufficient to describe her reaction to Chris Peterson's pursuit of the bottom line on behalf of Earl, who "drives everything." She saw Gray Reynolds as a calming influence. "When negotiations went south, Gray brought them back. He was instrumental in tempering a lot of Snowbasin's shenanigans at the end." By the time Snowbasin finally exchanged signed deeds with the people of the United States, Lori had grown so mistrustful of Earl and Chris that she held every single page up to the light and lined it up with her copy, to make certain that Sinclair had made no surreptitious changes.

———

After the announcement of the deal, all Mitt Romney could muster was "It's nice that Mr. Holding will be able to have a more complete resort to showcase." Environmentalists applauded the Forest Service's resolution in forcing Earl to capitulate on Taylor Canyon. But it was hard to be enthusiastic over the national forest's net gain of 10,000 acres without knowing more about these new forest lands.

The local press looked for silver linings. The *Ogden Standard-Examiner* noted that "the kinds of accusations and vitriol usually reserved for arguments over religion, homosexuality and the Second Amendment are over. . . . Earl Holding got the land he wanted for completing his world-class resort. But the people got something of great value in return. It's a good deal." The *Salt Lake Tribune* took a similar position, dismissing the "quibblers" and asking for a focus on "the wealth of new public lands and the coming coronation of Snowbasin into the royalty of Western resorts. It's a deal that everyone should support."

Janine Blaeloch of the Western Lands Project remained a proud "quibbler." Why should we support a deal, she asked, that is nothing more than "another great example of a few members of congress acting as brokers for wealthy landowners? We are left having to swallow something that became inevitable." The environmental community was ready to take a look at the new additions to the forest and appreciate their status as preserved public lands. But they had not abandoned their fundamental resistance to privatization of public lands and peppered their comments, still, with words like "tragedy," "lies," "scandal," and "detestable trade."

THE NEW LAND, now part of Wasatch-Cache National Forest and owned by the people, includes four parcels specifically mentioned in the legislation along with an additional ten, which range in area from 100 to 2,800 acres. When the Forest Service held an open house in June 2000 to describe these new lands to the public, only a handful of local folks attended. After a decade of meetings about the land exchange, people were worn out.

The Forest Service displayed maps and graphs comparing what we-the-people had acquired from Earl with what we used to own at Snowbasin. The bottom line showed a net gain of 12.4 miles of perennial stream, 15.5 miles of intermittent stream, and 14.5 miles of trail access, in addition to re-duction in boundaries by 21.5 miles, consolidation of ownership, and in-creased big game habitat.

The Forest Service did its best to describe a positive outcome, ticking off the list, describing the benefits of each new parcel. Taylor Canyon, of course. Lightning Ridge, that favorite of hunters named in the original land exchange legislation. Franklin Basin, 2,800 acres in the headwaters of the Logan River—the largest parcel of all, which included habitat for the en-dangered and threatened lynx, goshawk, and Bonneville cutthroat trout. Jebo Creek, above Bear Lake—still more lynx habitat on nearly 2,000 acres that had been slated for development. A waterfall in Providence Canyon. Additional land along the Ogden River Scenic Byway. A full square-mile section along lower Wheeler Creek that would save a population of Burke's draba.

More than two years later I asked Chip Sibbernsen about the new lands. After his Snowbasin and Olympic service he had been appointed Ogden district ranger, and yet he didn't have a lot more information than the initial charts had provided. The Forest Service had not diverted many resources to the new lands, but Sibbernsen pointed out that most of these additions to "the green" weren't for anything in particular. They are simply forest lands valuable for habitat and "dispersed recreation."

The Forest Service had moved on to other issues, other crises—above all a disastrous fire season in 2002 that sucked all the oxygen from the budget and left no funds for fieldwork on the new acres. Indeed, the agency's recre-ation budget has been shrinking for years, forcing the agency to turn for fi-nancial partnership to the very corporations that want to develop its lands.

Chris Peterson summed up the final Sinclair position: "The decision has been made to make Snowbasin into a place that can accommodate a whole lot of people. Will there be negative effects on living things there? Yes. Can these effects be offset by the lands in trade? Yes."

Two days after the land exchange was signed in May 2000, workers started digging foundations for Earl's base area buildings. During the summers of 2000 and 2001 Earl's crews created the resort's public face, the lodges and restaurants that made Snowbasin look like "Sun Valley, Utah." With each new layer of infrastructure the price of lift tickets increased, more than doubling from $29 in 1998 to $62 a day in the winter of 2007–08 (comparable to other high-end Utah and U.S. resorts).

Over time Snowbasin began to shed its burden of controversy and scandal. With each year's distance from the finalization of the land trade, more citizens grew comfortable with the simple tagline that Earl Holding, the good businessman, had worked toward for all those years: SNOWBASIN, A SUN VALLEY RESORT. By 2007 the resort was earning high marks in annual industry ratings; the resort-oriented *Ski Magazine* gave it first place for lifts, second place for on-mountain food, and third place for service. *Skiing* magazine, more concerned with terrain than amenities, ranked Snowbasin tenth in the overall list of "best" American resorts.

Earl quipped in 2003 that Snowbasin was "the most expensive ski resort in the world without lodging." He needed 450,000 skier visits a year to begin to earn back his money. Each year visitation goes up; he was drawing more than half that number by the winter of 2005–06. Earl admitted to fatigue: "Building the hotel and condominiums, the health club, golf, tennis, and swimming pool is a big job and could take as long as four or five years. Sometime soon I'll have to hire a new construction boss."

When he made that hire, he took no risks. After Gray Reynolds retired following the successful 2002 Olympic races, Chris Peterson replaced him as general manager of Snowbasin. But just two years later Peterson left Snowbasin—and Sinclair. He had worked for his father-in-law for nearly twenty years and described the parting as "amicable" but implied that the older man's reluctance to move quickly toward completion of Snowbasin's resort facilities had placed him at odds with Earl.

Chris Peterson resurfaced in the news in 2006 when he proposed a resort of his own for Mount Ogden. He had purchased 1,440 acres in Malans Basin on the front side of the mountain, immediately above Ogden City on the trail system leading from Taylor Canyon to the summit. This was land the Forest Service had long coveted. Chris proposed an elaborate development scheme, which would link a gondola that ran from downtown Ogden to Weber State University with a gondola running through a new, high-end development to a small ski area in Malans Basin.

Mayor Matthew Godfrey of Ogden was thrilled—and did everything he could to line up support. He stacked the planning commission that would sign off on Peterson's resort and partnered with his own father-in-law in a campaign promoting "Lift Ogden."

Not everyone was persuaded. Trail and open-space advocates were flabbergasted. The Ogden city council delivered 184 tough questions to Chris Peterson. The director of planning at Snowbasin in the '70s and '80s pointed out the critical difficulties posed by a small, low-elevation, steep-terrained, avalanche-prone resort for advanced skiers only. Snowbasin made it clear that they had no interest in collaborating with Peterson's operation, confirming Peterson's insistence that he was acting independently of Earl, though he remained married to Earl's daughter.

Chris Peterson built his dream on support from Ogden Mayor Godfrey. In the summer of 2007 the mayor withdrew a crucial portion of that support when he decided not to sell city land to Peterson. The dream was left "in a precarious state," Peterson admitted. But he's a developer, with an investment, and he won't easily give up. It's yet another round in the war for the mountain's soul.

"IS THE SNOWBASIN LAND TRADE A GOOD DEAL? By what measure?" Ranger Chip Sibbernsen asks the crucial but frustrating question. In looking for an answer, he sees "more green" on the map. He sees the number of Snowbasin skiers more than doubled, the trails busy all the time, lots of recreation use on the mountain. He sees high water quality. He focuses on the end product rather than the means used to achieve it and concludes that "the public was well served. It's wrapped up. It's got a bow on it."

Ogden conservationist Robert Smith launched his evaluation of the land trade in the local press with a disclaimer. The new lands are valuable in many ways, but Snowbasin is irreplaceable: "It's apples and oranges."

Susan Giannettino, the former Wasatch-Cache Forest supervisor who had represented the national interest in the 1990 mediation, believes that not a shred of "natural-resource-based" data supported exchanging more than the originally proposed 220 acres at Snowbasin. "Do I feel good that that land went from public land to private? No, I don't." But when the process moved beyond resource-based decisions, when the Snowbasin exchange was politicized, Giannettino believes legislation was appropriate, "given the times and personalities involved." She favored a Congressional directive if the natural-resource-based process could only yield a foreordained political outcome.

John Hoagland, chief Forest Service Olympic planner, wonders whether public land in fragile alpine environments should be exchanged at all. Are high-quality meadows and woods ever better served by private development than by management for the public good? "Every time you put a bulldozer on a mountain," said Hoagland, "it's like a meteorite hitting the face of the earth. It can never go back. The compromises are always risky. Mountain environments are one of the most finite resources we have."

Former Ogden District Ranger Randy Welsh remains proud that the Forest Service protected the integrity of the Wheeler Creek corridor through every iteration of the trade. "I can't tell you how many times Chris Peterson would come up with plans to dig up those meadows on the approach and create a water feature. Protecting this key watershed, recharge area, and Flammulated Owl habitat was our greatest success."

These western mountains you look down upon from transcontinental air flights may look trackless and limitless, but logging roads fragment them, developers covet them, and wildlife corridors between islands of wilderness grow narrower and more tenuous with every construction season. The Rocky Mountain states still claim plenty of counties with a population density of less than one person per acre, but we live on a tide of change powered by increasing population. In the 1990s Utah, Nevada, Arizona, Colorado, and Idaho exploded with the fastest growth in the union.

At the root of the problem lies a viewpoint so "deeply institutionalized in our culture" that it brings Janine Blaeloch to despair: land—both public and private—is nothing more than a commodity. Blaeloch founded her Western Lands Project on the opposing belief that public land is "land apart." It is land "We don't own." She calls herself a "fundamentalist" about The Commons, about NEPA, and about the process of public involvement. She believes we should embrace conflict and celebrate those "unorganized, inexperienced, scrappy grassroots activists who cobble together a small ad hoc group to save a place they love." Blaeloch insists we must protect our right to public comment: "It's one of the only real manifestations of democracy we have left."

Wendy Fisher, the director of Utah Open Lands, also sees Snowbasin in a larger context. "It's the classic struggle for control of land in this nation, a classic David and Goliath story, but David lost. Sometimes, it doesn't matter how much community support gets rallied—the power brokers win.

Ultimately Snowbasin poses the question of whether the good of the many is better served through development or preservation."

SNOWBASIN STANDS, FINALLY, as a fable in the contemporary crisis of the West—where democratic ideals about land and citizenship confront the forces of population, development, and political power on the hallowed stage of public land.

We concentrate in a few cities, circling our wagons around oases of water, infrastructure, and private land. Beyond, we pass into the vastness of millions of acres of National Forest or Bureau of Land Management land, where we can walk virtually anywhere, camp anywhere, drive existing roads without permits or requests for permission. National parks and wildlife refuges have more rules, but they too add their acres to our common ground. Throughout the West, public lands are out there—simply out there—a vital and dependable bedrock for our lives.

Students in Joan Degiorgio's University of Utah public lands class hear her words differently than do students in a classroom in New Jersey or Nebraska. About 40 percent of America is public land, but no state east of the Rockies has more than 13 percent public land; most have less than 5 percent. Out West things are different. Federal land managers administer so much land in western states that communities necessarily acknowledge the bureaucrats as essential players. The tension between private and public interests supercharges western politics and fuels antienvironment, antifederal uprisings like the Sagebrush Rebellion and the Wise Use Movement.

Degiorgio's students, most of whom were raised in Utah and surrounding western states, live on islands of private land embedded within the public domain. Nearly 65 percent of Utah is federal land, the second highest total in the nation. Next door in Nevada, 83 percent of the state is owned by all of us.

I have always believed in public lands as our permanent common ground. I use the word *community* more than I use the word *property,* the word *conservation* more than *commerce,* the word *planning* more than *profit.* I often use the word *wilderness* to capture the magic and freedom of public lands, and I'm astonished and thrilled to own land that borders proposed wilderness in southern Utah. Like so many of my generation I have carried the catchphrases of the first Earth Day in 1970 in my catalogue of truths:

Thoreau: "In wildness is the preservation of the world."

Aldo Leopold: "I'm glad I shall never be young without wild country to be young in. Of what avail are forty freedoms without a blank spot on the map?"

Our attitudes about the public trust and public lands are entwined with our social history—and how each of us sees the land trade at Snowbasin depends on which current of history we ride. We wonder: what is ownable? Water? Wildlife? Habitat for that wildlife? How do we balance the private and the public, liberty and equality? Is private property a God-given right or a flexible social institution defined by the law, generation by generation? Which rights belong to the commons and which are privileges? Who pays for the purchase of public rights? To whom do we give the power to answer these questions?

Once a week, from the mid-1980s to the mid-1990s, a new land trust began its work somewhere in America. Initially this work was motivated by the government's abdication of federal conservation responsibilities under Reagan. As the twenty-first century begins, the pace has accelerated to two new land trusts each week; thousands of community land trusts are saving open space where ten years ago there were just a few dozen. Former President Bill Clinton and his secretary of the interior, Bruce Babbitt, created enormous national monuments to protect whole ecosystems. Former Forest Service chiefs Jack Ward Thomas and Mike Dombeck made ecosystem management the keystone of national forest policy and tried to protect remaining roadless areas.

Dale Bosworth (Forest Service chief from 2001 to 2007), more a forester than a politician, worked for the agency for nearly forty years; he had grown up in government compounds where his father served as a ranger and forest supervisor. He sees collaboration as the key to moving beyond the conflicts of the past that freeze us in "process gridlock." Bosworth sums up the fundamental concern: "I really believe in the *national* part of national forest lands. At the same time, how do you balance the national good against the local good?"

George Bush and Dick Cheney and their petroleocracy have set us back. They sanction destruction of public lands in the name of free enterprise and national need. But they are behind the curve of progressive American values, stuck with the same narrow views of natural resources as commodities that Charles Wilkinson calls "the lords of yesterday." Americans who look to the future are poised to enter a new New West—a twenty-first-century West, where the watchwords are ecology, ethics, relationship, collaboration, community.

JACK WARD THOMAS HAS DEFINED three Forest Services over the last century. From 1905 to 1945 the agency emphasized consolidation and protection; this was the custodial era. The post–World War II era through 1987 emphasized timber cutting, which peaked in 1988. The environmental era followed, when the Forest Service came to grips with the great body of reforming land legislation of the '60s and '70s.

Thomas hopes that a new era is beginning now, the period of ecosystem management. Here is his blueprint:

> Give the Forest Service even a glimpse of a clear mission and the resources to do the job and they will come through to the extent possible under current laws and regulations. There lies the future. Coordinate the laws and regulations to make it possible for them to perform. There lies the future. Maintain clear lines of authority. There lies the future. Make certain that the professional leadership can surface issues of law and resource needs and allocations. There lies the future. Bring decision-making closer to where the trees and grass grow and the water flows. There lies the future. Move as many people and funds to the lowest levels in the organization. There lies the future.

Thomas predicts that we will reach equilibrium, with sustainable levels of timber harvest and public lands grazing (the latter stabilizing at half to two-thirds of current levels). "The alternative is even more rapid development of the private lands adjacent to the public lands and intolerable fractures in the social fabric." He lists the astonishing changes he has seen in the course of his career, ranging from the establishment of wilderness and old growth reserves to the creation of new national monuments, the successful blocking of proposed dams, and a series of important victories in the courts.

"Come on! Life is good," Thomas chided me when I admitted to dwindling hopes. "There are new elections every two years. No new administration, to date, has been able to turn back the clock on environmental concerns and attendant legislation. I began my career as a pessimist and have, as I come to the end of life, morphed into an incurable optimist."

———

In this Next West, the People's West, where wildlands are no longer remote, where 60 million people live in the once lightly settled interior West, and where public lands interfinger with all varieties of private lands—including my own—we have the opportunity to redefine the individualistic view of ownership in a new geography of conservation. That's the future. Despite our losses in the Bush years, Earl Holding and his tycoon-takes-all entitlement belong to the past. In the bureaucratic present the Forest Service must find a way to mediate between the two.

PART III: THE MIDDLE-AGED WEST

FINISH LINE, MEN'S DOWNHILL RACE, WINTER OLYMPICS, SNOWBASIN, UTAH, 2002.

NINETY-NINE SECONDS

Whatever you can do,
Or dream you can, begin it.
Boldness has genius, power, and magic in it.

JOHN ANSTER, PARAPHRASING GOETHE, 1835

FIRST, EPHRAIM'S FACE, *fast,* curl in a tuck, seventy-five miles an hour, carry
speed into the John Paul Traverse dropping away to the left, off kilter. Twenty
seconds in—a jump, Flintlock, a wall that leads into the sky. Aim for that
bump on the horizon, turn right, land and turn hard left into the three
turns of Bear Trap, climbing the side of the ridge, falling away again, then
diving into Hibernation Hole, pushed back on the skis—*hold on, hold on.*
Legs ache. *Breathe.* Arrowhead Jump, a roller coaster of bumps, then into
the air and a soft whistle of wind, two-second respite from crunch and chat-
ter. Down, edges bite, legs lay out almost horizontal for Three Toes, three
gates, long and smooth, falling away again to the right, then a quick right
into Muzzle Loader Jump, blind, uphill, airborne, stay small in a ball, down
for tight turns in Offtrack Canyon, riding, carving up the side hill off Sling-
shot and over Buffalo Jump, blind again, thrown forward. Muscles nearly
used up, heart booming, the mountain falls away to the right—but the
course goes left, ninety miles an hour down Rendezvous Face, and done, the
crowd roaring.

Ninety-nine seconds is a line—*this* line—3 feet wide and 1.87 miles long, dropping 2,900 vertical feet, with a margin of cheers and cowbells and kathunking motor drives and the bright blur of 26,000 spectators. Every downhill racer in the 2002 Salt Lake City Winter Olympics could measure those seconds with eyes squeezed shut, envisioning perfection, owning the Mountain.

NINETY-NINE SECONDS IS PRECISELY how long it takes me to read aloud the two paragraphs that you have just read. It may take you a moment less or a moment more. But the variation between us in reading speed certainly will be greater than the differences in finish times for the downhill racers.

In the 2002 Olympic downhill, fifty-three men started at the ridgeline of Mount Ogden, on the "Grizzly"; this is the course you ran in the first paragraph. Thirty-eight women started just a little lower, on the "Wildflower." Eyes open, will focused, nerves aflame but steady, each racer clicked into skis, glided forward, planted poles as far as arms can stretch, then launched into the free fall—the controlled chaos—of the Olympic downhill course at Snowbasin. The racers skied so well, so fast, so precisely, that only subtle differences in smoothness and clean lines distinguished them.

"Extraordinary" wins. "At least twenty people out there are *good* enough to win," former U.S. ski team racer Carrie Sheinberg told me. "The winners are the ones who are extra something. They might be extra mean, extra crazy, or extra dumb. Or they draw energy from some other event in their life that can distract them from the task at hand—the death of a family member or friend. Self-awareness almost hinders the racers. They can turn off their analytical side. The race is programmed into their bodies."

Fritz Strobl of Austria won the men's race at 1:39.13. All three medalists in the men's downhill clocked times just over ninety-nine seconds. French racer Carole Montillet won on the Wildflower course, coincidentally in ninety-nine seconds plus, at 1:39.56. The silver medalist was five hundredths of a second behind her.

This particular ninety-nine seconds, where a few hundredths of a second can make a life-changing difference to an Olympic racer, could never have happened without five years of construction, thirty years of politicking, sixty years of skiing on Mount Ogden, and two hundred years of American colonialism and pioneering in the Rocky Mountains—an entire span

FRITZ STROBL OF AUSTRIA WON THE 2002 OLYMPIC MEN'S DOWNHILL AT SNOWBASIN. U.S. SECRETARY OF INTERIOR GALE NORTON SMILED ADMIRINGLY AT THE PODIUM, WHERE STROBL, SILVER MEDAL WINNER LASSE KJUS (NORWAY), AND BRONZE MEDALIST STEPHAN EBERHARTER (AUSTRIA) RAISED BOUQUETS IN JOY.

of converging human history. These ninety-nine seconds, centerpiece of the spectacle of media and commerce and sport we christened the 2002 Winter Olympics, replay the paradox of massive changes that happen in the West over astonishingly short times.

By contrast, the John Paul Ridge has a backstory measured in billions and millions of years, a historical saga ending with Mount Ogden—pyramidal, powdered with drifts, fluted like a mother goddess Himalayan peak, sheer like the north face of Switzerland's Eiger.

LIKE THE RACERS, I brought my own fantasies to the mountain. I was a senior in high school, watching from Denver, when Jean-Claude Killy won the three alpine events in the 1968 Grenoble Olympics. When I dreamed of celebrity, I dreamed of skiing like Jean-Claude and winning the downhill. One year later I watched and yearned and envied as Robert Redford's character rode his passion and his skis out of Idaho Springs, Colorado, to the

Olympic gold medal in *Downhill Racer*. I drove through Idaho Springs every weekend on the way to my local ski areas, Loveland Basin and Winter Park. I could imagine myself in this story. Killy and Redford were doing what I was doing—only they were doing it better, faster. But we were on the same continuum.

I went off to college, where the Sierra Club poster for Tom Hornbein's classic book *Everest: The West Ridge* loomed at me for years from the wall of my dorm room, carrying with it that inspirational couplet I quoted at the head of this chapter, which the Sierra Club's director, David Brower, lived by. Brower's exhortation to dream and to act can be taken to heart by any passionate seeker, any risk taker. It could be the inspiration for a downhill racer or a mountain climber, for an entrepreneur like Earl or a romantic like me. And these aren't exclusively guy reveries. When Henriette d'Angeville climbed Mont Blanc in 1838, she carved her motto into the ice at the summit: *Vouloir, c'est pouvoir*—"To will it, is to be able to do it."

Much has changed in these last forty years. Today's racers—those big, thick-muscled Austrians and Norwegians—ski so fast, so precisely, laying themselves almost horizontal on their edges at eighty miles per hour, that it's hard to envision being one of them, even in dreams. Especially now that I'm a middle-aged man with a sixteen-year-old son who can outski me. Skiing was hip in 1968 America. In the twenty-first century, the hip factor has passed to the snowboarders and aerialists. Indeed, I saw Jean-Claude Killy at the Snowbasin Olympic downhill race, looking more middle-aged and weather-beaten than I am, telling reporters of his own new love of snowboarding.

I still have fantastic dreams of downhill racing, of flying. But my age in these dreams is a little vague. I can no longer tell whether I'm screaming down mountains with elegance and grace as myself, a man in his fifties, or as myself recreated, with the endurance of imaginary youth.

At the age of seven my son asked me if I could do a flip off the pool diving board. I can't, but I told him the truth, that I'd always dreamed of doing it. I could *feel* myself walk out on the board, take a deep bounce, and whirl through the air in a tight tuck. I could previsualize the perfect dive, but I'd never done it.

My son listened, walked out to the end of the board at our neighborhood community center, and *just did it*—like in the Nike ads. He imagined his dream, and then he acted it out. He has teased me ever since about my unfulfilled fantasy life. And now he's as tall as I am, a big-mountain skier, calm and confident about leaping off cliffs or adding a trick in the air on his descent.

We reserve the word *crazy* for dreamers like downhill racers. And for radicals—for citizens on fire with the absolute necessity to preserve liberty and freedom. And for driven and obsessed CEOs. At the same time, though, these crazies are our heroes.

Dreamers may be timid. Doers may be aggressive. Perhaps it takes selfishness to achieve success. But where is the proper balance that yields grace?

GALE AND HAYNES FULLER, EVERGREEN RANCH, EDEN, OGDEN VALLEY, UTAH, 1998. HAYNES HOLDS HIS BALE HOOKS—PERFECTLY DESIGNED AND IRREPLACEABLE—A UNIQUE VALLEY TREASURE CRAFTED FROM THE TINE OF A HAY RAKE YEARS AGO IN THE FULLER BLACKSMITH SHOP.

FARMERS IN EDEN

Eden ... is not a place. Eden is ... a pattern of relationships, made visible in conversation. To live in Eden is
to live in the midst of good relations, of just relations
scrupulously attended to, imaginatively maintained
through time.

BARRY LOPEZ, "EDEN IS A CONVERSATION," 2006

THE MONKS ARISE IN VELVET DARKNESS to recite Vigils, the night office, at
3:30 A.M. Sixteen mostly elderly men—their average age is seventy-five—
bunch close to the altar on facing banks of wooden choir stalls, intoning
back and forth. Variations in voice and timbre transform their antiphonal
chorus into the organic chords of a pipe organ, a heartbeat, a river.

It's Psalm 68 on this May night: "You poured down, O God, a generous
rain." Outside it's raining and thundering, quickening the 730 acres that
the monks farm. They chant:

Why look with envy, you high-ridged mountains,
At the mountain where God has chosen to dwell?
It is there that the Lord shall dwell forever.

Above the deteriorating Quonset huts of the Abbey of the Holy Trinity in
Huntsville, beyond the rain-soaked fields of the monks, Mount Ogden rises
in darkness.

One of seventeen Trappist-Cistercian monasteries within the United

States, the monastery at Huntsville was founded in 1947 when the monks moved to Ogden Valley and erected Army-surplus huts as a temporary home. Thirty-four men came to the Valley to balance isolation and cooperation, prayer and charity, "solitude and silence, a life of fraternal love and voluntary poverty." Everywhere I look I see holiness reflected in ordinariness, from the glorious stained glass of the chapel reflected in the linoleum of the church floor to the crosses perched atop weathered barns that lean toward Mount Ogden.

In idyllic Ogden Valley, the fastest-growing village is named Eden. When the Olympics came along, billboards sprouted in Salt Lake City, luring city dwellers with tantalizing promises that "Eden is within reach." The ads promoted Ogden Valley's densest development, Wolf Creek, and the valley's first condo and golf community. The tagline—"minutes from Snowbasin"—assumed that Earl Holding's new resort was sufficiently well known to attract new homeowners.

The seven thousand citizens of the valley, monastic and nonmonastic alike, relish a sense of living in a private paradise. They harbor a fierce love for the place, and the names they give to their towns capture these feelings: just down the road from Eden is its satellite village, Liberty.

WHEN THE CITIZENS OF THE SWEET VALLEY of Eden and Liberty speak to me of their home, they often break into tears. They have a spiritual relationship with this sheltered thirty-six-square-mile circle of quiet, and the accelerating pace of growth and change unsettles them.

"The people *need* the monastery here as a spiritual center," Father Charles Cummings believes. Father Charles, who came to the abbey in 1960 as a young man of twenty, spends much of his day simply, in the minute-by-minute experience of his vocation. He is one of the most learned men at the abbey, a noted medievalist, longtime editor of *Cistercian Studies,* and author of two classic books, *Monastic Practices* and *Eco-Spirituality: Toward a Reverent Life.*

Reciprocity grows between a place and its people. In Father Charles's words, "Nature—with all of its seasonal variations, wildlife, vegetation, and physical aspects—assimilates the people. The rounded shapes of the hills that surround us envelop us with a tenderness and protectiveness, and unconsciously affect the people who live here, if they are open to it."

The Trappist brothers live on nearly 1,900 acres and support themselves from their land, running eighty cows and making fruit-flavored honey. Though they own the largest working farm left in the valley, the aging

FATHER CHARLES CUMMINGS, LONGTIME TRAPPIST MONK, 2003.

monks now lease to a local operator. The abbey, which started with 1,500 acres, purchased the additional acreage to preserve solitude and create a buffer of open space—what one brother calls a "perimeter of silence." Beyond the peeling paint of their outbuildings, beyond the roll of their fields, past the waves of homes filling in the valley, the monks look to the Mount Ogden massif rising regally on the western rim of their lives, just ten miles away.

"Mount Ogden is our horizon, every day of our life," Father Charles told me. "The mountain is always there. It is a symbol, a constant reminder of God's compassion, greatness, stability, protection. It's taken for granted that this tremendous view—the sun rising in the morning and lighting the upper tips of the mountain—is part of the landscape of our life."

Father Charles can emphasize the "eco" content of his book *Eco-Spirituality*, but, as he makes clear, "I have a faith perspective. God is worshipped here, praised here, day after day, week after week, for more than half a century. It builds up an energy, a spiritual energy. People sense this and feel it on a deeper level. It's being in the presence of the Holy. . . . This is not to say we're any better than anybody else. We just happen to be crystallizing a tradition that makes this energy palpable. It happens around all monastic centers. It's a concentration of spiritual energy that draws people, heals people, even transforms people." That transformation takes only an hour of walking on the farm, listening to the monks chant.

No matter their own faith or lack of it, the citizens of Ogden Valley feel a special affection and reverence for the abbey. They speak of "our" monastery—an instance of private land adding to the public good—and want to make sure I've visited. When the Trappists say that they pray for us all, their neighbors clearly believe them.

Thomas Merton, the best-known twentieth-century American Trappist, wrote of the cloistered life. "The monastic vocation is . . . by its very nature a call to the wilderness, because it is a call to live in hope. The monk carries on the long tradition of waiting and hoping."

The hopeful monks of Ogden Valley are raising funds to replace the worn-out Quonset buildings. Together with the conservation group Trust for Public Land, the abbey is considering protecting most of its land from development through conveyance of a perpetual conservation easement, which fits the Cistercian model. Traditionally, monasteries have had to maintain themselves by farming. The monks are here to pray. They aren't about to build a golf course on the back forty.

I CAME TO THE MONASTERY for a three-day retreat, as all men, Catholic or not, are welcome to do. I lived in my eight-by-ten cell, which had a bed, a desk, and a window canted through the Quonset hut cylinder. I spent my quiet hours writing and editing, trying to match the circles and rhythms of the monks, who pray together in the chapel seven times each day. They retire at 8:00 P.M., rise at 3:15 A.M., then withdraw to their rooms after Vigils for two hours of silent prayer and meditation before the 6:00 A.M. celebration of Lauds and Mass and the beginning of their workday.

An irony of the cloistered life is the need for clocks. To maintain this precise daily round of prayers, clocks are everywhere, in every room. For our interview Father Charles asked me to meet him in the abbey's library at 2:23 P.M.—just after None, the afternoon prayer chanted at 2:15.

The monks take a vow of stability, agreeing to remain at the abbey for the rest of their lives, but only four men are now moving through the six years required of a monk-in-training. The community of twenty-five needs new members, but, as Father Charles says, it is "a calling for the few; we don't expect many." The lack of younger men in the abbey "puts a question mark at the end of every sentence about our future."

Over time the contrast between the monastery and the surrounding land grows ever more stark, the abbey's acreage ever more valuable (it would bring between $50,000 and $80,000 per acre on today's market). Father Charles admits that there may be a need to sell their land and move, perhaps to Arizona, perhaps to Hawaii, but "it would be like pulling a tree out of the ground by the roots or a tooth out of your mouth." The same emotional wrench threatens everyone in the valley as change encroaches on their communal sense of this place as a retreat.

Father Charles leans back in the monastery library and looks out toward Mount Ogden. Birdsong floats in through the open window. "Like anything that's meaningful, the mountains grow on people. They become friends, part of oneself. And so when some people hear that they are going to lose what's special in this valley, hear about these plans for development, they get anxious. They fear change. They ask: 'Am I going to lose my landscape?'"

One afternoon, as I stand in the little archway outside the gift shop where the monks sell honey, books, and rosaries, I meet the fundraiser helping the abbey to raise the $8.5 million needed for new facilities. He is excited by the architect's lovely design, by the views of Mount Ogden, by the clarity of the need. As much as he respects the monks' dedication to vows of fidelity and obedience, he finds it frustrating that these prayerful, quiet men won't pursue their cause more aggressively out in the world. The monks have invested $2 million they had set aside for medical needs to start construction of the first phase of new buildings; as for the rest, the abbot has said, "we, of all people, have to trust in divine providence." The fundraiser believes in the abbot, but he also knows that the monastery's land could sell immediately.

The first potential buyer he mentions is Earl Holding. Most everyone who worries about the monks' future names Earl as the likely inheritor of this land steeped with sixty years of prayers. No one seems to know whether he has been making offers. His identity as the inevitable buyer is part of his myth.

And then the fundraiser takes leave, returning to the secular world of his Park City office.

Father Charles uses words like *hope, compassion,* and *reconciliation.* In his book *Eco-Spirituality* he writes of humans as caretakers of creation. "For a caretaker the issue is not mastery or control but harmony. A caretaker does not impose order from outside but from within, guarding the existing integrity of the whole interdependent system."

I am no Trappist monk. I'm not even a Christian. But most of what Father

Charles says and writes makes sense to me. The monks here hold the world in the same embrace as the Pueblo Indian people I've watched emerge from round kivas to dance in circles through the packed earth of their plazas—dancing for us all. The monks retell the story of their savior; they loop through the round of Psalms every two weeks, circling in prayer within the sheltering circle of Ogden Valley. They cycle through the rounds of seasons with their farm and fields and livestock.

These revolving rhythms of the abbey are the polar opposite of the rising growth charts of American progress, the antithesis of Earl's vision of change and accomplishment at Snowbasin. The monks' take on the divine stands in stark contrast to that of the developer of Ogden Valley's Wolf Creek Resort, a man who loves to quote Romans 8:31 in support of his plans for booming sales: "If God is for us, who can be against us?"

Some consider the choice to live as a monk to be extreme, a commitment far beyond the norm. It's demanding and intense, yet simple and quiet. It's a little crazy, yet full of grace.

SUSAN MCKAY LOOKED DOWN at the photograph in her hands, my picture of her sheep farm on page 110 of this book. She looked at the view of Ogden Valley, the dearest place in the world to her, and teared up. "It's just so perfect. It's this little round valley surrounded by these hills that aren't very far away. It's so self-contained. What's beautiful is the checkerboard," a mosaic of pastures and streamside groves, farmhouses and communities, reservoir and marsh—the hills and the Rocky Mountain peaks of the public lands above. Crooked Creek flows through my pasture, and I have my great-grandfather Angus McKay's signature on the Crooked Creek Irrigation Company papers." She paused: "Everybody in Huntsville has stories like this, you know."

One after another, her grandparents, parents, and brother have died, and McKay has become the sole operator of the fourteen-acre pasture that has been in her family for 150 years. For her this is now "an indispensable haven, a wellspring of restoration and renewal."

The McKay pasture lies along a curve of state highway on the Eden side of Huntsville. This foreground roots the viewer in an intimate, pastoral landscape that humanizes the wild ramparts of Mount Ogden on the horizon. McKay began identifying buildings in my photo, moving on from those I could see to others shielded by spring-green trees—each structure with its own ties to her personal history. "That red barn, that's the old McKay barn, built by my grandpa and his brother. It's very old. And over here, they are building *really big* houses. Through those trees you can see my grandparents' house, and, right here, the David O. McKay house."

David O. McKay, perhaps the most beloved of modern Mormon Church leaders, was born in Huntsville and for twenty years until his death in 1970 served as president and prophet of The Church of Jesus Christ of Latter-day Saints. Susan's great-grandfather was his first cousin, and she is proud of being a McKay. Susan thinks that it is family rather than religion that ties her and her neighbors to the land. She defines the old-timers as the "homesteading families. They are all still here—as much as the land could be divided and the kids could build houses."

With one PhD in linguistics and a second pending in French, McKay carries that old identity even as she teaches at Weber State University, over the mountain in Ogden. Fully aware of "the wrenching need to choose between two parts of oneself," she puts her animals first. "We came from Scotland and we had sheep, that's who we were." The first thing she said when looking at my picture of her farm was, "That's Misty—when she was gray!" Her mare—since grown lighter with age—grazed across my photo; some of McKay's 185 ewes surrounded the horse.

Shy at first, cautious about eye contact, McKay gradually dropped her physical defenses and emotional diffidence as we talked. She wore no-nonsense, earth-colored clothes that hovered between campus and country in style. She presented herself unadorned, with no make-up, allowing her feelings to pool in eyes of intense cadet blue. With her cropped brown hair flecked with gray, she had the same warm overall brownness as her cinnamon-colored sheep.

McKay feeds her sheep from a dooryard along the road. Here the grass has disappeared and eager hooves have churned the earth. "That's what a real ranch looks like. It's not a petting zoo. People want a caricature of agriculture, not real agriculture. A working operation is not Kentucky bluegrass and white picket fences." She loves the winding five-mile drive up through Ogden Canyon—for her this is "the passageway between the two parts of my life, a corridor which gives me time and distance to transform myself from one persona into another. People don't have to go seventy miles per hour *everywhere!*"

———

Every time Susan McKay walks outside, she looks up to Mount Ogden. "I know every slope and patch of trees on the mountain by heart. It has a thousand different faces and moods. It isn't summer until the snow is off

Snowbasin. It was horrifying to watch those new strips appear the summer they cut the new ski runs. It was heartbreaking. We're used to the scars now, but we hate Earl Holding. He could have had his world-class resort—that's manageable and offers some benefit to the local communities. But the destructive proliferation of condos and hotels is an unjustifiable intrusion."

The pressure to sell accumulates daily in requests to turn her farm into a subdivision, a ranchette—converting land, which anchors lives, to overnight riches, to "money that's gone like water." Rooted in her family heritage, in the lessons—"responsibility, stewardship, steadfastness, harmony with nature"—that she has reaped from her land, Susan McKay knows where she stands: "All Earl Holding wants is to be left alone and have his millions. All I want is to be left alone and have my sheep."

A TRAVEL-GUIDE VISIT TO OGDEN VALLEY does not include the McKay sheep farm. The traveler on an itinerary starts at Snowbasin, proceeds to Huntsville for lunch at Utah's oldest saloon, and goes from there to the monastery.

I follow the banked curves of the Trappers Loop Highway, pass the turn to Pneumonia Road, and wheel down into the valley. On this trip I'm headed for the saloon.

In 1998 the turn into the center of Huntsville from the state highway was completely rural. These days the town entryway leads between South Fork Village (tenanted by a gas station, a Subway franchise, and a gallery selling Western art priced in five figures) and a new Huntsville post office, a beamed building skirted with river rock like a miniature Earl Holding ski lodge. Away from the highway the homespun nature of Huntsville reasserts itself; its 1861 pioneer layout of eight lots per six-acre block remains intact. Each large lot in every Mormon village was designed by Brigham Young to accommodate house, farmyard, orchard, and garden—and many lots here still include pastures, corrals, outbuildings, rusting horse trailers and farm implements, and treehouses in venerable cottonwoods.

The road leads to the town square, a full block of grass much like a village green, which has ball fields, tennis courts, and picnic tables. Several signs announce, HUNTSVILLE PARK: NO VEHICLES, HORSES, GOLFING, OR ALCOHOL. Surrounding the green with its old evergreens are Ogden Valley's sole elementary school, the LDS ward house, and a branch of the county library with a modern design that contrasts mightily with the weathered wood of the Shooting Star down the block. This 1879 bar is famous for the mounted head of the world's largest St. Bernard and for its Star Burger, a double-pattied affair layered with grilled onions and Polish sausage.

The wooden boardwalk creaks, just as it does in our fantasies of the Old West, when I enter the Shooting Star to have a beer and chat with the long-time owner John Posnien in the amber half-light of Budweiser signs reflecting off varnished tables. Posnien and his wife, Heidi, have managed the bar for more than twenty years, but it had been an institution for seven decades before John came to Huntsville in 1948, when he was ten. The local tall tale goes like this: the pioneers came to the valley, looked around, and said, "What do we need?" Well, the answer was, clearly, "a saloon." So they built the Shooting Star. Then they put in the mountains.

Posnien told me that he has been on every planning committee and run for mayor: "I'm a Catholic, and I run the saloon. I'll always tell you what I think and treat everyone exactly the same. And so people are terrified of me, and I lose—yet I get 40 percent of the vote in a town that's almost 80 percent LDS." I suggested that, given his gray beard and eagle eyes, he should play up his resemblance to Brigham Young, but he wasn't particularly pleased by the comparison.

"You always hear 'Growth is inevitable; change is inevitable.'" Posnien was vehement. "It's a lot of hooey. It's only if you allow it—in an unorganized manner. You don't have to be a rapist to accommodate growth." Trying to rally people to be more thoughtful has worn him down. "You can't go to every meeting, be on every committee, write to every publication. And then the politicians, they just go around you at the end—sneakin' and creepin' things in."

Posnien shows the same independence in his other role, as real estate agent. He'll often discourage a potential buyer of a large parcel of land if he thinks the client just wants to turn Ogden Valley into the next boomtown and move on. He worries about wars over water and about installing a valley-wide sewer system that will open the floodgates for development. He worries about his land-rich, cash-poor neighbors like Haynes and Gale Fuller, whose Evergreen Ranch in Eden is, he figures, probably worth $15 million.

"THE VALLEY HAS GONE FROM BEING A REFUGE for the poor to being a refuge for the rich," says Haynes Fuller, who is both appalled and amused. This new era arrived when "Olympic fever" hit in 1995: "Now we have a lot of absentee owners—virtual owners. Showing them a shovel to clean out their irrigation ditches is like showing a cross to Dracula—scares them to death!"

A woman approached Fuller about buying his pasture to build a house. He said no. She scolded him, "You are selfish. This valley is too beautiful to farm." His pragmatic response: "At $3,000 an acre, she's wrong. At $60,000 an acre, she's right. We live in ridiculous times."

Haynes's brother, Gale, chimes in: "Our kids want the land—for one day. Then they'll sell. They don't want to farm. The marvel is, why don't *we* sell?" Haynes gives me the answer: "Our farm was just good enough not to starve us off." The two brothers constitute the fourth generation of Fullers to farm in the valley. They are storytellers and observant commentators on the local ironies. Haynes tells me, "Our family was Republican, but we got so poor about twenty years ago that we turned into Democrats." Haynes knows what's coming. "There hasn't been any farmland here for more than twenty years. There's just land being farmed. In Eden district there are more llamas than dairy cows. I have more pigs than anybody does, and I have one!"

Farmers on this urban fringe must deal with increased traffic, which makes it hard to move equipment or livestock on the roads. They suffer vandalism and theft from the recreational use of fields by all-terrain vehicles and motorcycles. Clueless new neighbors clog irrigation ditches with lawn clippings. In 2000 three-fourths of the farms in the valley had annual sales of less than $10,000.

Haynes takes a long view, one that is turning toward fatalism in his maturity: "It's a transition that started when Peter Skene Ogden startled the Indians. The Olympics accelerated the changes, but it would have happened anyhow. In the end, money has its way."

Weber County planner Craig Barker sees the same barrier to progressive dialogue. The resorts draw people who want more services—"want to make it just like the area they escaped from." Others want to maintain the valley as a rural retreat and don't mind driving to Ogden to shop or go to a movie. The two groups are at loggerheads. With his thirty years' experience, Barker—"resident encyclopedia" for the planning department—believes that "leadership and education" will determine this county's future. He yearns for government leaders with the will to put their political careers on the line. "We will need to tax ourselves to buy open space—and leaders are afraid of the political outfall from that."

The growing number of urban professionals commuting or telecommuting, as well as retiring or spending as much time as possible at a retreat home, is creating a new dynamic in Ogden Valley and places like it around America. Though they may not work the land, some newcomers will stand with Haynes Fuller against the corporate schemes of big developers. And these newcomers have professional and societal heft that may allow them to win battles the old-timers might lose if they stood alone.

WE NEED TO TAKE A LESSON from the monks, whose vocation consists of living in hope. Jim Hasenyager is working to grow that hope. He is a founder of the Ogden Valley Land Trust, conceived in 1999 to save open space in the face of these changes. He had fought on the side of Save Our Snowbasin and lost to Earl. He ran repeatedly for the state legislature, losing each time by a smaller increment. But his faith in his neighbors remained.

When Hasenyager moved to the valley in 1978 he found surprising tolerance for the "young, bearded stranger" who came to live in Huntsville and practice law in Ogden. Recently, however, Hasenyager has seen the valley change, not only from an increase in homes and decrease in agriculture but from an influx of "me-oriented" people who are more concerned with their starter castles than with their community. He looks up to Mount Ogden at night and sees the lights of the resort where he used to see "a mountain, looking over the valley." In protest, the Hasenyagers refuse to drive up that new road; "we will never spend one nickel up there."

Not a conspicuously religious person, as well as being non-LDS, Jim nevertheless uses the word *faith* a lot. "You have to have faith in the concept of conservation easements if you are going to set them aside in perpetuity. They are an act of faith for the future, just as America as a country was something you have to have believed in on faith."

More than 1,600 local, state, and regional land trusts are now working in America. As of 2005 they had protected almost 12 million acres. National land trusts have preserved an additional 25 million acres. Between 2000 and 2005 the total area encumbered by conservation easements held by local, state, and regional land trusts tripled, to more than 6 million acres, and the Nature Conservancy holds conservation easements encumbering an additional 2.7 million acres. One by one, thousands of individual landowners have chosen to protect their land through perpetual conservation easements by donating or selling development rights to land trusts like Ogden Valley's. In acquiring those easements, land trusts agree to enforce all restrictions that have been written into the agreements—in perpetuity.

"It's going to be another Park City in a decade, unless . . ." For Jim Hasenyager and his wife, Charlene, this sentence ends with "we start a land trust in the valley." He figures they have maybe five to ten years to preserve the available open space. In 2000 the Ogden Valley Land Trust acquired its first conservation easement, which protects sixteen acres. The trustees have since taken on the responsibilities of a conservation easement restricting development on 120 acres of pasture and ranchland right at the base of the old Snowbasin road and another protecting a 5,000-acre-plus mountain ranch/hunting preserve in the Monte Cristo area east of the valley.

National organizations like the Nature Conservancy and Trust for Public Land have worked in Utah for twenty-five years, but smaller, community-based land trusts are new. In 1990 a single land trust was operating in Utah, the Summit Land Conservation Association, predecessor of what became the state-wide Utah Open Lands; by 2007 there were four more—including Ogden Valley's. Collectively, the five have protected more than fifty-six thousand acres. Nationally, California leads, with 173 regional land trusts. The largest conservation easement protects 762,000 acres of Maine woods for traditional public uses like hiking, camping, and hunting—taking nearly $30 million of development rights off the table.

"It's like fishing," says Hasenyager of his land negotiations with his neighbors. "You put out a lot of lines; over time you hope for bites."

————

The West has seen Ogden Valley's style of trade-off before. When Averell Harriman came to the Wood River Valley of Idaho to build Sun Valley in 1936, the little town of Ketchum was instantly transformed. In the beginning, visitors bypassed Ketchum in their single-minded desire to reach the resort. Decades later the resort began spilling back toward town, gentrifying the western village in the process. Hal Rothman could have used the same words for Snowbasin and Ogden Valley that he applied to Sun Valley in *Devil's Bargains:*

> Sun Valley revealed the characteristics of modern tourist economies. It served visitors ahead of residents, attracted neonatives who embraced its transformed ethos, grafted a new power structure onto the community, relegated most locals to the lower levels of the economic ladder, and linked the resort more closely to the nation than to its surroundings. . . . Soon there was little local about such places except the cachet of their name.

WHEN ENGAGED OGDEN VALLEY CITIZENS read quotes like these, they cry. Then they act. They act because "Snowbasin belonged to the community in every conceivable sense of the word," as Sharon Holmstrom puts it. "Third and fourth generation skiers go up there most any day."

Holmstrom was Utah Teacher of the Year in 1998. Her love for her home permeated her curriculum. One year she helped her eighth-graders interview old-timers and create a book that lovingly traces the history of Snowbasin. On the afternoon of our interview in 1998 she made sure I knew what was happening at that moment: the remaining foundations of a nearby Civilian Conservation Corps camp used by the young men of the Depression (who reforested Mount Ogden and built Snowbasin ski area in 1939) were being ripped away to make way for a subdivision.

Since then she has moved her energetic and thoughtful self from her Eden classroom to the Weber County Planning Commission, where, she says with some amazement, the commissioners do listen. As a planner, Holmstrom never forgets the emotional complexity at the heart of the issues in her home landscape: "Our valley is unique because it's a circle. There's a magic and a power about that circle. It's like living on a cul-de-sac, a dead-end street. This isn't a drive-by, it's a settle."

Holmstrom's neighbor Shanna Francis took her passion for the valley a step further: after serving on the Eden Planning Commission, she returned to college for an advanced degree in land-use planning. Francis yearns for a big "bible of planning" that a community could consult for formulas she knows do not exist but that would ensure happy endings. "I want the recipe!"

Francis grew up on her family's farm in Eden. Farmer-storyteller Haynes Fuller is her cousin. She remembers "a fairy tale childhood—playing in the creeks, building the forts"—and because she wanted to re-create the experience for her own four children, she and her husband moved back to her grandfather's place and built their dream house. She is a slight person, even and clear in her thinking, her quiet, slightly formal manner belying her fierceness.

Motivated by her despair at the perennial crop of disappointing candidates, Francis ran for county commission and lost. She founded the *Ogden Valley News,* the local biweekly that gives her a bully pulpit and keeps her close to the pulse of her community. She recounted the sequence of planning initiatives for me, one step forward and two steps back, all aimed at the "good ole boy ladder of white LDS men" who are determined to make Ogden Valley into "Anywhere, America." "How can you fight development," she asks, "when *all* your political systems are packaged to promote development?"

In 1996 Ogden Valley came close to instituting a visionary master plan that would have clustered development in existing villages on one-acre lots, with the surrounding countryside zoned in five-acre minimums. At the last minute newly elected Weber County commissioners, deferring to aggressive developers and property-rights advocates, killed the plan. When the county subsequently lifted a moratorium on building permits, housing units doubled in six months. In the five years ending in 1997 Weber County lost an astonishing 68 percent of its remaining farmland.

The commissioners looked for compromise. Shanna Francis credits the county with a sign ordinance that requires the use of natural materials, a dark-sky ordinance (which curbs light pollution by regulating exterior lighting), architectural guidelines, and a master plan for pathways and trails. In 1998 the commissioners established a three-acre minimum for Ogden Valley lots.

Longtime Weber County planner Craig Barker told me that the three-acre minimum came from "reasonable" numerical answers to two questions: "How much degradation to the water supply is acceptable?" and "How much traffic can Ogden Canyon safely absorb?" The planners submitted their data to their computers, and the modeling programs responded with a maximum of one dwelling per three acres. Voilà!

Analysts of the 2000 census figures for rural America have acknowledged the effects of decades of exodus from farming country, but they also describe the new resurgence of rural America, the revival of small towns, the rural demographic rebound. The pattern was clear: the population of "recreation counties"—whose natural amenities, despite their remoteness, drew migrants—grew 20 percent through the '90s, twice the rate for rural counties overall. The opposite was true for "farming-dependent" counties; over half of them lost population in the '90s. Ogden Valley boasts a reservoir, three ski areas, and the mountains, as well as proximity to Wasatch Front cities. Valley citizens have seen what the explosive growth of amenity migration can do. The constant refrain runs, "We don't want to look like another Park City—a sea of roofs."

John Wright puts it bluntly in his *Rocky Mountain Divide:* he describes Park City, forty miles south of Ogden Valley, as "the Hong Kong of Utah. It is an insular, expensive recreational and retailing colony surrounded by a vastly different culture." Ogden Valley could become the neighboring resort-studded island, Macau to Park City's Hong Kong.

How does a community cope? Shanna Francis's reaction when developments at Snowbasin begin "trespassing on my childhood" is to choke up, regroup, and move on.

In 2002 the battle in Ogden Valley shifted to the possible incorporation of Eden. Shanna Francis watched the debate: "*Everybody* is fearful, ensuring their own personal interests will be protected." Even more appalling to her than fear was the widespread apathy. Nearly all the people who were attending incorporation meetings had been in the valley less than two years. Where were the old-timers?

Wendy Fisher, director of Utah Open Lands, has an answer: "Here in Utah, everybody wants to be on the same page. It's more an avoidance of conflict than a lack of passion. People care passionately, but they avoid confrontation."

Dave Livermore, state director for the Nature Conservancy, has been working in Utah even longer than Wendy Fisher. His theory about how theological roots play into environmental philosophy starts with the Mormon tradition that "we are different." People assume that difference surely will save Utah and keep everything the same. "People are so traditional," Livermore believes, "that their long-term vision is to expect little change. Many haven't traveled widely, they haven't seen sprawl. And so they simply don't see change, they don't see the loss of open space as a crisis." Sprawl is relative, of course, but one look at the army of large automobiles carrying one passenger each on eight-lane freeways slowed to a crawl during daily rush hours would suggest that sprawl has definitely arrived in Utah.

Nostalgia can motivate concern. As Livermore notes, this is after all a Jeffersonian state with an agrarian heritage, where many people remember visiting their grandparents' farm. You can't worry about the future, however, until you admit that change is happening—and realize that you may not like what change will bring.

Shanna Francis argues that the mostly LDS long-term residents are kept so busy—and so exhausted—by their church obligations that they don't have time and energy to inform themselves and attend public meetings. "It's the public's fault. They don't study the issues. They see a candidate running whom they don't really know, but they say, 'Well, he's LDS, he's respected in the ward, he must be a good guy.' People in power take advantage of that."

THE CHURCH OF JESUS CHRIST OF LATTER-DAY SAINTS is the monster in the closet, the matrix not everyone wants to acknowledge, lurking inside any discussion of the politics of growth in Utah. Most people I've asked say that the divide in Ogden Valley isn't Mormon versus non-Mormon. It's urban versus rural, or developer and politician versus planner and conservationist. Worn-down activists say it's the people who care versus the people who don't care. But the fact remains that the Church influences the beliefs and values of some two-thirds of the citizens in the state, all of whom have at least nominal connection to their Mormon roots.

Mormon culture celebrates progress and growth. Money and success are blessings, signs of worthiness and of God's love. Mormonism is a faith that likes the word *burgeoning*, and this is reflected in its missionary work around the world, its approval of large families (who bring waiting unborn children down from Heaven for their earthly experience), its drive to fill Zion with suburbs and highways and franchises and ward houses. Brigham Young envisioned a *City* of God in Zion, and to Mormons the explosive urbanization of the Wasatch Front feels righteous.

Even so, currents of stewardship move almost invisibly beneath the developers' juggernaut humming along in tandem with the dominant culture. Both the founder and the director of the Glen Canyon Institute, an exuberant organization working to decommission the dam and restore a free-flowing Colorado River, are Mormon. Neither man yields to the charge of inconsistency in being a church member and an environmentalist, though both understand that they have few soul mates in mainstream Utah.

Open-space advocate Wendy Fisher has worked with citizens all over the state for fifteen years: "Part of being Mormon is being a Utahn, and part of being a Utahn is having a tie to the land. The people who have had the greatest conservation ethic that I've worked with in Utah Open Lands have been LDS. The doctrine may be different than the spirituality."

George Handley makes the same point. A humanities professor at Brigham Young University, Handley finds support for stewardship running through Mormon doctrine. He points to a line like "All things which come of the earth, in the season thereof, are made for the benefit and use of man, both to please the eye and gladden the heart"—an entirely human-centered teaching—and finds encouragement in these words. Handley is an optimist; he concludes, "Such pleasure leads to care and devotion." And he points to another passage from LDS scripture, which admonishes us to remember to use the creation "with judgment, not to excess, neither by extortion."

The Shoshone people who lived in Ogden Valley before the arrival of Anglos understood their place in the world through stories. Gods and animals and people shared the land, time was circular, and life was good. When Anglo settlers came to the home of the Shoshone, they dreamed of what they could do to change the place, to transform it into Zion on Earth.

The Mormons came to Utah in a grueling trek across the continent after their prophet, Joseph Smith, was murdered and they were driven from their Midwestern homes. In Utah they carved a haven from the desert, creating villages and towns in inhospitable places. Here they found a place safe from terror and made a refuge for themselves.

Professor Handley believes that non-Mormon environmentalists all too often forget this history. They forget that their saga of trauma and escape—the "American diaspora"—tends to make Mormon people defensive and distrustful of the federal government that now manages their public lands and administers laws aimed at conserving their natural resources. Rural Utahns, especially, cling to these antigovernment feelings and continue to favor politicians and developers and "wise-use" fundamentalists who drown out the calmer voices in government science and LDS scripture that plead for stewardship and restraint.

There is another kind of eco-spirituality embedded in the Mormon faith, and that is a belief in the inherent goodness of domesticating the West—an unflagging desire to honor the symbols of the heroic farmer, the sacred plow. Farmers and ranchers love the land because it gives them sustenance. They tend not to see the earth as a place with a rich nonhuman life; they don't see themselves enmeshed in a world of nature. The fervor of fresh converts remains, along with an underpinning of what rural Mormons call "custom and culture." They tend still to define themselves as God's troops in a challenging wilderness, carrying out a mission from the Lord.

Mormon pioneers instilled their faith into everyday agricultural life in a way that rings still in the culture, extending even into the dense suburbs along the Wasatch Front. The catch here is that the culture and the land are no longer continuous: Mormon Country has been urbanized.

The doctrine of stewardship that runs through LDS scripture remains deeply buried. As Handley points out, "even simple environmental ethics . . . are rarely mentioned over the ward house pulpit." This silence is the operative ethical contribution from the Church to dialogue about the environment.

Other unspoken assumptions help define Mormon identity, among them that to be a Mormon is to be politically conservative and procorporate and to equate growth with "divinely sanctioned progress." *Dominion* is a more common word in LDS vernacular than *relationship*. While preparing for the return of Christ, Mormons, in the words of Brigham Young, "handle the temporal elements of this world and subdue the earth" so that it will, in the words of Joseph Smith, "resume its paradisean glory, and become as the garden of the Lord." Each Mormon follows the teachings of the Church to reach "godhood."

George Handley notes that "Mormonism isn't very well codified. It is quite improvisational, without a rigid theology," and that enables "zealous cultural norms" to flourish though they have "weak spiritual foundations." Sustainable city planning can be found in the writings of Joseph Smith and Brigham Young—and modern city planners give some Church officials high marks for understanding the principles of New Urbanism —yet suburbs and highways are filling in the valleys of the Wasatch Front. Though Mormon families are smaller than they used to be, most growth in Utah is internal, and the Wasatch Front still looks like a population bomb to geographers.

William Smart, the former editor of the Church-owned *Deseret News* and a board member of the Grand Canyon Trust, coedited a book on Mormon environmental stewardship that is full of eloquent pieces from Mormon activists deeply disappointed by their maverick status. Smart sadly notes that he "can't see that the book had *any* impact in places that count." He is devastated by the lack of environmental leadership he sees in his church. "If only one of those divinely inspired men would raise the issue, it would make a huge difference!"

George Handley calls for "more restraint. We need an environmental fast." Don Adolphson, another LDS professor who emphasizes stewardship, admits that sustainability is not a key ethic for Mormons: "Accountability to God is more powerful than accountability to those who will live in the future."

You can find in the writings of Brigham Young such surprising lines as "There is life in all matter, through the vast extent of all the eternities; it is in the rock, the sand, the dust, in water, air." And "Let us all learn that the earth is not ours." He preached that "it is not our privilege to waste the Lord's substance. There is only so much property in the world." But the next step is crucial: this world we don't own has "been bestowed upon us for our action, to see what we would do with it . . . to beautify it and make it glorious."

What thoughtful Mormons like Bill Smart and George Handley hear today from the divinely inspired men in charge sounds more like what Second Counselor James Faust wrote in 1995, "Those who argue for sustainable growth lack vision and faith. The Lord said, 'For the Earth is full, and there is enough to spare.' That settles the issue for me. It should settle the issue for all of us. The Lord has spoken."

What Faust neglected to mention is that the same passage holds "every man accountable, as a steward over earthly blessings."

SHARON HOLMSTROM BELIEVES that "the source of all the conflicts in our valley isn't LDS/non-LDS but rather the huge philosophical difference between dominion and stewardship." Not everyone falls predictably into place along this continuum, however.

Liberal voices within the Mormon community continue to speak for stewardship. The more than six hundred national members of Mormons for Social Equality and Justice urge "all citizens to reduce their impact on the environment," and they call upon "corporations to engage in more environmentally sustainable practices" and request "national and local leaders to promote responsible policies which reduce pollution, protect biodiversity, and conserve resources for future generations."

Another hopeful voice arose in 2005 from an unlikely constituency. The National Association of Evangelicals included a plank on "creation care" in their "Evangelical Call to Civic Responsibility," but their more liberal members couldn't quite push through a statement on global warming.

Sharon and Dave Holmstrom have thirty acres tucked away in Eden, where they live in a house that started as a barn and grew, addition by addition, into a rambling lookout, eaved and bedecked, that opens to the mountains. Dave sits on the board of the Ogden Valley Land Trust. Sharon is proud that the five wild turkeys that moved in nearby and chose River Road as their winter territory, have been treated with tenderness by potential hunters and harried drivers and are still there a year later.

Holmstrom sees the valley as a particularly fragile place, a bowl that could fill with air pollution. She worries about an Ogden Valley with "quarter-acre lots all over the valley and every one with a fireplace. It would be Thneedsville, in *The Lorax*—home of the people who cut down all their trees."

I look back at Dr. Seuss's book, where the Lorax speaks for the trees and lectures the thoughtless who believe that "business is business! and business must grow." The people of Thneedsville, intent on "biggering and biggering" and "crazy with greed," cut down all their lovely Truffula trees as they set out to make as many Thneeds as possible. Dr. Seuss leaves us with hope, though, with one last Truffula seed and a call to action: "Plant a new Truffula. Treat it with care. Unless someone like you cares a whole awful lot, nothing is going to get better."

OFF-SEASON CHAIRLIFT, SNOWBASIN RESORT, UTAH, 1998.

CRAZY GRACE

There is a cloud on my horizon. A small dark cloud no
bigger than my hand. Its name is Progress.

EDWARD ABBEY, *DESERT SOLITAIRE*, 1968

EVER SINCE HENRY DAVID THOREAU earned Concord's disapproval by going to jail
for his principles and wandering away to Walden Pond to live by himself,
we have been quick to assume that the essential environmentalist is always
a little nuts, a little crazy.

Today we value these loonies, these unsocialized fringe elements screaming into an empty darkness. The Salt Lake Olympic Committee flashed
quotes from Thoreau on the Jumbo-tron at the 2002 Winter Olympic opening ceremonies, co-opting the solitary writer as proof of their environmental sensitivity and wittingly or unwittingly connecting the slightly crazed,
obsessed athletes and the celebration of Olympic and American values with
the sage of Walden. Environmentalist radicals, however, turn out to be more
conventional than one might think. Thoreau may have seemed unsound to
his neighbors, but at his contemplative core he was a naturalist, a philosopher, a diarist. The fiercest activists in mainstream environmental organizations often turn out to be masters of arcane regulatory detail and relentlessly
orderly fundamental believers in the law.

Dave Foreman, cofounder of Earth First! is a preacher at heart and bookish by practice. Ed Abbey, patron saint to a generation of environmentalists, was profane, sexist, lecherous, and humorous, but he was also a shy man who studied philosophy when he was in graduate school and was happiest alone and quiet in the middle of nowhere. David Brower, the archdruid himself, also was a deeply shy man.

I bumped against the image of the demon enviro one morning when I talked for a spell with Larry Fletcher at his home in the Kodachrome badlands on the outskirts of the little Mormon village of Cannonville, Utah. The wind swept down on us from the west, whistling through the pines and firs shading the breaks at Bryce Canyon and swirling through slickrock narrows where I'd been hiking with my family in the new Grand Staircase–Escalante National Monument.

Folks in town had referred me to the Fletchers. Having rattled the bike rack to pieces on the back roads of the Colorado Plateau I needed a place to store our family's mountain bicycles until I could return for them with a repaired rack—and I'd been told that the Fletchers had an empty shed that might be available. Larry was generous and accommodating and neighborly. His face was as wind-chafed as the barn wood of his outbuildings. And then he cocked his head and asked me a question. He wanted to know if I happened to be a member of the Sierra Club.

It seemed Larry had never met such a character. He had grown up in Cannonville. He imagined every Sierra Club member, every environmentalist, to be his enemy—a faceless Other from New York, who would never come to his town or to his home territory, much less to his driveway. He was convinced that these people hated him and wanted to destroy his way of life.

Larry looked at me with wonder when I admitted my identity. I didn't fit his caricature. Sure, we had plenty of differences. But we could talk without fisticuffs; we were even enjoying each other's company. I knew a few of the places that he knew, a few of the same people. By the time I left, he was bemused by the whole situation—bemused that I had turned up, and that I didn't seem to be crazy.

JIM KILBURN, A MAINSTAY OF SAVE OUR SNOWBASIN, walked this shadowy line between fierce grace and old-fashioned craziness. He had his emotional problems, including alcoholism. But he believed that Snowbasin was his salvation. Born in Ogden in 1948, he had grown up fly-fishing the Wasatch streams and skiing the local mountains. In fact, he said that if his mother had not taken him to Snowbasin to ski, maintaining a year-around exercise program after his childhood bout with polio, he might not have been able to walk as an adult. He walked with a limp forever after, but he *walked,* and on skis his limp disappeared.

————

In 1995 Jim lived out a dream. He designed and built a log home in Valhalla Estates, a cluster of cabins on the tiny floodplain in Ogden Canyon nestled against the steep ridges of spruce and fir leaping upward toward Mount Ogden.

One year later the politics of the mountain swept him away. He hated feeling trapped in Earl's world, a world beyond his control. He hated seeing the destruction of the place he loved. Jim stayed away from the front lines, afraid his temper would flare inappropriately. Instead, his contribution was artistic: a graphic illustrator for the U.S. Air Force, he photographed the mountain from the air and assembled the "battle book" that the Huntsville conservationist Jim Hasenyager took to Washington when Save Our Snowbasin sent him to lobby Congress.

The intensity of Jim's personality always made an impression. Roberta Glidden, an artist friend, told me that "you *knew* when he was in a room. He had these amazing eyes—blue, almost the color and depth of turquoise. He didn't seem to blink. It wasn't scary; it was almost like you could see through his head into a spiritual side." Mary Ellen Yonkee, a fellow Save Our Snowbasin activist, was struck by his kindness.

Yonkee had stood up at one public meeting "on fire" in opposition to Earl's Snowbasin land trade. She had said things like "By supporting this bill, you are supporting a lie." She talked about her fear that septic tank leakage at the Snowbasin development would turn wetlands into "open-air poop ponds." By her own admission she was "pretty out of control." Chris Peterson, who spoke immediately after Yonkee, looked at her the whole time he spoke. When Congressman Jim Hansen's representative stood up, she couldn't stand "any more lies" and walked out. A man she didn't know had followed her. She walked faster, uncertain of his motives. He asked her to wait; he just wanted to thank her. "I was in tears; he calmed me down. He made me feel so good."

The man who thanked Yonkee, who soothed her with his kind words, had been Jim Kilburn.

————

NEW LIFT TOWERS PILED LIKE BONES IN THE PARKING LOT OF THE OLD SNOWBASIN DAY LODGE, 1998.

In 1998 the mountain still had its beauty, but Jim had lost to Earl Holding, and now he could see the results as an aggressive fleet of track hoes began to reshape Snowbasin. Kathleen Hession, Jim's fiancée, told me that the construction unnerved him; he could see development overwhelming the solace of the place. After years of sobriety he started drinking again. For help he began taking the alcoholic's powerful punishment drug Antabuse. On August 4, 1998, Jim drank a half pint of scotch with the pills. He didn't die, but he landed in the hospital.

When he returned home the following Sunday, everyone was worried about suicide. On Tuesday Jim called Kathleen to say that he was going fly-fishing. He also told her, "I want you to know that I've had the best nine months of my life. I want you to know you've been loved." She didn't realize until later that this call was Jim's good-bye.

Tuesday evening, Jim's brother, Bob, called the little cabin below the mountain three times to suggest meeting for a hamburger. Jim said no, he'd already eaten, he was just fine. After hanging up for the third time, Jim left his house. He drove up the winding road to Snowbasin. He sideswiped his Subaru on some obstacle along the way. He parked next to the Snowbasin equipment shed, where no one could miss the vehicle when they came to work in the morning. He pocketed a photo of himself with his son and left identification in the car, as well as a box of shells on the front seat. His fishing pole and vest rested in back. He walked up the Wildcat Lift for a steep half mile until he found a chair stopped next to a tower. Tower number 8. Chair number 92. He clambered up the ladder on the side of the steel post and climbed out onto the chair.

He smoked three cigarettes, dropping their butts to the ground below, inhaling, exhaling, thinking. Then he pulled out his new .38, unbuttoned his shirt, and tied himself to the chair with his right sleeve. With the barrel resting against his skin immediately over his heart, he fired once. His heart shattered. He died within a minute.

Jim shot himself at first light, facing southwest, looking up the mountain. The team of summer laborers clearing brush on the ski slopes spotted him at 9:30. From the parking lot below they could see someone sitting in the chairlift silhouetted against a streak of clouds across the morning blue. They approached hesitantly and saw a figure slumped like a rag doll, leaning over the inside bar of the chair. He looked unbearably lonely.

The young men who found him had to close the approach road and shut down construction for several hours until the authorities could evaluate the area as a potential crime scene. While they waited, deeply unsettled, they were transfixed by the dead man suspended on the chairlift over the halcyon green of the hillside. When the officers reopened access to the mountain, the surging drone of Earl's helicopters resumed, ceaselessly building, stopping for no one.

The only press coverage of Jim Kilburn's death appeared two days later, on August 14, 1998, in a sidebar of short takes on local news in the *Ogden Standard-Examiner;* the column got Jim's age wrong, gave a garbled timeline for his last night, and was sprinkled with misspellings and typos. Jim's friends, deeply saddened by his passing, wanted more. They absolutely believe that when he chose Snowbasin as the scene for his suicide he intended to send a message to Earl Holding.

Bonnie Cookson, the retired teacher who helped organize Save Our Snowbasin, had been Jim's neighbor and friend. She understood Jim's message even if Earl did not: "All of this is dying, and I'm going to die, too." Right here, on your land, in your face. Margot Smelzer, too, maintains adamantly,

"He was totally dedicated, totally upset about this Snowbasin thing. Yes, he was drunk; yes, he was an alcoholic. He just didn't want to die in vain. Nobody who knew him could believe anything else."

The women of Save Our Snowbasin cherish his memory and wield his final act of defiance as a shield and a declaration. To counter anyone who says, "He was just looking for peace," they say. "There's no way Jim would find Snowbasin peaceful the way it is now." They say—and I believe them—that he wanted to have his poor dead self land on Earl's desk.

Earl, of course, wasn't there below the Wildcat chairlift to receive Jim's cramped body into his arms. But he knew something about his death. I know this from the most unlikely source.

In the summer of 1998 Mary Ann Bolinder woke up every morning at about 2 A.M. and left her trailer on the north slope of the Uinta Mountains, along Black's Fork in Wyoming mountain man country. Her husband worked on a nearby oil rig. She would drive twenty miles north to Interstate 80, and another thirty miles east across the austere Wyoming Basin, to start her waitressing job at Little America at 3 A.M.

One morning not long after Jim's death, Mary Ann found herself waiting on the boss himself, Earl Holding, at the coffee shop counter. She overheard him talking to the local Little America managers about the recent suicide at Snowbasin. She nearly fell apart. For Mary Ann Kilburn Bolinder is Jim Kilburn's sister.

THREE MONTHS AFTER JIM KILBURN'S DEATH a literally inflammatory protest against ski area expansion lit up the night at Vail. In October 1998 members of the nearly unknown Earth Liberation Front (ELF) took credit for igniting lodges, buildings, and lifts in a blaze that cost the huge Colorado resort between $12 and $26 million. It was the single most destructive act of eco-terrorism in our nation's history. "On behalf of the lynx," began an anonymous e-mail received by the press after the arson. The messengers declared that "putting profits ahead of Colorado's wildlife will not be tolerated."

The attacks on Vail were ELF's first big action. A series of tree spikings, arson at McDonald's restaurants, and attacks on BLM wild-horse corrals, SUV dealers, timber companies, megahome developments, scientists, and firms involved in genetic engineering followed. The FBI estimates that the 600 ELF actions in the United States between 1996 and 2002 resulted in damage of about $43 million. The Senate Environment and Public Works Committee estimates the total at $110 million.

After Al Qaeda's attacks of September 11, 2001, the FBI's sudden increase in funding for antiterrorism activity allowed thirty agents to work on the ELF arson cases. With the cooperation of one crucial insider, the Feds homed in on suspects who began informing on each other with details that led to multiple indictments. These weren't kids who had gone out for a single prank. They were young adults who were philosophically committed to radical action. The ELF cell responsible for $45 million in losses—including the destruction at Vail—was based in the Pacific Northwest and led by a young man named Bill Rogers.

Rogers had spent his childhood in upstate New York, learned about Deep Ecology at Prescott College in Arizona, and worked out of his truck as an Earth First! activist, hoping to save western forests from logging and development. He had moved on to a "family" of other thirty-somethings devoted to animal rights, who began taking action far beyond what Earth First! advocated. Rogers became the expert fire starter. He wrote that we are "predators, seeking to change the established order and create a more just society—by whatever means necessary."

Rogers's lookout and protégée on Vail Mountain was twenty-one-year-old Chelsea Gerlach. The two carried out the Vail operation alone and two days later drove to the Denver Public Library to write and post their e-mail to the world. Gerlach, who wrote the message, eventually had the chance to compose another missive when she pleaded guilty in a Eugene, Oregon, courtroom in 2006. Before receiving a ten-year sentence she told the judge:

> These acts were motivated by a deep sense of despair and anger at the deteriorating state of the global environment and the escalating inequities within society. But I realized years ago that it was not an effective or an appropriate way to effect positive change. I now know that it is better to act from love than from anger. That it is better to create than to destroy. That it is better to plant gardens than to burn down buildings. I have taken responsibility for what I have done and will make amends by being a voice for peace in an increasingly hostile and polarized world.

When the ELF cell began to implode (in part, because the targets they burned—including the Vail lodges—were quickly rebuilt), Bill Rogers moved back to Prescott to hide. He was arrested in 2005 and accused of having masterminded the Vail arsons. In his jail cell, disgusted by his friends' betrayal, Rogers left a note for his family before suffocating himself inside a plastic bag: "I chose to fight on the side of bears, mountain lions, skunks, bats, saguaros, cliff roses and all things wild. I am just the most recent casualty in this war. But tonight I have made a jailbreak—I am returning home, to the Earth, to the place of my origins."

SNOWBASIN HAD CAUGHT FIRE METAPHORICALLY when people's emotions reached full blaze. Vail burned literally. On both mountains the powerful had their way, and their vision of Mountain as business and commodity overwhelmed the people's vision of Mountain as community and ecosystem.

At the end of *Powder Burn,* his book about the Vail attacks, the journalist Daniel Glick wrote of the remarkable hatred he found in the Vail Valley for the corporate owners of the resort, emotions so intense—much as those I found expressed toward Earl Holding—that they poisoned the local community. The depth of antipathy startled him: "Many people believed the current owners of the ski area somehow *deserved* to be burned."

Totting up millions of dollars in budget items—profits from one business venture plowed into a new venture—is one way to measure the cost of development. Here is another, from Thoreau: "The cost of a thing is the amount of what I will call life which is required to be exchanged for it."

What are the costs in Thoreauvian "life" of each conflicting dream for the North American landscape? In *Downhill Slide,* his investigation of the power wielded by the ski industry, Hal Clifford poses a question in the chapter title "What Is Land For? A Theological Schism." In *Powder Burn* the same conundrum brings Daniel Glick up short; a quote from a spokesperson for corporate Vail haunts him: "Who gets to decide what's enough? That's the heart of it."

Jim Kilburn's answer was clear: "I have no power to decide what this mountain is for, and I'm depressed and angry about it." Jim was no eco-terrorist, but the Thoreauvian costs built into our exchange for the New may have included his life.

Who determines the limits of development on Mount Ogden? The answer—the final answer—is Earl Holding. His goal is to develop the mountain and achieve elegance and grace—as he defines them—in every concrete slab and high-vaulted beam, every petunia bed and prime rib buffet. He has so much power and influence that many people, cities, agencies, politicians—indeed, the United States Congress itself—willingly do his bidding.

But not every person. The most passionate citizens react. The craziest citizens overreact. They all seek to make a difference.

When I was a teenager I loved the Arthurian legends. Watching the 1967 film musical *Camelot* I struggled right along with Arthur as he tried to understand how his two best friends, Guinevere and Lancelot, could have betrayed him. When he apologized to King Arthur for the tensions he had brought to the court, Lancelot's explanation didn't seem sufficient, but it seemed true: "All fanatics are irritating."

Like Lancelot, fanatics accomplish things—by their passion, their single-mindedness, their tenacity. They may be crazy, they may disrupt community, they may be criminals, they may be repellent or admirable, but we are impressed by their ability to change the world.

AT THE SAME TIME EARL HOLDING was transforming the mountain at Snowbasin into his vision of an ideal resort, he was creating another mountain from scratch in Salt Lake City. Grand America Hotel was rising, a chunky gray monolith that would anchor the southern rim of Salt Lake City's downtown.

Earl scrutinized every construction detail. At a Vermont quarry he chose each of the fifty-thousand-pound blocks of Bethel White granite that would sheathe Grand America and shipped the lot of them to his favorite stonecutters in Spain. Earl favored the Vermont source, in part, for its proximity to Joseph Smith's birthplace; the LDS Church also favors Bethel White for its new temples. The dressed granite slabs returned by boat via the Panama Canal to Los Angeles, from where they were trucked to Salt Lake City— along with cherrywood furniture from France, crystal and bronze chandeliers from Austria and Italy, English wool carpeting, and marble from France, Italy, and Portugal. Over and over people say of Earl: "He is obsessed with quality." A former employee says, "Earl believes if it's worth building, it's worth over-building."

You could wager Earl's fortune on the fact that he and Carol have personally chosen all of these "finest materials from around the world," as his promotional literature describes them. Carol has said that "Earl knew from the very beginning what he wanted and what tile he wanted and what marble he wanted." The Holdings traveled often to Europe, choosing the furnishings for Grand America and bargaining with suppliers. Before allowing the installers to proceed, Earl is said to have laid out every marble tile, vanity, and shower sill in the basement of the rising hotel and to have rejected most pieces.

The completed Grand America quickly became a venue for banquets and proms, but it does not say, "This is your building." Grand America is grand only for those who can afford it.

———

MAC LIVINGSTON, MANAGER OF THE FLOWER PATCH, BELOW GRAND AMERICA, 2004.

The extravagant monument to Earl's enthusiasm for hotelkeeping fills nearly an entire oversized block. The granite walls and courtyards of Grand America trace a perfect rectangle, except for one corner where they must make a jog around a slightly seedy florist's shop.

I knew from newspaper accounts that the owner of the Flower Patch, despite intense pressure, had refused to sell out to Earl. Earl had wanted the whole block, but he couldn't have it. And so he had to build around this little outlying building. The press had loved this story. K. McCoy Livingston—who managed the Flower Patch and spoke for its owner—was the little guy, Earl was the Big Guy. Both were eccentric fanatics out to change the world.

When I called Mac Livingston I told him I was working on a book about Earl Holding and his mountains—the mountain he had developed and the mountain he had built—and that I wanted to understand the effects wrought on our lives by both. After my introductory spiel there was a long pause on the other end of the line. And then, intense and exultant, relieved that a writer had finally appeared to tell his story, he said evenly: "I've been waiting for your call."

A FEW DAYS LATER I CAME TO MAC'S OFFICE at the Flower Patch headquarters in the industrial interstate corridor of Salt Lake City. Maps highlighted in red covered the conference table. Mac had asked his assistant, Julie Brewer, to photocopy every article and document relating to his battle with Earl. With a joint flourish Mac and Julie slid two overstuffed blue binders in front of me; when I balanced them on my bathroom scale later, they weighed nearly seven pounds.

"Exhibit A" was penciled on the first document in the binder. Mac waved it at me. It was a letter from Sinclair's Chris Peterson to Alice Larkin Steiner, the executive director of the Redevelopment Agency (RDA) of Salt Lake City, and it was dated March 31, 1994. Chris stated that Earl (in the corporate form of "Sinclair") owned twenty-eight acres of property on four blocks in downtown Salt Lake City and asked the agency to designate these blocks as a "blight survey area to determine if blight exists and a redevelopment project area is feasible."

The neutral-sounding language veiled Sinclair's bald request for public money to help pay for development the company intended to pursue anyhow. If his four blocks could earn the necessary designation of blight (a broad, loosely defined term that could apply equally to areas with hazardous waste, inadequate open space, dilapidated buildings, or poorly platted lots), Earl could receive money from the Redevelopment Agency—as well as breaks on his property taxes.

Earl and his people said that they would be happy with "assistance" comparable to the $24 million tax credit provided to another recent RDA project. Earl may have intended this figure as a total. Mac multiplied the figure by the acreage of the blocks that Earl deemed blighted and concluded that "comparable" assistance to Sinclair would amount to $450 million. Either way Earl would become the beneficiary of tens of millions of dollars from public funds.

A month after the blight study was announced, Mac sent a five-page letter to property owners within the affected area, proposing an alliance to fight the RDA: "Together, we are involved in a classic confrontation involving government bureaucracy and big business versus the small property/business owner." He noted that any business within a "blighted" area that declined to sell could be condemned, and that the enforced sale price could end up being far below real value. He also pointed out that Earl's corporation had for some time been tearing down buildings in the area, blighting the very neighborhood they now wished to declare blighted! Sinclair was asking for public money to reclaim its own neglected lands. Mac was outraged.

The South Downtown Alliance born from Mac's first meeting was a coalition of owners—mostly women—of small businesses and office complexes that included the flower shop, motels, banks, electronics stores, pawnshops, and auto-repair and parts garages. The Alliance mounted a formidable campaign. They educated themselves in the law. They politicked for reform in the state legislature. They confronted the city council with obvious conflicts of interest. They attracted national press attention.

MAC'S DOCUMENT FILE OPENED WIDE the passageway that led me into the inner workings of an astute man and carried me beyond his droopy eyes, delighted smile, and Sonny Bono moustache. He thinks in outline form, and he reveled in the organized compendium of paper that traced his fight with the powerful.

Mac's actions are consistent with his heritage; he gives credit to his childhood home for his fundamental belief in liberty. Freedom, Utah—where Mac was born in 1936, in the depths of the Great Depression—doesn't exist anymore as a village. Today it's a lane, a few blocks long, at right angles to a country road in a classic Mormon agricultural landscape; it lies at the base of the craggy little San Pitch Mountains, along the edge of the San Pete Valley. Freedom was settled after the Civil War by immigrant Mormon converts. *Utah Place Names* suggests that these pioneers chose the patriotic name because "many of the early immigrants had experienced oppression in the tyrannies of their home countries in Europe."

Mac Livingston is still ready to fight tyranny. He cares more about the philosophy of John Locke than either flowers or money. Greg Parrish, who owned the Flower Patch, felt that Mac made a better warrior than he did. And so Mac took to the field for his team.

In Salt Lake City, Mac was journeying from Freedom into what old-timers in Utah call the Web. Spun by the powers that be, the Web inseparably entangles money, politics, and the Mormon religion. Wealth buys power and political connection, and then the powerful retain control by corralling all the decision making within their tight group. Property works pretty much as it does in a game of Monopoly: whoever owns the most wins the game.

The Flower Patch stood in Earl's way. He tried to make it go away. In May 1995 he offered to buy the shop for $266,000—a figure he described as

"140% of the appraised value of $190,000." Ten years earlier the Flower Patch had purchased the site for approximately $400,000 and spent an additional $100,000 on renovation that considerably improved the former "go-go" bar. Facing condemnation by the RDA, the Flower Patch placed plans for further renovation on hold.

The site was one of the most profitable and most productive of the twelve Flower Patch branches, an irreplaceable store on a conspicuous downtown intersection, catty-corner from the glorious castellated City & County Building. Earl's initial offer made no allowance for the contribution that this location in the secular heart of the city made to property values. According to Jim Boud, the Flower Patch lawyer, even Sinclair eventually acknowledged that this had been a "phony, lowball appraisal."

The Flower Patch refused to sell. Ever. Flower Patch owner Greg Parrish threatened to chain himself to a bulldozer if Sinclair condemned his shop. But Mac, on Parrish's behalf, extended a counteroffer to Sinclair: The Flower Patch was ready to buy *all* the Sinclair land on the "blighted" blocks at their appraised value, which totaled $16.5 million, and to redevelop the land without "extending our hand to the public trough" or "employing an unjust law to harass, intimidate, frighten and tyrannize our neighbors."

In October, with no resolution in sight, Mac Livingston and Julie Brewer met with the RDA director and board chair, Alice Larkin Steiner and Keith Christensen. Julie's notes on the meeting gave out after seven pages: "At this point I felt it absurd to continue taking notes as Keith and Alice kept repeating the same thing, like a mantra: Meet with Sinclair, meet with Sinclair, meet with Sinclair. . . . To which we kept saying: We don't want to move, we don't want to move, we don't want to move."

Mac was aware of the deadlines in play here, those of the RDA process and the coming Olympics. He told me, "My strategy in all of this was to stall. That's why I protested to the city council. That's why I challenged Alice Steiner, the director of the RDA, with conflict-of-interest connections to Sinclair. That's why I put off meeting with Sinclair. That's why I sent my assistant to meetings, that's why I did everything I did. Nearly everyone was opposed to my strategy, but I was insistent. I knew that if I stalled long enough, Earl had to cave in."

His strategy drove the powerful to rage and distraction. Mac wrote letters in response to every detail in every document, and he sent copies to tiers of officials. He asked that every statement be clarified, challenged the dates of hearings, objected to the size of meeting rooms. He charged officials with collusion, forcing them to respond, and then responded to their responses—generally by quoting the Founding Fathers. He assigned three Flower Patch employees to do research and supply ammunition for his fight.

The lawyer Jim Boud says that "if Mac had Earl's money, he would try to solve poverty in the United States. He is as obsessed with his principles as Earl is obsessed with accumulating." Eccentric and obsessive are words that I hear applied to both men. But Mac appears to have acted totally selflessly. Boud told me, "Did you ever see *Man of La Mancha?* Mac *is* Don Quixote."

On December 16, 1995, in an exhausting hearing that lasted eight hours, the city council (which acts as the RDA board of directors) dutifully, and with little comment, listened to the blight consultant, the expert witnesses, the protesting property owners, and the lawyers. They passed every motion unanimously and verified the RDA consultant's findings by declaring 22.46 acres of land—more than half the contested four-block area—to be blighted.

Two weeks later the *Salt Lake Tribune* ran a lead editorial suggesting that Sinclair should have kept its redevelopment in "the private sector, where it belonged" and should never have involved the RDA in the first place.

In January 1996 Mac employed the ultimate stalling weapon. Together with the owners of the neighboring pawnshop and autoglass repair service, he sued the Redevelopment Agency of Salt Lake City, alleging conflicts of interest, violations of open-meeting statutes, and abuses of constitutional property rights. The suit asked that the courts throw out the blight designation. Mac and his lawyer, Jim Boud, insisted that with the lawsuit in place, all activity must halt until the courts resolved the issue. The RDA continued to schedule hearings that Mac and other representatives of the Flower Patch refused to attend.

At the next hearing Earl himself narrated a three-hour slide show that unveiled his detailed plan for Grand America, including the $185-million price, the 905 planned rooms, and the 100,000 square feet of conference and ballroom space. The RDA used its allotted time chiding the press for inaccurate reporting and insisted that eminent domain would not be used to condemn properties. This represented a crucial shift in their position. They continued to ask the two sides to consider compromise and sacrifice—for the good of the city.

On February 12, 1996, the Flower Patch received its first letter directly from Earl, who increased his offer to what many people would have judged acceptable. In a subsequent series of letters Alice Steiner at the RDA tried to clarify and mediate the dialogue between Earl and the Flower Patch team.

———

On March 20 Mac and his allies had their one and only meeting with Earl, who was accompanied by Ken Knight and one of the Sinclair lawyers. Earl was ten minutes late. When he arrived, everyone rose to greet him except Mac, who remained seated. The meeting mostly consisted of a series of questions posed to Earl by the owners of the pawnshop, auto glass shop, and flower shop. With the help of their lawyers, the small businesspeople played offense, proposing full participation in the development of twelve stories of office suites on their corner of Grand America. Earl answered most questions himself. A query about cost led him off into a long monologue about engineering, earthquake protection, and Salt Lake Valley geology.

As he left, all once again stood—all except Mac Livingston. He wanted to force Earl Holding to reach far across the conference table to shake his hand, and he told me that he had never seen quite so much hatred in anyone's eyes as in the glare Earl turned on him.

———

On June 17, 1996, Earl Holding unilaterally terminated the RDA applications. The Olympics were looming; he couldn't wait any longer. Sinclair requested permits for the construction of Grand America. Earl would build his mountain of a hotel without public funding. He would persuade the owners of the auto glass shop and pawnshop to sell. But not Mac and the flower shop.

Ken Knight said that Earl withdrew because the lawsuit would have been a lengthy process and the delays costly for Sinclair. Delays would have been unavoidable, for they were required by law, as Mac and his team had pointed out: a year earlier the RDA had missed a thirty-day notice requirement; the entire process after that was illegal. By statute the city would have had to wait a full year to begin again. This had been Mac's ace in the hole, "the small pebble that felled Goliath," as Mac's lawyer put it. Mac had won.

IN 2002, AFTER THE OLYMPICS, after the opening of Grand America—after, indeed, Mac had moved on from the Flower Patch to his own consulting business, I met Mac and Julie on the front steps of Grand America. Neither had been in the building.

We strolled the halls, cocooned in Earl's personal world of cut glass and stone, brocade and polished wood. Here Earl finally superseded the legend of Little America. His personal legacy would not be a place steeped in local tradition and regional history; instead, Earl brought to the community a collection of imported elite objects entombed in marble.

The kind of perfect order Earl strives for strikes me as the ultimate contrast to the spirit trail that Navajo weavers build into their rugs. The weavers create this deliberate break in the lines of their pattern with a path of contrasting yarn that leads from center to edge and allows the weaving to breathe. They know that humans cannot confine the spirit of their art within rigid boundaries. Letting go, allowing that exit to chaos and freedom, is the weaver's act of grace and wisdom.

Earl patterned the Grand America after the Ritz in Paris. He wanted to be a great hotelier, so he brought the cultural symbolism of Europe to Salt Lake City. Earl's version of a grand hotel is not the Mirage, the Venetian, or the Paris of Las Vegas. It's not a wacky hedonistic fantasy; rather, it's Little America on a grand scale, a straightforward convention hotel with an ornate veneer of tapestries and chandeliers. Church members have told me that it looks not unlike the interior of a Mormon temple.

At first, Grand America left Mac nearly speechless. Once he regained his voice, Mac was proudest of the fact that "we didn't pay for this with taxpayer's money. I firmly believe that if we hadn't interceded, he would have gotten $450 million from the RDA."

Over lunch at Earl's Garden Café, Mac contemplated the craving for power over other people that drives his opponents. "They are full of rage—typical of insecure, dominating males. It's a sickness. It is not confined to Utah, it's a sickness found around the globe. What happened to the humanity that's supposed to dwell inside of them? People like Earl Holding are being born as you and I sit here talking, people who will take advantage of other people, who are born in a culture that stresses the making of money. It's a plutocracy: money rules the law." Mac paused, catching his breath. "Earl is not my enemy. The issue is not really Earl Holding, it's not the politicians, it's not the judges—it's the awful system. The tragedy is our ignorance. It's us, paying no attention to politics while those we elect to defend us against tyranny pass and support tyrannous laws."

Complacency rules. When researchers asked Utahns what they value about their home, they answered: "Peace of mind . . . which emanates from a feeling of safe haven based on living among people who prize and share a common sense of honesty, morality, and ethics." That safe haven is all-important, and diversity, change, complexity, conflict—and fanatics—all threaten it.

———

In 2005 the Utah RDA reform movement succeeded in persuading the state legislature to pass a bill that removed eminent domain from the powers of city redevelopment agencies, limited the number of eligible projects, and placed a moratorium on new RDAs. The driving force came from citizens who had been horrified by the diversion of property tax money from education and schools to public funding of big-box retail malls and sports arenas. This was a real accomplishment in a legislature whose leaders in both houses often come from the real estate and land development industries.

The Grand America has gone on to achieve its coveted "five-diamond" ranking. When President George W. Bush came to Salt Lake City to address the American Legion convention in 2006, he stayed in the Grand America presidential suite, which costs $4,500 per night.

Mac Livingston, meanwhile, still has one unfinished proposal for reforming the shape of Salt Lake City civic life. "Here's what I'd do with the Flower Patch if I owned it." His eyes sparkle, his moustache dances. "I would raze the building. I would put up a high wall along the boundary with Grand America and leave the street side open. I'd call it Liberty's Place, or Liberty Plaza, and have people come to roller-skate and ice-skate. It's small—but think of Rockefeller Center. . . . And on the high wall I'd put a memorial to our whole fight, tell the whole story from first to last, so people could understand our political birthright. I would really sparkle that place—and tell this story as a lasting legacy to Earl Holding."

Whether or not Mac builds Liberty Plaza, this kind of democratic response to power lives deeply within the American soul. Mac wouldn't approve of Jim Kilburn or the Earth Liberation Front arsonists. But these quirky and intense people share more than they might think. All of them hate what they see when they look at our culture of inequity. They just differ—dramatically—in their responses.

Mac and his band of ordinary citizens succeeded where others failed. They hijacked the complacent hierarchy and prevented the powerful from having their way. With unquenchable spirit they chart the path to good citizenship: become a partisan, face conflict, and exercise the power of the individual while honoring community. Each of us must follow this same path as we strive to sustain, to re-create, or to create our own personal Edens.

THE HENRY MOUNTAINS FRAMED BY THE AUTHOR'S CONTRACTOR, JOHN
SAMMOND, AS HE POSITIONS A WINDOW IN THE BEDROOM OF THE HOUSE,
TORREY, UTAH, 2002.

DEVIL'S BARGAINS

By means of the house we become friends with a world,
and gain the foothold we need to act in it.

CHRISTIAN NORBERG-SCHULZ, *THE CONCEPT OF DWELLING*, 1985

MY WIFE, JOANNE, WAS BORN the day after April Fool's Day. I was born the day before Halloween. When our intensity cranks up beyond what's appropriate, we remind ourselves of the inherent silliness of our beginnings.

Joanne isn't a consumer. She isn't a collector. She is happy with the clothes she loves and the few possessions she defines as treasures, and she has little need to acquire new ones. Joanne is also decisive. When she knows something is right, she goes for it. Absolutely, resolutely.

She keeps asking hard questions. We both do. Even when the questions have no simple answers. Especially when the questions have no easy answers.

Right in the middle of my work at Snowbasin we landed in a thicket of hard questions that mirrored the issues circling about Earl Holding. But this time they swirled through our own lives. The parallels and the ironies taught me to see the Snowbasin story in a new light.

———

My small-scale equivalent of Earl's saga begins in March 2000. I step from a curb in downtown Salt Lake City to rush across Main Street to my truck; I'm late for the next family chore. I look left, I look right. In the middle of the wide street, crews are laying the new light rail train line. As I run, I trip on the rail, torque into the air, and come down hard on the metal rail, with all my weight on the outside of my right foot. After a sleepless night I turn myself in at the doctor's office and discover to my chagrin that I've broken my fifth metatarsal in two places. I spend the next six weeks in a boot cast. I joke with worried friends that I've had a light rail accident.

Two weeks into my convalescence comes the first weekend in April—Joanne's birthday. We had planned a family ski weekend at Alta. Since I can't ski, we go instead to southern Utah canyon country, to a cabin that belongs to friends. For years, whenever our friends are not in residence this has been our vacation retreat. It's outside Torrey, near Capitol Reef National Park, where I worked as a ranger nearly thirty years ago. We—and the circle of families who use this cabin—are able to live this classic privileged American vacation life with no investment of our own, no need to grapple with the ethics of second home ownership. We have a cushy deal financially and a free ride philosophically—and we know it.

We take one small assignment with us to Torrey. A friend has sold a ranch in Montana—a working ranch, with cows and considerable acreage. Now, for tax relief, she needs to reinvest quickly in new property. When we tell her we are heading south, she asks us to check with the local real estate agent and find out if anything interesting is for sale. We know her request is casual, that the Rockies and New England own her heart. We almost forget to do what she asks.

Torrey, the gateway community to Capitol Reef National Park, is a Mormon pioneer village shaded by grand old cottonwoods lining the ditch that flows with the lifeblood of this irrigated society. At one end of Main Street lie an RV park, a youth hostel, and two first-rate restaurants. A few blocks away, at the other end, stand three art galleries, a burger joint, and the log-cabin office of Cathy Bagley's Boulder Mountain Realty.

Fiftyish, Cathy is finally living the boom after many lean years. She runs the dominant real estate operation in the area and, with her husband, a high-end art gallery, but her best friends are ranchers, and she serves as Torrey ditchmaster. Cathy's eyes twinkle at the shenanigans of Torrey's small-town politics, but you never learn everything that's going on behind her smile. She acts as a kind of gatekeeper, choosing by instinct buyers she believes will be a good match—"crafting the community," in the words of one of her clients. Her grandmother was from Taos Pueblo, and she reminds me of the Pueblo women I know from New Mexico, not just in the opacity of her black hair but in the way she speaks her opinions with care, keeping much to herself.

I'm not sure she thinks much about the irony in selling back to white people for large sums of money the land they took from her ancestors, but I enjoy that undertone to all the modern contracts she arranges between sellers and buyers. You could argue that she is the most powerful person in the county, for she is the sentry, making first contact, interpreting local culture for the newcomers, and making decisions that affect both the old guard and the newly arrived.

Joanne and I explain our ranchless friend's position and ask Cathy blithely, "Do you have anything really expensive for sale?" Words dear to a real estate agent, words that have never before passed our lips. Cathy knows of us, and we pass her test; and as surrogates for our more affluent friend she passes us along to a seller. In her laconic, low-key way, Cathy says, "Well, there's a piece of land just out of town that's nice. It's just barely on the market. There is no sign, but you could go out and knock on Al's and Anna's door and see if they're home. They'd be happy to show you around."

As lovers of the area, as part-time members of the community, just having the chance to see this "nice" piece of land intrigues us. Curious, we drive out to take a look—for our friend. We are shopping vicariously.

AL AND ANNA *ARE* HAPPY to show us around. Al Schmierer is a charming sixty-year-old optometrist who has retired from the U.S. Army and Indian Health Service. Bearded, pony-tailed, a bit of a beatnik, he is also a tinkerer and proudly displays a darkroom off his living room, a woodcarving shop in the basement, and projects all over the property. In the chest pocket of his work shirt he keeps a pencil and index cards covered with notes in neat, tiny letters. Anna is a painter, entranced, ironically, by the very flowers that trigger her terrible allergies.

Al and Anna lived for a time at Zuni Pueblo and know my books about Southwest Indians. The four of us share a love of the local landscape. This feels like a visit to friends.

The Schmierers bought and sold property in seventeen places as they moved around the country, becoming successful small-scale real estate entrepreneurs. Fifteen years ago they purchased eighty acres here from the Curtises, a pioneer family that had listed their property with Cathy Bagley. Al and Anna camped on their mesa top and pondered building sites, planted a field with more than two thousand tree seedlings, and took to leaving meat scraps from a friendly butcher on the point of the mesa. Turkey vultures, red-tails, merlins, and ravens landed to scavenge.

Eventually, they built a house on their favorite perch and retired here. They piped drinking water from town and subdivided the northern portion of their eighty-acre rectangle into five lots. All sold, for about $20,000 per acre. Al and Anna made a killing. They kept forty-seven acres of Moenkopi Sandstone bedrock and Indian ricegrass meadows, along with the ditch-watered tree farm and views toward the local landmarks—Boulder Mountain, the Cockscomb, the Henry Mountains, Capitol Reef, Thousand Lake Mountain, as well as, on clear days, the blue smudge of the La Sal Mountains beyond Moab more than one hundred miles to the east.

Now the Schmierers again have itchy feet. Much as he loves messing about with his trees and his vintage tractors, Al's back is bothering him. An impassioned birder, he is bored with the 116 species he has tallied here. Anna, faced with a suite of health problems, is worn out from the ill effects of the pollen blowing through the piñon-juniper woodland that surrounds them. Al is ready for new birds, Anna is ready to risk new flora, and they have decided to move to the Oregon Coast, where the seabirds will fly for Al and the rain will wash the air clean for Anna.

The mesa is for sale.

WE TOUR THE SCHMIERER HOME, moving from window to window, one a perfectly framed view of the highway running south toward Boulder Mountain, another banked just right to catch sunsets blazing in the west. It is a solid, lovingly designed custom log house, but it is not quite right for our friend's reinvestment. Joanne and I are enjoying Al's stories of his evolving relationship with this land. Anna has just pulled muffins from the oven, and we sit and drink coffee and talk until our kids, bored, retreat to the back seat of the truck with their respective portable CD players and check out from the adults.

Al wants us to know how he came to give something back to this community that had enriched him and his wife. In 1999 he learned that his neighbor across the highway had protected ninety-six acres of pastureland through the conveyance of conservation easements to the Nature Conservancy. With this donation, the land could be farmed but never developed. The easements would run with the land, no matter who owned it, in perpetuity. Why not do the same, thought Al and Anna, with the roadside acreage of their own land?

The Schmierer place was smaller than most Nature Conservancy preserves, but it enhanced the still-rural feeling of the curving approach that leads travelers through fields and piñon-covered hills, across the Fremont River, and up and over the high country to the new Grand Staircase–Escalante National Monument. This state highway was one of America's great drives, a designated National Scenic Byway and All American Road. Now rapid growth and development—the sudden erection of new businesses and motels next to freshly subdivided ranchlands and pastures—were coming to the corridor, as they were in Ogden Valley and most of the rural West.

Al and Anna worried about the vulnerability of Wayne County, the remote expanse surrounding Torrey, and about the open-space future of their highway corridor. Some of the local old-timers worried even more, for they saw the people of Torrey and its lovely valley preparing to trade the old for the new. As Hal Rothman defines the downward spiral of change in *Devil's Bargains: Tourism in the Twentieth-Century American West,* a community can begin to crumble when some catalytic moment arrives, a drought that brings agriculture to its knees or hard economic times that force a sawmill to close. Next thing you know, young people leave, and outsiders discover the lovely but ailing place. Hoping for a boom, believing in tourism as savior, the real place sacrifices its distinct regional identity only to find that it hasn't landed quite where it had hoped.

Descendants of pioneer families can become wealthy overnight by selling their land, but in the process they trade their personal and community identities for nothing more than a new real estate market. The national tourist industry gains a new recreational venue to promote to nonlocal affluent second-home owners. We reach in the hat and pull out—*shazzam!*—the New West.

Al had come to terms with his bargains and harvested his share of profits, but he felt that this was enough development for any one family. The Utah chapter of the Nature Conservancy liked his offer to protect much of his remaining land—and they liked the symmetry of saving both sides of the highway. So the Schmierers donated two conservation easements to the Conservancy, thereby encumbering—and protecting—twenty-eight acres (60 percent) of the land they loved.

To explain how the parcels fit together, Al pulls out a map. The first easement limits use on eighteen acres of mesaland rising from the highway and wrapping around the rims. Here the Nature Conservancy restrictions are comprehensive: no grazing, no agriculture, no structures, no roads, no motorized vehicles, no hunting, no parking. The second easement encumbers the ten-acre roadside field once farmed by the Curtises, now Al's tree farm and full of Japanese black pine and Douglas fir and Engelmann spruce and Scotch pine. Here the Schmierers retained agriculture and grazing rights but permanently prohibited development. Nearly twenty acres surrounding the house remain unencumbered.

AL MENTIONS OFFHAND—by the way, an afterthought—that there is a second building site along the rim. Do we want to see it?

We are absorbed in the Schmierer story, but my broken foot needs a rest. Joanne walks to the second house site with Al, listening to his running patter of natural history, and I return to the truck to wait with my children, Dory and Jake, and their cooped-up high spirits.

When Joanne returns, she is quivering with excitement. Our lives are poised to begin a new chapter.

She had taken one look at Al's second-favorite house site and had fallen under the spell of the place. There's a primary view down a small canyon, past an alfalfa field, and on toward the crags and mountains to the south. Al has figured out how to bring power and water up onto the mesa, where to carve footings in the bedrock, and where to site the septic system in a meadow below. It's easy to imagine a house there.

A scenario, full-blown, has struck my anticonsumerist wife: what if *we* buy the whole forty-seven acres and split it immediately—sell the house on a few acres, sell the tree farm, and recoup most of our money? We take on two new identities: stewards of the mesa preserved by its conservation easement, and owners of the spectacular building site. Here we could construct our own retreat.

———

We had briefly explored the notion of a second home when the owners of the cabin that we had used for ten years retired. This cabin suddenly became the *home* of our friends, who lived there fully half the year, and we had been lucky to find it free on this weekend when we turned into house hunters. In imagining the consequences of this shift in their—and our—lives, we had always reached the same conclusion: we could stay countless nights in every bed and breakfast in southern Utah between camping trips and still only spend a fraction of what it would cost to purchase our own second home. We were comfortable with this decision. Any plans we had for looking for land or a cabin had faded, or so we thought.

Still, using our friends' cabin brought the rejuvenating experience of a second-home sanctuary into our lives. We were getting older. In a few short years our kids would be gone, and we, too, might be able to spend more time here.

Wait a minute—what happened to our friend and her Montana ranch money? We were looking for that "really expensive" land for *her*. We will tell her about this land, certainly. But we know this wouldn't be her top pick. As it turns out, we are right. This land makes us dream. Her dreams take her back to her New England childhood; she has since reinvested in a Connecticut beach house.

———

We retreat to our friends' familiar cabin across the valley. High on exhilaration and possibility, we call a half dozen friends and family, looking for advice, reassurance.

We would never consider buying and keeping the whole parcel. We would not want the tree farm; we have no interest in being farmers and irrigators—and we don't love the existing house. We do believe that the house would quickly sell, however. Few homes of such quality turn up on the local market. The full acreage would just pass through our hands, and we would be left with thirty acres—our own house site and the preserved open space of the mesa-top—a remarkable piece of land for a remarkably small investment. I know this even before I've seen the house site, because I know this territory well.

At least for a moment I am thinking strategically, like a good businessman.

Like many of our contemporaries, we are the beneficiaries of our parents' hard work and restraint. We have invested that money. For years we managed our savings with benign neglect, which fit my self-image: since I never worked in the business world, I always thought of myself as living outside the economy. Freelance, nobody's man, an unaffiliated independent, with no permanent boss or employees of my own. I have tended this image with care, and it has allowed me to feel distinctly separate from Earl, even while that separation began to decrease as we got older and, like all those other baby boomers, started spending our inheritances and saving for our retirement.

The financial cushion is there. And now we're poised to draw on it.

When Joanne and I return to the land in the morning with the kids, I walk gingerly over to the building site, a ledge of rimrock perched on the south edge of the mesa, surrounded by a bonsai garden of piñon and juniper trees twisting out of the rock like dancers. The world sweeps away to views in every direction. It is thrilling to be here, above the whole valley, with a sense of standing plumb with the sky.

The road is there, right below us. That concerns me. The noise from our street in Salt Lake City ruins my enjoyment of the backyard. A house here will not be a wilderness hideaway but rather a lookout, rimming wild country yet engaged with the flow of community. A house here would perch midway between town and wildland; it would look down a curve of road to our neighbors in Torrey and in every other direction out over wild canyons and mesas. Other houses roost on the ridges nearby. This is a frontier, an ecotone, connected with both the land and its human community.

The highway hum comes from Roger Oyler turning his truck into the alfalfa field below to move sprinkler pipes, from ranchers Emmett and Viola Clark on their way to town, and from German tourists passing through paradise. I realize that the highway knits this world together —and reminds us all to be engaged citizens, to keep talking with our neighbors.

We have fallen in love with this place. Do we want to own it? At another moment, we might have said no. But at this moment, enthralled with its magic, we say, to our own astonishment, yes.

ONCE MORE JOANNE AND I WALK into Cathy Bagley's realty office. It is only twenty-four hours since our first visit. We don't actually make an offer. We imagine a couple of numbers, a grand total and a down payment. We ask Cathy to pencil them in while we decide whether or not our yes is absolute.

The next morning Cathy calls us at home in Salt Lake City during breakfast. We expect her to say that the rough draft of an agreement is coming by fax. Instead she says, "I ran your offer by the Schmierers, and they'll accept." Joanne and I are speechless. Our next thought, of course, is "Surely we offered too much!"

Reeling, second-guessing ourselves, we proceed; at every hurdle we believe our risk is worth taking. We know the land is desirable; if we were to back out at any step, the market would take over. Within two days calls begin to come in that verify our confidence: "We hear you've bought land in Torrey and have a house to sell. We are interested." Some inquiries come from friends, some through the grapevine. Though the Torrey Valley is neither Aspen nor Park City—and definitely not the golden land of California— Wayne County is teeming with pilgrims looking for property.

Meanwhile the members of the Wayne County Planning and Zoning

NEIGHBOR'S HAY BARN AND THE COCKSCOMB AS SEEN FROM THE AUTHOR'S HOUSE, 2007.

Board still have to agree to our splitting the land. The County Commissioners must approve the decision. Our saltbush and bunchgrass meadow needs to pass a percolation test for a septic tank. And the Town of Torrey must grant us a water hook-up. Cathy and Al see no problems in any of these hurdles. They are our "people," our advisors, just like Earl and his circle of people.

———

It all happens quickly, and Joanne and I sign on for the voyage. This is the rural West, where real estate actions don't require lawyers, and documents are little more complicated than written handshakes. We buy the land. The county officials grant our request to subdivide. Within a month we have split off the house and its surrounds along natural boundaries into a separate seven-acre lot. Arthur Adelmann, a painter and professor retiring from Weber State University, has seen the house and fallen in love with it—just as we did with the rest of the mesa. He *has* to have it. He *has* to live here. He is obsessed.

Arthur buys at our asking price. Within a year Joanne and I have sold our agricultural land to the owner of the pastures under easement across the highway. Each step of the story goes without a hitch. The powers of the universe seem to align to link us to this land.

Though we hold title to about one thousandth of 1 percent of the amount of land Earl holds, we, too, now own our private piece of the West. My spouse and I, like Al and Anna Schmierer before us, become land developers by navigating a series of options available to all citizens.

At the end of our land rush, our title describes the thirty acres that belong to us in nearly indecipherable survey language. The twelve acres surrounding our house site, completely unencumbered, allow us to build a structure and a road; to civilize and reconfigure; to do most anything with the land, water, and mineral rights we possess. This is traditionally called a "bundle" of property rights.

Our remaining eighteen acres are protected by the conservation easement that Al and Anna granted to the Nature Conservancy, which prohibits all development on our southern boundary in perpetuity. Arthur's house and the already sold small lots of the Schmierers' subdivision enclose us on the west and north: so our views will not fill in with still denser housing. Public land—Bureau of Land Management (BLM) land—begins thirty feet to the east of our imagined house and runs through wilderness-caliber country continuously for five miles to Capitol Reef National Park.

Three hundred miles from Mount Ogden, in May 2000, our sale to Arthur closes the day after Earl Holding finalizes his Snowbasin land trade. As the irony of this coincidence sinks in, I feel a tad more empathy with Earl. On vastly different scales, we are both dealmakers.

I TRY OUT THE DECLARATIVE STATEMENTS. My family now owns land. I own land. I am a property owner. Simple phrases, but with momentous consequences. Our title to thirty acres of mesa and cliff feels quite different from owning a house on a tenth-of-an-acre city lot. Our Salt Lake City neighborhood has been urbanized for a century and a half. Our family is simply passing through, investing for a time in the right to live in a two-story foursquare brick home built nine decades ago. People lived there before us. Another family will follow. Our little backyard, grassed, gardened, and fenced, has been thoroughly incorporated into the human-dominated world.

On the mesa we own eroded rimrock ledges and potholes and piñon-juniper forest and cottontail hideaways and Great Horned Owl roosts. The rains bring wildflowers. Drought matters. Bark beetles consume the piñons. Charcoal under a ledge marks a prehistoric campsite. Mule deer bucks bound away at sunrise. We are the stewards of a living ecosystem.

We love the little patch of furrowed field in our view from the mesa. We would rather see hayfields there than rooftops. We know all the cracks about NIMBYs, the not-in-my-backyard folks who want to shut the door behind them. We are acutely aware of just how privileged we are.

Like the other newcomers, I would be happy to slow the very development I've just accelerated. Just like the writer Mary Austin, who arrived breathless in Santa Fe in the 1920s, I simmer with visions of my new home's future. And I wince when I come across a passage in Hal Rothman's *Devil's Bargains* describing the self-important Austin who had hoped "to maintain the special character of the place" by appointing herself "keeper of traditions and arbiter of what was appropriate for the 'real' Santa Fe."

The only traditional resources our land might yield would be forage for perhaps one cow for one month each spring or decorative flagstones. No humans have ever before built a permanent structure on our share of the mesa. And now we've subdivided this wild land, increasing density by a factor of two; we have become accomplices in the domestication of the open space of the West. I mourn the loss while I celebrate what I've gained—a home.

Drawn by the thrill of living so close to wild country, with each step toward the creation of our home here I add a wrinkle to the social fabric, tweak the economy, and nudge the environmental balance of the mesa and its surrounding communities. The changes bounce back, too, and I must reorder my self-image accordingly.

I've struck my deal with the devil.

I KNOW THAT MY FAMILY has an impact in the Colorado Plateau backcountry, but I can tolerate this threshold level of disturbance because this is indeed public land. I have harangued my kids since toddlerhood about how to avoid crushing the living plant crust that shields the soil, that unique black cryptobiotic surface. They can repeat the riff back to me, with affectionate sarcasm. I always believe that since we are surely gentler than more mechanized users, we can't do much real damage. I have a powerful sense of sharing with all who follow us, whoever they may be.

Americans have two competing attitudes about owning this astonishing continent of ours. We treasure our public lands; indeed, the wisest of Western writers, Wallace Stegner, called national parks America's best idea. Public lands are the fundamental source of energy as well as solace, the altar of daily worship for the American environmental movement. At the same time, those famous lines at the end of *Gone With the Wind* ring in our ears. In the last scene ghostly voiceovers from the men in Scarlett O'Hara's life restore her will by speaking of the power of her land, reminding her of the place she loves: "Tara! Home! Land's the only thing that matters, the only thing that lasts. It's from this you get your strength, the red earth of Tara."

———

Camping on land that is "ours," we drive up the track to the top of the mesa on Labor Day weekend, 2000, and step out onto "our property," onto a piece of the Earth that we "possess."

We will want to engineer our road. Make it passable in winter. Cut through the ledge rock. Maybe even blast. . . . Should I pioneer the road to the building site though I don't know precisely where it will be?

I realize that I am not ready. After half a century of acquisition, Earl knows what he wants to do with his vast acreages. I have yet to establish protocols. I don't know when to say yes and when to say no, don't know how to limit our impact within my comfort zone. So I torment our kids, admonishing them every time they veer their mountain bikes six inches off the road. I see Jake practice skids, and it makes me nervous even when he *is* on the road. Photos from years of newsletters from the Southern Utah Wilderness Alliance light up in my brain—illustrations of tire tracks through cryptobiotic soil, cleated treads wounding the earth, single-track gouges that, when the next rain rips into them, broaden to arroyos.

I sound like a neurotic sitcom character, continually overreacting, but I'm trying desperately to be responsible about having taken on this wild land. My family can't believe the intensity of my feelings. It will be another year and a half before I can laugh at myself—and permit Jake to ride his bike off-road on our land, designating a corridor of ledges for him to bounce down. Why has this become okay? One answer comes from my father, when I bring him to the mesa. He looks around with his geologist's eye and then, incredulous, at me: "That's not 'soil,' it's two inches of coarse sand over bedrock!" He liberates me from my fussy perseverating with an amazed shake of his head and convinces me that our bike trails will disappear when we quit using them, to be swept clean by the wind.

When we take Joanne's eighty-three-year-old mother to the mesa, we want her to come to the view fresh and relaxed. We drive right to the rim, taking our truck between the trees, bumping over the ledges and weaving between the buffalo berry and blackbrush for a hundred yards. We leave a mark, but by the time we come back a few weeks later, rain and snow have washed it away.

We drive to the house site on most visits after that first nervous-making journey. Once we start driving it, the route becomes a road. The tracks remain. Our impact is accelerating.

On a trip to the land in June 2001 Joanne and I begin to settle in to this notion of ownership. We walk in from the highway with the man who will complete our site work. He hands us a business card. I recognize the graphic—a silhouette of a track hoe. Just like Earl, I am about to hire earthmovers to reshape this land to suit my own needs and to engineer the entrance road from a rutted track to a graveled, well-drained roadway. Fill in the dips, control the water, make the land conform to my desire to drive easily up a hill with an automobile.

Joanne and I move a woodpile that had been collected by Al. In living with a piece of property, at least a few of its resources seem to inevitably become commodities, destined to be used.

I STAND ON A RIDGETOP, a deer head in my hand, my tripod shouldered like a rifle, looking for all the world like a poacher. I hear a truck approaching. I prepare to explain myself.

Our dog, Tika, and I have picked our way around a rimfall where flash floods have poured over the red sandstone, fluting and molding the slick-rock in those rare, intense moments when rain pummels the desert. We are exploring the BLM land adjacent to ours. I can see Arthur's house, still two drainages west. Just before reaching the dirt road that snakes the ridgeline out to Beas Lewis Flats, we stumble on a nearly complete mule deer skeleton with a five-point rack attached to a skull mostly clean of flesh—a picturesque Old West treasure. I collect the trophy, holding on to the smooth antlers. Tika periodically tries to nibble at the scraps of fur on the skull's snout.

I'm always amazed at what turns up when I extract myself from the truck and start walking, keeping an eye out for objects composed for a photograph, waiting for rainbows. I find sunstruck cliffs, cactus blossoming crimson, moonsets in lavender skies. I hear canyon wrens. I smell cliffrose. I find deer skulls.

Then I see the pickup—not a sleek black SUV but clearly local, a rusting rattletrap white truck with an empty bed. There is something vaguely threatening about the way the truck noses down washes where no roads exist. I wave, but the driver is too distant to look in the eye, and the truck never reaches me. Unable to block the unease that comes, unbidden, I turn and head back toward my own vehicle. On this soft November day, alone again, the peace of immersion in redrock returns to calm me.

I park along the highway in the mouth of the little canyon below our house site. I leave the pavement and walk up the wash, headed for our woodpile, where I plan to leave the skull. Suddenly I intersect fresh tire tracks where there is no road. I know I tend to be self-righteous about off-road vehicles—my youthful park ranger persona resurfacing. But wheels damage the land and invite further trespass. At first merely irritated, I simmer easily into my youthful impersonation of a full-fledged authority figure defending the land from destruction.

I hear a motor, and the same rusting white pickup emerges from behind the piñons. The driver must have come in from the highway, as I had on foot. We are on my land, now, or close to the boundary. I am in control. I am not just The Ranger; I am The Owner.

The truck pulls up; I see a jittery man, sixtyish, scrawny, with a hard edge that the warm and forthright local ranchers never have. I talk to him through his open window: "What are you doing back here?" Clearly nervous, he replies, "Just driving around."

"Why?"

"Looking for rocks."

I respond without hesitation, "Well. This is my land. The land coming up here is also private. And this is *not* a road. Please don't drive up here *ever again.*"

He's quick to say, "Okay," quick to escape.

————

I listen to myself, nonplussed. When I saw him at a distance on public land, I granted power to this man, seeing *him* as the insider. Now I have the power, fueled by the outrage automatically conferred by the complicated myth we call ownership, by the landowner's peculiar self-granting of authority. My role reversal stuns me. I sound just like one of those too-fierce defenders of private property rights who have always aroused my suspicions. And normally I don't even feel comfortable describing our place as "property." I prefer "land."

Now, on my land, without pausing to consider the irony, I have acted as imperiously as the wealthy, the powerful, the insider—The Man.

THE LAND IS WILD. We drive in past Arthur's gate one summer afternoon, and a desert bighorn ewe stands at the foot of the mesa. She looks hard at us, then melts upward along the ledges and disappears. We see her only this once. Arthur sees her several times. Presumably the bighorn wandered over from the Fremont River Gorge, a straggler from the reintroduced herd in Capitol Reef National Park. The gorge, less than a mile away, is included in the Utah Wilderness Coalition's master proposal for designating wilderness on BLM land. The coalition hopes to include all the BLM land adjoining the park, which would bring designated wilderness on the American Commons right up to our property line.

The following winter, mountain lion tracks mark the snow around Arthur's house.

Another trip. Dory and I camp on the land, parking at the house site. An antiphonal chorus of coyotes sings out just as we click off our headlights and let the ebony night flow over us. Nighthawks work the updrafts along the rim as we drift in and out of sleep, their cries punctuating the bass-drum booms that their feathers draw from the wind.

Sunrise the next morning hits the top of the Cockscomb, a brilliant white-gold flare rimming the Navajo Sandstone cliff. I'm partial to the monumental, transcendent stripes before me: red Moenkopi ledges in the foreground, piñon-green hills and mesas midground, then the sea-monster ridge of the Cockscomb spotlit by shafts of sunlight from the Fresnel lens of moving clouds. The green-black mountain rises beyond these as backdrop and finally gives way to blue sky, with strokes of cloud swashed across the firmament.

And that's just the view to the south.

Maybe it's this predilection for stripes that has always made me so sympathetic to the landscape of Capitol Reef. The long, rolling cliff face of the reef, its monoclinal tilt eroded in hogbacks and ridges, color by color, formation by rock formation, runs across the horizon in what the Paiutes call a "sleeping rainbow" for a hundred-plus miles.

In the still cool air I write these thoughts in my journal as I listen to the ravens and Red-tailed Hawks that nest on the cliffs within a couple of hundred yards. I hear the croaks and cries when the adults flap off their nests to hunt and return to eggs and fledglings—generation to generation, here, sharing our ledges. Dory sleeps in the back of the truck; the drone of vehicles on the highways is nearly constant. Once more I grapple with the paradox of wildness and civilization.

The conservation easement protecting our mesa captures that paradox.

––––––––

The land under easement is wondrous open space, but it is worthless as developable real estate. According to the easement deed this land "currently remains in a substantially undisturbed, natural state and has significant ecological and open-space values . . . Protection of the Property will contribute to the agricultural, archeological, open space, scenic and relatively natural features and values of the property." Indeed, the document continues, "all of these natural elements, ecological values, and agricultural values are of great importance to the Grantor [the Schmierers] and to the people of the State of Utah, and are worthy of preservation."

When Al and Anna donated this perpetual conservation easement to the Nature Conservancy, they significantly reduced the market value of their newly encumbered land. We wrote that appraisal figure—$5,000 for all eighteen acres—into our contract when we became the new owners. Al and Anna had made a charitable gift, and they were rewarded with a charitable income tax deduction based on the value of that gift, the decrease in the market value of their land resulting from the easement restrictions. The Nature Conservancy, having accepted the easement as trustee, agreed to monitor and enforce the easement restrictions in perpetuity for the benefit of the public.

And then, in 2001, the Wayne County assessor raised property taxes. Not just on houses and unencumbered property but on every piece of property. Convinced that open space does have market value, county officials decided to ignore the existence of the conservation easement. They looked at the comparable sales figures for agricultural land and valued our land—even though development is prohibited—at $4,000 an acre! We protested and submitted letters of support from Cathy Bagley, our Torrey real estate agent, and from the Nature Conservancy. We repeated our argument that these eighteen acres were worth no more in the marketplace than their appraised value of $5,000, just $290 per acre. But the county held firm.

The tax bill on the newly assessed value of our eighteen acres was just a few hundred dollars, and most of it would go to support the desperately poor county schools. But this would be a bad precedent because it undoes one of the tax advantages of a conservation easement and ignores its legal effect, the permanent prohibition on development.

The county assessor is apologetic. She explains that the State Tax Commission is continually admonishing her because Wayne County land is undervalued—indeed, property taxes on homes in unincorporated areas of the county are the lowest in the state. The tax commissioner wanted her to raise all the assessments, so that's what she did. She tells us that she has no experience with conservation easements. The federal laws that provide tax incentives for conservation easement donations date back only to 1976, and the Utah law that validates perpetual conservation easements dates only to 1985. She encourages us to appeal her ruling to the state. She is looking for guidance, and this will be an exercise in fact finding, one way to have the Utah Tax Commission focus on Wayne County's issues.

When our appeal comes before them, the tax commissioners tell us conversationally that they have never considered a conservation easement case before. We are flabbergasted. Though we certainly haven't come prepared to create a precedent, we tell our story. Joanne, who is an appellate attorney, fears she may have to represent us in court if we need to appeal the case beyond the commission, a role for which she has no appetite. I begin research, just in case. We alert the Nature Conservancy, as we may need their help.

CONSERVATION EASEMENTS HAVE BECOME the most widely used mechanism for preservation of family lands and open space because they so beautifully meet the needs of both landowner and community. By carefully phrasing the restrictions, owners often can continue to use the land as they always have. They can leave their land to heirs or sell it, but all future owners will be bound by the restrictions as written.

Tax reforms passed by the United States Congress in 2006 both expanded tax incentives, particularly for farmers and ranchers, and limited abuses, such as the exaggerated appraisals that can inflate the allowable charitable income tax deduction of an easement donation—a loophole the national press had highlighted.

When landowners encumber their land with a conservation easement, the community gains from the permanent protection of open space, wildlife habitat, historic resources, scenic views, agricultural landscapes. Communities also dodge an economic bullet, since building a house on the same ground would increase every citizen's tax bill to pay for the infrastructure needed to support development.

Though the term *conservation easement* dates back only to 1959, the first effective application of the idea came in the late 1880s when Boston took steps to protect the parkways designed by Frederick Law Olmsted (who also designed New York City's Central Park). Later the National Park Service used easements to preserve views along such scenic drives as the Blue Ridge Parkway. Wayne County's highway corridor fits right in with this tradition.

Wendy Fisher, the founder and director of Utah Open Lands, notes that people understand that open space is a treasure. They understand about the rewards of positive action and leadership. But "doing *nothing* as a legacy?" That's a tough one for many folks, she finds. She could look to Thoreau for pithy philosophical reassurance: "A man is rich in proportion to the number of things he can afford to let alone."

The property-rights fundamentalists look askance at conservation easements and say, "We're locking in the fate of the land forever." They see in "preservation for perpetuity" the same hubris that conservationists see in greedy development. They ask: How can we know the needs of a community in a generation, much less in five hundred years? What if our definition of "development" changes? Even conservationists can imagine reasons to reexamine easements in the future: What if the land itself changes, evolving dynamically in natural processes or with climate change to some state that degrades or destroys the conservation values for which the encumbered land was protected? What if it makes sense in fifty years to permit in-fill of easement-encumbered land to prevent development from leapfrogging to even more environmentally sensitive areas?

When someone wants to extinguish or modify a conservation easement in the future, the courts have a protocol in place. When conservation objectives become "impossible or impracticable," a legal safety valve called the doctrine of *cy pres* can terminate or modify an easement, redirecting any proceeds from subsequent sale or development to similar conservation purposes elsewhere. Oversight lies with each state attorney general, who has the responsibility to ensure that the wishes of long-dead easement grantors are respected.

Wendy Fisher notes the paradox: allowing random development hinders our choice of options for the future; establishing conservation easements preserves them. Eighty percent of the ranches in the West will change hands in the next twenty years. This is a moment of change and opportunity. She is well aware of the challenge "to ensure that we are up to the task of forever."

———

Three months after our hearing, the Utah Tax Commission rules that Wayne County had no reason to raise property taxes on our easement-encumbered mesa. The original appraisal stands. The Commission narrowly limited the scope of their decision, however, noting that we have made no general argument for conservation easements. Though it is the most powerful tool in our legal system for preserving private land and open space, conservation easement law is young and still has remarkably few judicial precedents.

The future seems clear. To guarantee a reasonable income stream, Wayne County will continue to tax second homes heavily. This is entirely appropriate. However, county authorities will also have to recognize that conservation easements, in permanently prohibiting development, really do reduce the market value of that land. And even small land trusts will need endowment funds to monitor, enforce, and defend the conservation easements they hold.

Second homes will fill in open spaces all over rural America during the next ten years. At Snowbasin Earl Holding is banking on this trend to turn his investment to profit. Land trusts are working desperately to counter the same trend and save as much private agricultural land as they can before it all fissions into subdivisions and big-box malls.

Demographers predict that the steady increase in the purchase of vacation homes will peak at five million in 2013. In that year the youngest baby boomers will be on the cusp of fifty. The huge intergenerational transfer of wealth from their parents will be complete. And as boomers pass out of their peak consumer years, the second-home construction and resale market will gradually decline.

By then Earl will likely have sold his elite lots at Snowbasin and built his lodges and golf courses. The National Forest will remain, surrounding his newly private land. In Torrey we will have built our house between lands preserved by the people of the United States and by the Nature Conservancy. Other houses will have been built. Other conservation easements, I hope, will be preserving open space. Across America a new matrix of public and private land will evolve, a map of devil's bargains to remind us that we have a legitimate interest in managing our entire continent cooperatively. The catch, of course, is agreeing on our goal, our *communal* interest. How do we frame our decisions? How do we use this miraculous land? What is a mesa for? What is a mountain for?

NOVEMBER 2001. Our architect, a good listener named Kenton Peters, has asked us to plot every tree in the vicinity of the house site, an astonishing notion that reminds me of Earl's use of GPS at Snowbasin to survey roads and development grids. Kenton will embed these positions in his computer and design the house around the trees. I drive to Torrey on my own to work with the surveyor mapping junipers, piñons, cliff line, and bedrock. I brush my hands over the conifers, needing to feel the texture of the needles and reestablish relationship as the beeping electronics of the surveyors' technology assault me.

On a trip with Kenton in March 2002 we stake out the footprint of our house. Masonry string runs between the stakes, neon chartreuse on red bedrock. It's the most unnatural color imaginable, appropriate to this statement of human possession. But I remember lichens growing not so far away that have the same starting color.

We have discovered *A Pattern Language,* the classic architecture book by Christopher Alexander. I begin making lists of Alexander's patterns; I love this orderly approach to the relationship between humans and space. I am smitten: "Light on Two Sides." "Pools of Light." "Sleeping to the East." "Special Sunny Place." "Padded Window Seats." "Children's Beds in Alcoves." "Flared Outdoor Stairs." "Windows Overlooking Life."

Kenton stays with Joanne and me at our friends' cabin, the retreat we know so well that we have used it as the model for our own house. After good food and wine I want to read through my lists with Kenton and Joanne, to ensure that we have attended to all the crucial patterns. I begin citing summaries in Alexander's 1,216-page book. By the top of page three of my notes Kenton is visibly fighting sleep, Joanne increasingly exasperated. When I stop, well after 10 P.M., Kenton tells me good-humoredly that I'm the only client he has ever had who wanted to talk about architecture longer than he did.

Joanne and I spend several meetings with Kenton, trying to design an efficient kitchen. We want to be able to stand at the dish drainer, open a cabinet, and put dishes away without having to cross five feet to the opposite wall. I feel silly spending so much time on something so mundane, but the constraints of window, beam, corner, and counter make the undertaking remarkably complex. I am no longer so quick to ridicule Earl for his attention to detail.

Earl Holding is creating a business property. We will live in our house. But I am proving to be just as compulsive in choosing stucco colors for my walls and patterns for the brick on my floors as Earl is about every detail of Snowbasin's lodges and snowmaking and Grand America's chandeliers and stone.

I am learning that once you've committed to building a house, you're sucked into a vortex of decision making. The contractor and architect ask again and again: what do you want this to look like? "This" can be the detailing of trim, the number and position of light switches, the finish on doorknobs, the choice of shower tile, the precise placement of a window. Just like Earl, we care if these things feel wrong.

On our next trip we stake out the new version of the house, this time with screaming canary-yellow string. It's close to right and beginning to feel real, this maze of string. Dory notices that Joanne and I begin to talk about going to "the house," rather than the "house site." We have begun to possess this land with our grid and our stakes.

I am reminded of Ed Abbey's delight in *Desert Solitaire* when he walks by moonlight along the newly surveyed road into Arches National Monument, throwing away survey stakes, burying plastic flagging. That was public land. This is private land—my land, by gum. Sheepish, but determined, I know I don't want to pull out these stakes. They will remain, and they will be transformed into a house.

THERE IS A HOLE IN THE LIVING ROOM. Our contractor, John Sammond, supervises the first bites into the mesa with heavy equipment in late August 2002. A track hoe grinds up the road to the mesa. Just like the track hoes at Snowbasin, the machine wreaks irrevocable change on the land.

John takes out the few trees we must lose. Once we have given our final, final approval to his precise stakeout—after moving the footprint five feet west, two feet south, pondering, moving it back, and moving it again, trying to position the house sensibly in relation to the rim—he proceeds with digging the foundation. I blush at our dedication to getting this decision just right. I know this behavior; for years I'd been making fun of Earl for his compulsiveness. And yet the rim has an integrity we can feel, and we do not want to crowd it.

The track hoe scrapes against the rock, lifting out huge stones. The operator piles them around the house site, six feet high, for later use as walkways; no need for us to import just the right stone from Vermont or Idaho. Huge chunks of ledge nudge right up to the BLM line, around the trees we are saving, against the woodpile. The site looks like a quarry, but at least it doesn't yet look like a war zone.

At the end of the day I see the machine parked on the ridgetop, daylighted against the sky, just as at Snowbasin. After the builders have gone home, I climb into the cab and grip the shifters and throttles. Even with the engine still, it gives me a bracing sense of power and control.

In transferring decision making to first the architect and now the builder, I have conveyed a measure of responsibility to them. We chose to build this house on this spot. We carefully screened our contractor, John. Now it's his turn, and he is perfectly calm about it. John's only concern is for how I will react: "People aren't ready for how different it looks. This is a lot of change."

On my next trip down from Salt Lake City the outline of a house zigs and zags across the excavation. Footings have been poured, forms for walls built, and I can stand more or less at ground level, admiring the view from each imaginary room. I help hold the hose that feeds pulses of concrete from the clanking truck into the wall forms.

The pulses come a bit faster than once a second. Heartbeats. Thousands of pounds of pressure per square inch. It's definitely a macho experience, downright ejaculatory. Shaping wood and stone and concrete with these big machines—this has to affect the souls of the men (and it's mostly men) who do this every day.

Two weeks later the walls begin to rise. We are building with SIPs, structural insulated panels—six inches of Styrofoam-like insulation with a layer of aspen chipboard on either surface. The material provides superb insulation, reduces the numbers of trees consumed by our house, and goes up like Legos. As the walls rise, flanked by those of other houses along the nearby ridgelines, the low-profile silhouette on the mesa is reassuring. We haven't designed a castle. We won't feel like pigs.

"OH, SO YOU ARE BUILDING THAT HUGE HOUSE up on the ridge!" Marty Sammond, the wife of our contractor, runs into an acquaintance at the builder's supply store in Loa, the Wayne County seat. Marty protests, "It isn't a huge house—it's only 1,700 square feet!" The neighbor who made this comment lives across the highway in a 4,300-square-foot house. But she thinks ours looks big.

I am horrified when Marty tells me this story. Our unbroken north wall is thirty-two feet long and faces the highway. We hope the house blends in when the rock-colored stucco goes on. But the house is "substantial," as Marty puts it.

Marty means this as a compliment. She wants our house to be substantial. She doesn't want it to be flyaway or minor. Her husband, John, builds houses that matter. He is fast, smart, efficient, thoughtful. When we visit the house in January, enclosed now, sheetrocked, wired, ready for paint, we are overwhelmed by both its grace and its presence on the mesa.

In February we stand inside the house as the stucco goes on outside, a half dozen "stucco guys" smoothing on the compound in circles. They work fast. The sound from within is elemental. Their masonry tools scrape and shape the surface of the walls in a controlled frenzy, timed just so. It's the sound of a glacier grinding off the skin of a mountain. The sound of rapids. The fundamental sound of humans building, whether they work with Ndebele adobe in South Africa or European stone in Chartres. It's the sound of a blender concocting from earth and tint and acrylic the colored shell—the carapace—in which we will live for years.

We are daunted by just how "substantial" the house has become. We wanted "the not-so-big house," the small flexible space popularized by the writer and architect Sarah Susanka; we had budgeted for a few fine details rather than the standard suburban excess of square footage. But engaging

RAINBOW OVER THE AUTHOR'S HOME ON THE MESA, PERCHED ON THE FULCRUM BETWEEN
THE VILLAGE LIFE OF TORREY AND THE WILDLANDS OF THE REDROCK CANYONS, 2004.

an architect—even one concerned with sustainable building practices—
generates an unruly momentum. Our house hasn't turned into a castle, but
it has grown incrementally larger than we anticipated. It's close to being a
primary home rather than just a cabin.

Our contractor tells us that we process decisions more completely than
any clients he has ever had. John makes this comment just as Joanne and I
have been saying how painless it has been to build this house, how we have
felt reassuringly decisive and in tune with each other. We may not be as "violently eccentric" as Earl, but we too have a streak of obsessive control. Our
kids have perfected a parody of our relentlessly detailed decision making.

Even though the SIPs take longer than anticipated to frame around all
the corners in our idiosyncratic design, John finishes in six and a half months.
I sequence my slides to create a time-lapse story of walls rising, roof appearing, stucco applied, staircase to roof tower completed.

The house on the mesa is done.

The change from seeing a rock ledge where we camp and dream of a
house to standing *in* the house—looking out the windows, walking out the

French doors to the plaza with my morning cup of coffee, standing on the rim and looking back at the house, our house—astonishes me. From our bed alcove at dawn we see flares of orange light on beam and earthy stucco, with the snow-spackled forest of Boulder Mountain deep and dark behind. Watching the play of light move across the house equals the pleasures of contemplating a sculpture or an earthwork. The angles and framing lines interact with rock and horizon—*respond* to the landscape—and prompt us to think about our placement within that landscape as individuals, as a family, as members of a community.

This is one value of private land, then: to personalize a relationship with a place. It's reminiscent of the familiar feeling of creating a campsite on public land—the kitchen next to a ledge, the tent backed up between two junipers, camp chairs perched on the rim—an argument with comfortable predictability for the few days we live there. Only now the feeling of home is solid. Substantial. Our home is built to last for decades, into the next generation. This new permanence is moving; in its statement of ownership, of affluence, of dominion, it's also unsettling.

My crazed worry about change was superseded by engagement with the process. I took the trenching and tracks and compacted earth and lost trees in stride. We replaced the wild rim with a home, a domicile. We took a stand, created a physical presence to express our affinity with this place. And we're not done. I tick off an endless series of projects: laying rock walls, cutting firewood, managing invasive weeds, planting native seeds.

As we begin to use the house and dwell within its space, gradually our identities shift to incorporate our relationship with the mesa in our definition of home. After two weeks in the city, views from the mesa haunt our dreams. The warmth and light and freshness of the wind in this one place become fundamental to our definition of everyday joy. On the mesa we walk into a postcard and turn to look back at the rack of scenic views framed by our windows. As soon as we frame the view, limitless wildland becomes "landscape," "scenery," complicating nature with culture.

We have tried to create a house that engages us with the land we love. But we built on a mesa within sight of Torrey—not somewhere tucked away in the wilderness—and now we owe our neighbors something in return. We will need to explore the meaning and practice of good citizenship in our new community. Wayne County's measure of our bargain awaits us.

REAL ESTATE SIGN ON THE SHORES OF LAKE POWELL, GLEN CANYON NATIONAL RECREATION AREA, NEAR GREENEHAVEN, ARIZONA, 2002.

THE WOES
OF WAYNE COUNTY

Anyone who has lived on a frontier knows the inescapable
ambivalence of the old-fashioned American conscience,
for he has first renewed himself in Eden and then set
about converting it into the lamentable modern world.

WALLACE STEGNER, *WOLF WILLOW*, 1962

"WEALTHY, OVEREDUCATED SPOILED BRATS." A longtime resident summed up
local attitudes toward us move-ins, and a new acronym lurks in that one-
liner. Old-timers are jealous of WOES—those Wealthy Over-Educated
Spoiled brats—and they are fearful, too, of the power granted by financial
resources and education, angry at the shift in attitudes toward public and
private land that the WOES bring with them.

Stereotypes hurt. I can picture a cartoon of an overwrought face-off between the two factions—a couple of naïve but well-meaning, be-fleeced,
and Teva-sandaled WOES standing next to their mountain-bike-racked
SUV in front of their lovely stucco home newly built in a former alfalfa
field, righteously brandishing copies of Southern Utah Wilderness Alliance
and Sierra Club newsletters as well as a current *New Yorker*—toe to fence
line with an angry, cowboy-hatted, hardworking local mounted on an ATV
embellished with antienvironmentalist bumper stickers, a rifle strapped into
his gear, his machine flanked by ranks of hungry heifers searching for one
last clump of grass on a drought-starved range.

When you begin to turn over the rocks of casual assumptions, however, the conservative, resource-based local Mormon men and women may not match your expectations. The "wealthy, overeducated spoiled brats" may not either. Easy classifications like these form perfectly split kindling for western anger, whether aimed at Earl Holding or at the WOES in Wayne County. I'm convinced, however, that there is hope for the future and that dialogue can incrementally wash away the stubborn certainties and igno-rance of unchallenged generalizations.

WAYNE COUNTY LIFE IS A CLASSIC small-town, long-winter, droughty-summer western challenge. Ambivalence is born and bred; every native navigates be-tween love for the beauty and solitude of the place and resentment of its iso-lation and lack of economic opportunity. County Commissioner Allen Jones tells me, "My dad sent me off into the red rocks to work, not to play. When I came back after many years, I saw this land as beautiful for the first time."

This place of red rocks and hard work preserves the Big Empties for our imaginations. The nearest stoplight is still two counties and more than sixty miles away in Richfield. About 2,500 people live in Wayne County, scat-tered across 2,500 square miles—just one person per square mile in an area more than eight times larger than the five boroughs of New York City, which could absorb the entire population of Wayne County in less than ten Manhattan city blocks.

Homogeneity rules. The county is 99 percent white. Sixty percent of Utahns are Mormon; in Wayne County 80 percent belong to the Church.

Today, at the beginning of the twenty-first century, no more than five families in Wayne County are able to live on their farm or ranch earnings alone—and everybody knows who they are. More families in the county depend on earnings from art than from agriculture. Most wage-earners need to supplement the microprofits from raising alfalfa and running a few cows, sheep, or the occasional pair of llamas. Paychecks come from many other sources, including waitressing, carpentering, teaching and permanent or sea-sonal work with government agencies. In acreage farmed, Wayne County ranks third to last in Utah, a testament to the minimal amount of arable land.

There are three clusters of residences in the Torrey Valley, where the Fre-mont River flows between the 11,000-foot-high plateaus of Thousand Lake Mountain and Boulder Mountain. Teasdale is tiny; Grover—with perhaps a dozen full-time residents living in dispersed ranches and cabins where the scenic highway heads south, preparing to lilt up into the ponderosas and as-pen of Boulder Mountain—even tinier. Torrey is the valley's metropolis and only incorporated town, 170 citizens living in a grid four blocks by six blocks along the all-important irrigation ditch that parallels Main Street. Torrey is a crossroads, where the route coming north from Bryce Canyon and Grand Staircase meets the east-west highway bisecting Capitol Reef National Park just four miles to the east.

Torrey has a fine restaurant, whose chef trained at Deer Valley Resort and now serves organic veggies and good crusty bread from a back-to-the-land farmer who is proud of introducing his rancher neighbors to *bruschetta*. Galleries and bookstores are proliferating in town. This is gentrification, with all of its trade-offs.

This gateway town for Capitol Reef will never boom beyond imagining, however. It can't. Fred and Janet Hansen, who have taken turns serving as mayor ever since retiring here from northern Utah twenty-five years ago, worry about the Torrey water supply, which depends on mountain springs. Five years after we hooked up our meter in 2000, the town hit its limit, and currently no new home can connect to the city water system unless it has an existing meter. Fred has been mayor in recent years: "I'm sorry this drought caught up with us while I'm mayor, but it's good for the community. It woke us up. We just quit selling water; we can't sell something we don't have. That will determine the limits of our growth. Maybe that's why God set up the water situation—to let us know where the limits of the desert lie."

I FIRST LIVED IN WAYNE COUNTY thirty years ago when I worked as a Capitol Reef ranger; I've visited nearly every year since. I've met three generations of local residents. I don't feel like a newcomer, because I've loved this country for so long. But newcomer I am.

The rural sociologists who study "natural amenity-based growth" in the West apply scholarly analysis to the issues in this book. They support my conviction that if we can puzzle out a way to talk with each other we will find overlapping values that can lead us to higher ground; we can reach islands in the seething sea of antipathy, and from there, as a community, we can set a course for the future and stand strong against the grand development schemes of the Earl Holdings and others far worse.

Old-timers and newcomers—the "amenity migrants" who have lived in rural communities for five years or less—show similar levels of concern for the environment. Newcomers bond first with the landscape, reinforcing the "community of place." Old-timers are more invested in social networks, the "community of interests"; in rural Utah, membership in the LDS church guarantees instant connection. But the expected culture clash doesn't pop out from statistics. Strong opinions exist at the ends of the curve; in the middle, communities harbor common ground.

One friend who moved to Wayne County from the Northeast, in love with the enchanted wildness of the redrock landscape, found herself stranded at midlife in an isolated place that she wasn't sure she had actively chosen, living behind what one local calls the Alfalfa Curtain. At the end of one long winter she admitted that she had become obsessed with the question "How do you mitigate regret?"

Our whole community needs to address this question before we have taken too many actions that might require mitigation, before we approve too many steps toward homogeneity that will be cause for regret. I can feel the possibilities out there if we avoid these mistakes; I can picture a future filled with thoughtful dialogue, tantalizing us with hope.

Rural Utah has always been a culture of villages, but more than three hundred homes now lie scattered outside the three Torrey valley communities. Noisy newcomer WOES have been growing in numbers and shifting the culture. I can join the Wayne County community now without feeling quite so conspicuous. Indeed, one progressive grassroots land-use coalition—the Friends of Grover—has been working on threats to public lands in Wayne County since the mid-1990s, and I was pleased to sign on as a member.

Don't let me make too much of this. I perch on the rim of rural life without grappling with its most difficult daily realities. But I long for a chance to cooperate, for the satisfaction of protecting and ensuring a future that the community imagines together. I hope to work from what some call the Radical Center, the place where all factions come to talk. If we can move beyond our trenches, I'm convinced that we can find shared values in our mutual opposition to distant corporate and political powers refusing to listen to the people who cherish the land.

———

"I have no illusions," says Nan Anderson, a fellow newcomer, who came to rural Utah via Ohio, Washington, D.C., and Salt Lake City. "I'm a woman. I'm not LDS; I'm from the East; I'm a Democrat." And yet the county commissioners hired Anderson as director of economic development. "That Susan and I have these jobs tells me that there is an interest and a willingness to learn."

SUSAN SNOW, THE HARD-WORKING ACTIVIST FROM GROVER, 2004.

The loggers in Wayne County had turned to "Susan"—Susan Snow—for help when they felt endangered by environmental groups challenging every timber sale in court. In 2000 they asked Snow to take on the job of executive director of the Southern Utah Forest Products Association (SUFPA), to work to make community forestry sustainable in the Canyon Country.

At fifty, Susan hadn't been looking for a demanding, full-time job, but she was so honored by the risk the timbermen were willing to take that she couldn't say no. She became totally engaged by the work, passionate about promoting a transition from simple logging to restoration forestry. She attracted grant money and brought a level of enthusiasm and worldliness to her work for the small timber businesses of Wayne County that they would find difficult to replace. Susan has told me that "you're a hard worker" is the highest praise you can receive in Wayne County. Many of her friends would apply that accolade to her.

Like Nan Anderson, Susan Snow is an outsider. She is Asian American, Catholic, a woman, and an environmentalist. And yet the logging community of Wayne County trusted her. She had lived here for twenty years. She is a pillar of the High Country Quilters, women who gather regularly to "stitch and bitch," mixing tradition and innovation and generating mutual respect. She and her husband, the painter Doug Snow, had a daughter in Wayne High School.

Old-timers must expand their community identity to include newcomers like Anderson and Snow and others like them. Newcomers, for their part, must identify themselves as members of the community, not just part-time residents. Only through parallel transformations in both groups can we find a way to embrace our home landscape in a sustainable, healthy, reciprocal relationship.

What does it take to be a good citizen? This is the question to which I keep returning. For the people in power, it means, well . . . power. The elite admonish the rest of us: "Just sit down and shut up. We know best." An old LDS aphorism proclaims: "When our leaders speak, the thinking has been done." When Earl Holding acts unilaterally, the powerful honor him with corporate citizenship awards for his certainty. Mac Livingston and Margot Smelzer, Stan Tixier and Gale Dick, Joro Walker and Susan Snow believe otherwise. Now, in my new home in the rural West, I begin to look for effective pathways to citizen action.

"A GRAND OPPORTUNITY." That's what Bureau of Land Management planner Frank Erickson saw in his chance to create the first resource management plan revision in a generation for the sweep of southern Utah on his map. Beard streaked with gray, quick of wit, and bouncy of step, Erickson stood in the one-room chinked-log pioneer schoolhouse in Torrey for his first informal meeting with interested locals in December 2001. He explained the planning process to us. He listened to our concerns about privatization of public lands.

I love listening to Frank Erickson because he speaks like a visionary bureaucrat. The die-hard Wayne County old-timers hate listening to him because they mistrust both change and bureaucrats. Erickson has the right credentials—he grew up in Utah, has Mormon roots, and one of his grandmothers came across the Great Plains with the immigrant wagon trains— but he is a planner, a Fed who worked and lived away from Utah most of his career.

Frank opens the meeting: "It is the policy of the United States to keep the land, to keep the public domain. The presumption is—the land stays with the people." This presumption is written into the 1976 legislation that finally modernized and codified the BLM's jurisdiction over the public domain—and finally closed the frontier. On the wall Frank has hung a map

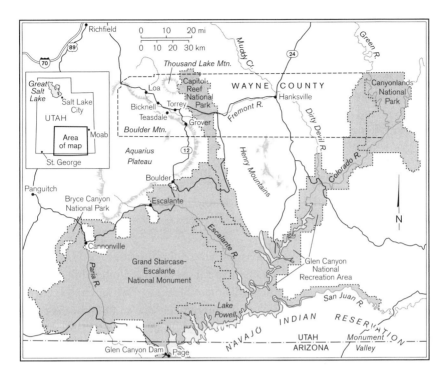

WAYNE COUNTY AND THE CANYON COUNTRY.

showing the 2.2 million acres of BLM land in his jurisdiction. The array of color-coded ownership stretches far beyond Wayne County, from Lake Powell on the Colorado River north for 170 miles to the southern flanks of the Wasatch Range, and from Canyonlands National Park west for 140 miles to the high plateaus rimming the Great Basin Desert.

Green marks the national forests, Fishlake and Dixie, and outlines the ranks of high plateaus above the river valleys. Purple follows the canyons of the Colorado and Green rivers and the cliffs of the Waterpocket Fold—the national parklands of Capitol Reef, Canyonlands, and Glen Canyon National Recreation Area. White outlines private land—mostly arable bottomlands. The rest—more than half the area of the map—is yellow BLM land, checkerboarded by an occasional section of blue-state land.

Almost every tally of public land includes state lands in the public column, as I do here, but in reality the isolated blue parcels are not public but rather "government-owned lands," "trustlands" that can be mined, leased, or sold. Since BLM land surrounds most of these lands, it is this game board of state and BLM lands that warms the hearts of developers eager for deals.

Starting with Ohio in 1803, Congress began granting incoming states at least one square-mile section per township to support public schools. Utah received four sections per township, a nearly 10 percent tithe, as compensation for the vast amount of land retained by the people of the United States. Just ten years before, Oregon had received only half this acreage; the lawmakers considered most of arid Utah to be worthless and figured the state needed all the help it could get. Thirty percent of Utah's private land started out as "school sections," mostly sold in the first thirty-five years after statehood in 1896. This pedigree includes a portion of our own land in Wayne County.

The School and Institutional Trust Lands Administration (SITLA) manages those blue squares to provide financial support for Utah public schools and universities, usually through oil and gas leasing or by selling parcels to new owners. School lands first earned more than $100 million for the trust in 2005. Though important discretionary funds for individual schools, the $18 million of interest generated by the trust endowment measures less than 1 percent of the budget for state schools. Wayne County's contribution to that total was just over one-third of 1 percent.

In the Torrey schoolhouse Frank Erickson waves at the wall map: "SITLA would like all their blue to be in one place. We'd like all our yellow to be in one place. We would like to acquire the land within Wilderness Study Areas. They want developable land." And so the school trustland agency trades for BLM land all the time. Many trades are noncontroversial. Some people see a request from SITLA to exchange land as automatically, by definition, in the public interest. For instance, a settlement negotiated by Secretary of the Interior Bruce Babbitt and Utah Governor Mike Leavitt in 1998 wiped all the blue squares from the map of Grand Staircase–Escalante National Monument, trading out 176,000 acres of school sections from the monument for BLM land elsewhere and creating a vast unbroken expanse of yellow public land. The trust, however, has remarkable freedom from oversight and regulation and makes deals that rival Earl Holding's for savvy and profit. Proposed exchanges can generate passionate opposition.

For every piece of land each of us sees a different reality—wilderness, parkland, homeland; grazing allotment, timber harvest, stone quarry, uranium mine. Beauty and challenge. We see real estate deals and quick profits. We also see public preserves and national parks, responsibilities to our great-grandchildren, lifetimes of local commitment, and Paiute Indian ghosts.

What we see is a mosaic of land tenure and fierce belief guaranteed to make the Torrey Valley a high-stakes battleground.

JUST 3.6 PERCENT OF WAYNE COUNTY IS PRIVATE LAND. Another 10.8 percent is state trustland, with mouth-watering potential for trade or privatization. The rest—85.6 percent of the county—is federal land owned by the people of the United States. This vast commons testifies to the sublime difficulty of the place—beautiful enough to warrant preservation as national parks and forests and arid enough to attract only a few pioneers to homestead on the public domain.

Those people who did come to homestead and hang on through drought and depression for 125 years created the infrastructure that now allows new-comers like us to build houses with water and power and telephones, to go to town to buy supplies and groceries, to procure services that ease our lives.

The school trustland administrators understand the lure of the valley. They know this is the hottest rural real estate market in Utah. They have already developed and sold state parcels near Torrey and keep looking for more blue squares that embrace a hotspot of biodiversity or that leave a hole in federal ownership of critical wildlands, eager to turn those squares yellow—hoping to trade for an attractive BLM parcel they can privatize.

John Andrews, the SITLA associate director, asked me a crucial question: "What do you do with these state lands if you don't want to see development?" You can turn to Utah Open Lands or the Nature Conservancy to raise funds to buy them. If there is no outside conservation money, you have to look at trade with the agency that administers surrounding acreage—usually, the BLM. Otherwise, if there is market demand, the lands will be developed and sold. It's that straightforward. Meanwhile, asks Andrews, "How do you maintain an economy that allows the long-term citizens to stay while avoiding schlocky development on private land, where alfalfa fields are subdivided into ranchettes without any thought of planning?"

After a dozen years as the trust's other progressive administrator, in 2007 Ric McBrier left SITLA. As assistant director for real estate development, he had worked with the public to prioritize swaps and create mini-regional exchanges; he describes the SITLA work as "engaging the community and building faith" rather than "cooking it up in the back room.

Just because we don't by law have to consult with the public doesn't mean it isn't in the trust's best interest to consult with the public." He favored making more money by getting things done rather than stubbornly fighting to win every transaction; and so he stood for incremental progress and compromise.

"Do we try to be opportunistic?" McBrier asked me. "Absolutely. Do we try to unfairly beat the BLM in the transaction? Absolutely not."

"GOOD FOR THE LAND. Good for the people. Legally defensible." Frank Erickson begins the series of official public meetings to gather testimony for the BLM resource management plan with a flip chart outlining his goals. The responses from fifty citizens in Loa on a cold March night don't compress into a few words so simply. Erickson and the BLM are out "scoping"— identifying the issues that matter to the people. Around the room we take turns voicing our positions, our hopes, and our frustrations.

Traditional westerners have grown more and more resentful of what they feel is a distant controlling hand, a force they see as imperial, colonial, paternalistic. The result? The property-rights, county-rights, Sagebrush Rebellion anger of the rural West that palpably heats the room at the Wayne County Courthouse. Guy Pace, a major rancher and landowner in the county: "The livestock business is becoming an endangered species. The Wasatch Front and California are moving in; you get one of those people in, and they are going to want another one." Sharon Lusco: "I have lived here all my life. Recreation is wonderful, but people have to make a living on something besides cooking hamburgers. Agriculture has kept this community alive." Her husband speaks of how their Fairview Ranch "has been there since before Utah was a state. I'm a land user, I'm an inheritor. We *are* the environment."

Others take aim at the idea of wilderness "locking up the land," insistent about their fundamental right to drive all-terrain vehicles (ATVs) anywhere they please. They speak in favor of "multiple use," a polite way of opposing wilderness. "Those ATVs, they are people too!" "Every ATV rider is one carburetor away from being a hiker." "A man's got a right to be here on this old earth, even if we leave a track."

"It's this *wilderness!*" The speaker, a woman, wails the word in anguish— though no designated wilderness yet exists in the county.

As I listen I realize that we need to shift the conversation from multiple use to sustainable use. Environmentalists need to see the impact of wilderness designation on ranchers. Ranchers need to acknowledge regional threats to biodiversity and the ecological effects of roads and off-road vehicles. We all need to concede the new economic reality: agriculture does not "keep this community alive." We desperately need conversation, reciprocity—and a sense of humor.

The Taylors speak next. Karl Don, only a little older than me, is a third-generation rancher. His son, Boone, talks about running cattle and working hard. He says, "I'm twenty-six, I love what I do; I want my kids to keep doing it." The Taylors' emotion is unmistakable. When I look them up later, I learn that the Taylors run 300 head of cattle on the east side of Boulder Mountain, moving their animals seasonally between the mountain and the desert, across 1,500 square miles of remote and rugged country. They hold the last grazing permit within Capitol Reef National Park.

Like so many people in Wayne County, Karl just wants to be left alone in all that glorious country, no matter what its designation, to do what he loves and knows how to do. He has no remaining trust for federal agencies. "They send out some new kid from back east where everything is green, who knows diddly shit about a cow, and who comes out to make a name for themselves. You can't take a college graduate who's been here for six months and have him tell a seventy-year-old rancher what's going to be done. It just doesn't work." But he shares some worries with environmentalists: "I'll be out at sunrise—about as far out as I can be—enjoying the beginning of a beautiful morning, and I hear a putt-putt-putt coming along. I think ATVs ought to have certain trails here and there and stay on them."

"From here to Lake Powell," Karl told me as we sat at a picnic table underneath the summer cottonwoods on Torrey's Main Street, "I've probably been around every rock and underneath every tree." His horses whinny from their trailer, waiting for him to resume the drive to work in his alfalfa fields. Karl lists the skills necessary to be a successful rancher: "You have to be a range con [a range conservationist, the term of art for a manager of cattle country], a part-time veterinarian, a weather forecaster, an economist. There is no aspect we can forget. It's born and bred in us."

Karl's son, Boone, has a daughter born in 2002; he loves to take her with him when he feeds his cows. Boone cherishes the land and the work: "You won't get rich doing it, but it's a rich lifestyle. It becomes just a love affair—baby cows on the ground, riding out through this pretty country—what more could a guy have? We're so protective of those public lands, we don't even like to see tourists down there."

Boone believes that the land needs to be worked, that grazing is good for grass and logging is good for forests. "If you take away the people that broke this country to what it is, the land will miss them. It won't miss the backpackers." And yet "you have to realize that times have changed. I'll do everything in my power to keep my cows out there, so we have to learn how to deal with influence from other parties."

Karl Don Taylor has seen decades of changing management unleash wild rumors; it makes people "a little hot. We're so jumpy about it, we hear one little spark and we start a fire. We've been burnt too many times." Boone, a rancher from a new era, can see both sides. "Look where we live: it's so pretty—and now people are finding out about it. Is this a trickle that's going to turn into a floodwater?" Boone is comfortable with his passion and well aware of his irony when he admits, "I'll allow change as long as it doesn't impact the way of life we've had here for 150 years."

PUBLIC MEETINGS LIKE THESE encourage monologue, not dialogue. We speechify, firing off rounds at the enemy and preaching to the choir. Ever since the '60s and Earth Day and debacles like the Exxon *Valdez*, environmentalists have felt justified in their pure, radical passion. We have felt righteous, but often we slip over the line and sound self-righteous. You can imagine how our words play along the line of worn stools at the counter of the Aquarius Café, where county old-timers come and go on workdays.

In a challenging critique the historian William Cronon has taken us to task for our certainties. His argument makes environmentalists wince. An avowed environmentalist himself, Cronon is painfully aware that celebrating wilderness has become the ideal of "elite urban tourists and wealthy sportsmen." Mainstream environmentalists have become paid professionals rather than volunteers on fire, and they have lost some moral ground in the process. We have set humans outside—and against—nature. We have disenfranchised those who work the land. "If we set too high a stock on wilderness," warns Cronon, "too many other corners of the earth become less than natural and too many other people become less than human, thereby giving us permission not to care much about their suffering or their fate."

Each time I loop through twentieth-century environmental history I reach the same two contradictory conclusions: that we have made astonishing progress toward achieving Aldo Leopold's land ethic and Rachel Carson's sense of wonder. And that we still rarely rise above the old destructive notions of unbridled development, of land as commodity.

When I visited Wayne County strictly as a pilgrim, as an unaffiliated environmentalist, I had a certain square footage of authority to stand upon—a platform constructed from my share of ownership in the public lands and my knowledge of the place gained by muscle power, sweat, and observation, by reading and conversation. By buying land and building a house I have changed the shape of that platform. I've cut away some of the sharpest idealistic edges and added some scuffed, old-fashioned plausibility, based on words like *property owner, taxpayer, citizen,* and *roots*—even if those tendrils growing from my feet are fragile and new. They are an unintentional by-product. I bought land not to infiltrate the community but because I loved it and was fortunate enough to be able to pay for it. For an environmentalist this was a sellout on one hand and subversive on the other. The county commissioners may resent me as a WOE. They may dismiss me as just another "Sierra Club extremist" down from Salt Lake City. In most ways I'll always be a powerless outsider. And yet they have to listen to me now because I am a landowner.

WHEN I CALLED THE MAYOR of Torrey after the next round of policy proposals, he hung up on me. On one level, his outrage made no sense. On another, it was predictable.

The Friends of Grover had written a joint response to Frank Erickson's resource management plan. Our biggest concern for the Torrey Valley was the potential loss of public lands in trades to the school trustlands agency. We knew that the aggressive administrators at SITLA were eager to crank up development without community discussion or planning, and the BLM had advised us that the most appropriate way to take public lands off the table for trade and "to protect the character of the land" would be to declare the Torrey Valley an ACEC, an Area of Critical Environmental Concern. And so we wrote a twenty-page proposal, asking for a special management area that would preserve the rural landscape of the Torrey Valley and maintain its scenic quality as a gateway to Capitol Reef National Park. We emphasized that this was not a bid for wilderness. We asked the BLM to maintain traditional uses—and to keep 34,000 acres of public land off the table for trade to state or private ownership.

But the words in the new designation were suspect. "Environmental" sounded like "environmentalist" to locals, and that nervous-making "critical" would scare traditionalists looking for hidden agendas. I remembered Wendy Fisher's warning: when she lobbies for Utah Open Lands in rural counties she reminds herself to heed "the politics of words."

As Ric McBrier of SITLA says, "The system wants to analyze who won and who lost, never how both sides won." As a result the barricades remain in place. Public discussion becomes impossible.

————

"This highly vocal, highly motivated minority took over the public process. And the silent majority doesn't get heard." That's how Kay Erickson (no relation to Frank) saw it when the locals and part-timers of the Friends of Grover led the fight to block trades in the Torrey Valley between the BLM and the school trust. Erickson, a local and for years the lands specialist in the Richfield BLM office, believed that the proposed trustland trade died when first proposed in the mid-1990s because his boss, the field manager, "decided he didn't want to mess with the Friends of Grover. You guys are vocal, had time and money, and seem to know the process better than we do." He was disappointed by his boss. And he was equally disgusted by us WOES with "money and power overriding people who have lived their whole lives there."

Erickson wanted to go forward with an Environmental Assessment and formally engage everyone. He claimed that "we never had an opportunity to go through the process"—the same phrase I had heard repeatedly from the members of Save Our Snowbasin when they protested Earl's move to legislate the Snowbasin land exchange. Down the road in Wayne County, development director Nan Anderson responded. She had good reason to support new development. But she is "absolutely committed to the concept of constituency. The people who lived out there said, 'We don't want this.' When the commissioners did not support the privatization of public lands beloved to their constituents, our elected officials heard the voice of the people. They took, in my opinion, appropriate action."

Kay Erickson resents all the interlopers messing about in his world. In the old days the BLM quietly served powerful constituencies in the resource extraction industries. Critics ridiculed the agency as the Bureau of Logging and Mining. Today "we manage people, not public lands," laments Erickson. "We've got Friends of Grover, SUWA [Southern Utah Wilderness Alliance], mountain bikers, four-wheelers, horse groups—everything has a friend, the Friends of Everything. How do you deal with all those and still walk through the middle and keep people happy?"

What rankles Kay Erickson, I think, has as much to do with affluence as with influence. Newcomers using the public lands for recreation tend to be people who earn their incomes elsewhere. Old-timers depend on those lands for basic sustenance. For them it's a workplace that produces little wealth but calls for considerable self-reliance. Erickson resents the "leisure class," those with the freedom to come looking for spiritual sustenance—whether it's the dirtbag Gen-X backpackers who come to the canyons to play or the retirees who can afford to teach themselves the basics of watercolor while they admire the red rocks on long walks every morning. Much of the county shares his resentment, keeping the community at a simmer that complicates all of our land management and planning decisions.

———

"I have credibility," Rob Williams told me, as a partial explanation of the county's anger at our proposal. "You don't." Williams grew up in Teasdale, worked as a Forest Service planner in Idaho, and retired to run 125 cows on Boulder Mountain. He went to high school with two of the county commissioners. He is related to the third. When he speaks as a Wayne County planning commission member, the county commissioners listen. "It's ironic," he says. "We sell our property to people who move here, and then we don't want them to have a different opinion. People can't get past their mistrust of government, environmentalists, wilderness. . . ." He didn't admire this state of affairs, but he understood it.

Susan Snow, the charismatic and effective director of the Southern Utah Forest Products Association, helped draft the ACEC proposal in her role as copresident of the Friends of Grover. But the phrase "Friends of Grover" had become a red flag, equated with the hated environmentalists. We would need to submit the proposal to the BLM as individuals. Susan decided not to include her name. The county was too riled. Indeed, most contributors to the ACEC document felt that signing it would open them and their families to ridicule and ostracism.

And so the Fremont Valley Gateway ACEC proposal went to the BLM with three names on the cover: Charles and Judy Smith, retirees from Salt Lake City who recently had declared their longtime Teasdale second home as their primary residence, and Stephen Trimble.

———

Two weeks after we released the final document, Susan Snow's board came to her with a list of demands. They insisted that she sign a waiver, agree to take no political positions, and assume no activist role, essentially prohibiting her from consorting with environmentalists like us. Sad and angry, she resigned from her position as director. One more promising progressive path into the future had withered for Wayne County.

What locals opposed was any increase in federal oversight, any more meddling in their lives by BLM managers intent on "critical environmental" values. At the same time, they were willing to risk any future brought to them by the status quo. And so, when I made that call to Torrey's mayor, Fred Hansen, to ask if I could stop by to discuss his reactions to the proposal, he said, "It's full of traps. You guys are trying to screw us." I said, "What do you mean?" He answered, "I'm not going to argue with you." And he hung up.

We kept repeating that the ACEC would *save* public land and protect the relationship that the citizens of Wayne County had with that land. We kept insisting that this was more balanced than "locking up" land in private ownership after trade to the revenue-hungry school trustlands agency. But to no avail. We had lost the hearts of the old-timers before we ever started because of our rush to deadline, our lack of grassroots debate—and because of the "politics of words."

We may never have been able to turn old-timers into supporters, but they wouldn't have been so angry if we had taken time for listening, for local discussion, and worked toward broader support for protecting the lands that everyone valued. After things had cooled off a bit I went back to Fred Hansen to discuss these events. At that time he admitted that he really didn't want to see the BLM land traded out for development. But Fred knew that "people defy change" and it takes time for suspicious citizens to mull over something like the ACEC long enough to "wake up and think it's their own idea."

THE WEST THAT WALLACE STEGNER DESCRIBED as the Geography of Hope seems to be evolving into a Geography of Hostility.

Traditionalists rail against new federal designations and feel threatened by the culture of new people. The move-ins like us tend to conclude that they—we—understand what's good for the place before spending enough time listening to fish hatchery technicians and truck drivers, waitresses and teacher's aides—all the people struggling to make a living in this beautiful, difficult country where there is so much more rock and sun than water and soil.

"Create a story that demonstrates public good." Stephen Goldsmith, the former director of planning for Salt Lake City, gave me this line when I asked him how a citizen can nudge the powerful to create change. "Feed the interest of the decision maker," he said, from long experience. "Make every commissioner, or council member, or legislator, think you have served his or her particular interest." Dave Livermore, Utah director for the Nature Conservancy, advises, "Have other people carry your water." If you can persuade an insider to tell your story, the other insiders will listen far more sympathetically.

Ric McBrier is worn out by Wayne County's response to his agency's efforts to earn money for Utah schools: "It's all negative and reactive. The way to get the good things done is to be positive and proactive." He has seen it happen in places where community members were just as eclectic but "loved each other. This might just be about love."

————

While we wait for a visionary risk taker who can move all of us forward together, directives from prodevelopment, antiplanning political appointees in Washington and Salt Lake City continued to arrive on Frank Erickson's desk in the Richfield BLM office.

After years of respectfully following the legal process dictated by NEPA, Erickson could barely cope when an interim state director assigned to Utah for only a few months gutted the core of his resource management plan. The temporary appointee was unwavering in his dismissal of process. He buried the conservation goals wherever they appeared, telling Erickson, "This isn't your plan, it's *mine*."

The interim state director moved on, but the meddling and undercutting just kept coming. Frank had carefully constructed his narrative—as instructed by law—with the guidance of field managers who knew the land, the chorus of comments from the public, and the best science the experts could muster. In a conference call the national director of the BLM casually dismissed his work. She wanted none of these balanced complexities but simply ordered Frank to "go back to the counties. I expect the counties to concur."

Erickson kept trying to salvage the integrity of the language and the process that would determine the future of this land. His beard turned white. In 2007 the powers that be finally removed him as author of the Richfield resource management plan, replacing him with a Washington insider who would create a more direct path toward the administration's goal of maximum oil and gas development.

Erickson thinks back wistfully to that "grand opportunity" he had seen in 2001: "It may take ten years, at $600,000 a year, to finish a twenty-year

FRANK ERICKSON, BLM PLANNER FOR MILLIONS OF ACRES OF PUBLIC LANDS, 2005.

plan. That's truly embarrassing; it's a travesty. I believe in federal agencies. I'm a company man. I can usually find a way to explain why we do what we do." But not this time. Frank Erickson retired from a thirty-year career in public service in the summer of 2007.

"I worry about us," Erickson frets. "Are we up to this task? You start with such idealism and such hope. And you get pummeled by changing directions. I was sure naïve. I had no idea of the *weight* of politics."

"A DECISION IMPOSED FROM THE TOP DOWN . . . the people had no say . . . a feeling of injustice." "The old-timers believe this wasn't done in a manner that was right. They will never forget and never forgive." The words sound distressingly familiar. They could be the voices of Ogden Valley locals talking about Earl Holding's disdain for public process in his drive to a Snowbasin land exchange. Or is this Frank Erickson talking about politically appointed administrators interfering with BLM field personnel?

Nope. These are the citizens of southern Utah reacting to President Bill Clinton's creation of Grand Staircase–Escalante National Monument in 1996. My own reaction to Clinton's proclamation was triumph and joy, a sense of validation for years of idealism and hope. Faced with reactions so at odds with my own, I've tried to decode my exhilaration.

In creating the new national monument, President Clinton ended a thirty-year debate about whether we should strip-mine coal on the remote Kaiparowits Plateau. He protected what was left of the Escalante rivershed—centerpiece of a national park proposal in the 1930s—and thereby reclaimed some of the philosophical and moral ground lost when the diversion tunnels closed at Glen Canyon Dam and Lake Powell began to fill. He acknowledged the presence of geologic and cultural treasures—first noted well over a century ago by John Wesley Powell—in this place that "glued together" Grand Canyon and Bryce Canyon and Zion national parks, as Bruce Babbitt put it. Clinton made the monument big enough to serve as a natural laboratory for research on genetic banking, speciation, and multiple migration corridors—acting on the authority of the scientists who need multiple habitats for their research (a faith since verified as the monument has yielded a wealth of new data and discoveries).

It had been a quarter century since the last major act of conservation in the canyon country: the national park bills that expanded Arches and Capitol Reef and created Canyonlands. Clinton's proclamation was a courageous act of policy, but he had acted unilaterally and without local consultation.

I hear the Snowbasin story ringing in my ears.

What had motivated the president? After talking with Katie McGinty, chair of Clinton's Council on Environmental Quality, and John Leshy, solicitor (chief legal counsel) at the Interior Department, who led the team that evaluated the region's potential for a national monument, I find their intentions remarkably honorable, exhilaratingly elevated above raw political calculation.

Clinton's decision to act in southern Utah grew directly out of policy differences with the Utah Congressional delegation. Katie McGinty pointed to the 1994 Republican takeover of Congress as the crucial moment. Before then the administration had "successfully staved off" attacks on wild Utah. When the numbers changed in Congress and people like Jim Hansen took over as chairs of congressional committees "they were just bound and determined to grab what they can grab, to repeal what they can repeal. The president understood the importance of not enabling a raid on the federal ecological treasures."

In late spring 1996 McGinty began to discuss with Clinton "the full suite of authorities" the president might use to counter the "rapaciousness" of the Utah delegation. The Antiquities Act surfaced quickly—the law signed by Teddy Roosevelt in 1906 that allows the creation of national monuments by executive order. The president took Interior Secretary Bruce Babbitt aside at a public ceremony to tell him that he had decided to take action in Utah. McGinty called Interior Solicitor Leshy to the White House just before the 1996 Fourth of July weekend and said, "The president wants to look at monument options in southern Utah. Put a team together and make a recommendation." Leshy would work in secret. The Utah delegation would know nothing of his work until the *Los Angeles Times* leaked the monument plan in early September.

John Leshy told me that once the story broke the Utah delegation insisted he meet with them. When he did so, he asked, "If the president moves ahead, what are the hot-button issues for you?" The Utahns ticked off their concerns: grazing, mining, off-road vehicles, water rights, hunting and fishing, and, perhaps most important, the managing agency. An "extremely pleased" Leshy realized that his regional experts had addressed every one of the delegation's issues. "We listened to the Utah people in advance, before we heard them." He sounds, depending on your politics, either prescient or paternalistic. "We had even decided to make it a *little* more politically acceptable to the locals by recommending that the BLM manage it—a deliberate experiment." Leshy gave Babbitt the credit for this innovative challenge to the BLM, the first time the agency had been charged with a real conservation mission.

Reaction to the monument proclamation in southern Utah was predictable: anger at yet another dictum arriving from Washington about how local people should live their lives. Senator Bob Bennett decried Clinton's actions as an "outrageous, arrogant approach to public policy." Leshy noted that much of the public outcry after the monument proclamation was about process, not substance. Others believe that Grand Staircase–Escalante was a response not only to Jim Hansen's Utah anti-wilderness bill but to his Snowbasin fervor. They knew that the Snowbasin land trade had angered Clinton's tribe, and they saw Grand Staircase, in part, as an act of revenge. I think the connection to Snowbasin was more atmospheric, part and parcel of the probusiness Republican approach to the environment. As McGinty summed up the climate in Congress: they felt like this was their moment, with Newt Gingrich in charge, and they were going for it. With the election looming, Clinton's people were also looking to distinguish his tenure with an act of conservation that would cement their green support. The Arctic National Wildlife Refuge and Utah's Redrock Wilderness were the biggest issues. Clinton's advisors figured that they could protect the former from drilling with the power of the president's veto. The defeat of Jim Hansen's Utah wilderness bill in spring 1996 had created an opening for action in the redrock canyons.

Both McGinty and Leshy emphasize, however, that this was not a "huge and easy political win." The most political members of the Clinton White House argued against proclaiming the monument because it would complicate relations with Congress and jinx the lone Utah democratic congressman (who indeed lost in 1996). Nevertheless, they chose to act.

THE PROCLAMATION OF GRAND STAIRCASE–ESCALANTE National Monument defies corporate use of national resources; the Snowbasin exchange enables that use. Katie McGinty warns against the troublesome "legislative mischief" of "riders in the dark of night that take the public out of these complex processes at Interior and BLM and the Forest Service," creating inappropriate exemptions from NEPA. In contrast—and she was fierce about this—Bill Clinton proclaimed Grand Staircase "in the light of day. It's the president acting under executive authority to proclaim an honorific designation of an area that has special cultural and ecological resources—where NEPA has never applied. The president cannot exercise the authority of the Antiquities Act in a sneaky way. It's very public."

With the establishment of Grand Staircase–Escalante, I have a sense of increased wealth. The riches of my life and the collective lives of all citizens both bumped up a few notches—the reverse of the loss of wealth I felt with the drowning of Glen Canyon and the privatization of Snowbasin.

I'm not defining wealth in terms of productivity or possession or con-

WILLIS CREEK NARROWS, GRAND STAIRCASE-ESCALANTE NATIONAL MONUMENT, UTAH, 2000.

trol. I'm defining wealth in terms of freedom, with a timeline of many generations. Clinton preserved our options. In setting aside passing preferences for burning fossil fuels and building roads, he acknowledged that we have more to learn from this land than we can know.

In the United States, where we have retained much of our wild country as public land, every citizen of the democracy shares in the wealth of this land. On this scale we all are wealthy. We are rich in freedom and acreage and rights to participate in planning for the future.

Just as the Ogden Valley community resented Earl Holding, so does the Wayne County community resent me and my cohort of second-home owners and would-be reformers of public-lands management. The more extreme traditionalists see us as powerful and pushy and insensitive—just as I see Earl. I'd like to think that this personal rejection horrifies me more than it does Earl.

There are differences, of course. Earl wanted public land for his own use. Grand Staircase heightens protection for lands that already were public and will remain so. As Katie McGinty said, "The Antiquities Act did not grab a single particle of dust that was not already federal land, but we never did win the public opinion battle as to who actually was doing the land grab."

Who knows what might have been if everyone who cared about Grand Staircase–Escalante had negotiated its future together? Given the scale— close to 2 million acres—it's hard to believe that we could have been as bold in committee as Clinton was as an executive. John Leshy acknowledges that "people feel like it was an act of political rape." But he doesn't believe that "it could have been done any differently. And what happened in the monument's wake is demonstrably good—to have the whole Kaiparowits coal mine business put to rest and to have those state lands out of there is going to have huge long-term positive impacts on the state."

In the mid-1990s Utah was so polarized that we essentially disqualified ourselves and allowed the debate to move elsewhere. Now it's clear that we must take back control of the conversation if we are ever to have a sense of real community. We must get everyone to the table. And once we are there, we can't walk away.

We aren't there yet.

"WE ARE AN URBAN STATE," says Frank Erickson, "and we live with the myth that we are rural. It's fine to have myths, but at what cost?" Ranching on public lands in the West no longer represents a dominant sector of the economy or the workforce. In the next ten years farming and ranching jobs will decline in numbers nationally more than any other occupation. Just 180 permittees run livestock on the 2.2 million acres of BLM land in Erickson's resource management plan, an area with a population of 50,000. Services and retirement income, not resource extraction, are the growth factors here. Welcoming new people and new skills will grow the economy. Agriculture, on the other hand, has declined to just 15 percent of the jobs in Wayne County, and manufacturing (including forest products) to less than 4 percent. Remote corners of the West that appear to be rural grow ever more tied to cities, just as the World Wide Web and the global economy link the far corners of the planet ever more completely.

All sides are beginning to acknowledge that the key to collaborative local decision making lies in recognizing our collective devil's bargains. I know longtime residents and newcomers who are acutely aware of these problems. I have a bookshelf of stories about groups around the West who have proven that former enemies can come together on higher ground.

The administration of George W. Bush pays lip service to collaboration but demonstrates imperial arrogance in its relentless drive to turn public lands over to corporations for profit. The Bush agenda aims to privatize everything from campground management and archaeological research to the operation of dams. Citizen collaboration must wait for a more collegial administration to be tested. In the meantime westerners are looking for models. Janine Blaeloch at the Western Lands Project has called for a moratorium on all federal land exchanges. A series of federal audits of government land exchanges and appraisal procedures is gradually coming to the same conclusion.

Dan Kemmis, the former speaker of the Montana legislature and past mayor of Missoula, has imagined the creation of gigantic land trusts that would turn whole watersheds over to local compacts of states, Indian tribes, and citizens. He insists on two provisos: that the lands remain public in perpetuity, and that trustees manage them for ecological sustainability.

Janine Blaeloch remains dubious: "There is a seduction in that process: the purpose is for everybody to be able to hold hands at the end of it. When you sit down at the table, you've already set a goal that by definition is not necessarily what's best for the land." Gale Dick, after years of shuffling towers of EIS binders while directing the actions of Save Our Canyons in the Wasatch Mountains, shares her doubts. He suggests that "long-term bickering may be the *solution,* not the problem. After all, protection of the land, not harmony among stakeholders, is the goal."

Jim Lyons remains skeptical as well. He is loath to turn these lands over to local control without ensuring that there is a broad perspective on their role as national assets. Lyons is from the East. When western senators asked him, in his role as agriculture undersecretary in the Clinton administration, "What the hell does a guy from New Jersey know about managing public lands?" he would tell them, "Senator, the one thing I do know is, in places like New Jersey where we don't have them, we have come to appreciate what you have in the West and how valuable these public lands, these national natural resources, are."

I think back to Stan Tixier's abortive effort at collaboration at Snowbasin after the 1990 decision to trade two hundred acres to Earl. Mediation failed because competing interests refused to find common ground, opening the door for Earl Holding to bypass process, manipulate Congress, and wield his power to the full. Frank Erickson, too, has seen these moments "where process ends and values begin."

Forest Service emeritus chief Jack Ward Thomas reminds us that 10 percent of the American people control 90 percent of the national wealth. He asks, "Is that not enough?" Thomas wants to make sure that "devolvement" of public lands management won't trade "our heritage and inheritance for a mess of pottage. These lands are part of America's culture—the only such lands that the vast majority of us will ever own."

AS I BEGAN TO IMAGINE sitting across the big table from people who are feeling embattled and defensive, I thought about how best to distill my principles before blundering ahead. I tried to list what I believe to be true, an inventory of issues that newcomers and old-timers alike must grapple with and within which we must find bridges to take us to a sustainable future together.

I'm not the first to attempt to articulate the bedrock of my creed. Victor Scheffer, the eminent marine biologist, stated environmentalism's "Articles of Faith" a few years ago. To me Scheffer's words seem like simple declarations of truth.

1. All things are connected.
2. Earthly goods are limited.
3. Nature's way is best.
4. The survival of humankind depends on natural diversity.
5. Environmentalism is radical.

These are radical notions. They demand fundamental change—in political systems, law, agriculture and industry, the structure of capitalism, internationalism, and education. They constitute, as Scheffer acknowledges, "a morality of life or death for civilization."

I first encountered Scheffer's manifesto on an antienvironmental "wise use" web site, where it was cited as a missive from the enemy, a distillation of "eco-ideology"—a word best said with a sneer. The wise use countermanifesto places humans at the center of the natural world, with all other beings servicing their needs. When I compressed wise use principles in a paragraph, I realized, with distress, that they match the core beliefs of mainstream society: A free market system provides the greatest good for the greatest number of people. The natural world is not fragile but, rather, inexhaustible. Technology can meet any challenge, solve any problem. Growth equals progress, and, so, accumulation of material goods measures success. Individual liberty always trumps community rights. Humans stand at the center of the universe, and "man's" reworking of the earth is inevitably benevolent.

What I've always thought of as a fringe statement turns out to be a swatch from the fabric of America. The good businessman, that devout practitioner of Harold Bloom's American Religion, has come back to haunt us.

———————

Manifesto is a fightin' word. Dogmatic by nature. Perhaps what I'm after is a credo: "This I believe." I want to take a stand based on introspection rather than a knee-jerk reaction, a stand that challenges dogma and articulates an ethic to live by as the middle-aged West fills in and rushes toward maturity.

Like our lives, my credo remains a work in progress. I offer it here now as a statement of what I believe today about land, community, and honor after fifty-odd years of living in the Imperial West and learning from the past, from my mentors, from the Snowbasin story and Earl Holding, from Mac Livingston and his like-minded band of frontline warriors, from the mountain, and from the mesa. A statement, too, of my dreams for the future.

My bulwark against regret.

CREDO:
THE PEOPLE'S WEST

LIFELONG LOCALS KNOW THEIR HOME. They understand the land's intimate cycles from decades and generations of living in place, a miracle of stability and identity.

We can never hope to restore or sustain landscapes and watersheds without the cooperation of local citizens. They rightfully resent and subvert any management scheme that excludes them from decision making.

We need mutual trust, respect, empathy, and accountability. The hits and misses of long-term elders can teach us all, while passionate newcomers—community members by choice—brandish a fierce love for their new home that can reinspire old-timers. Honor every skill and talent in the community. Involving too many people is always better than leaving someone out.

Economic health is essential for community health. If we don't create affordable housing and decent jobs for full-time residents, the community will lose its multigenerational roots. The working rural landscape will collapse into parody.

Ecological health is essential for community health. Conserve land *for* the land, and good things will come to people and community, as well.

Rapid, unplanned growth profits only the boomer, rewards only the developer, and will in the long run fail citizens and destroy their sense of place. Leadership must come from within the community. A master plan is the key to the future for each landscape—an inclusive, place-specific vision conceived in the broadest possible dialogue.

Proliferating roads and off-road-vehicle use fragment the integrity of surviving wildlands. Concentrate development where it already exists. Preserve agricultural land and the wild habitats it holds.

Ranching on public lands contributes to the American cultural quilt. But cows should have no special rights. Where cattle and sheep damage the land, eliminate grazing and manage for restoration.

That public lands make up most of the rural West is a positive—an asset. Keep public lands public to create a buffer between village and wildland. With privatization of the commons, we lose community access.

Refuse to drown in the deluge of change. Channel those floodwaters to power community dialogue. Continually reassess any plan for a specific landscape and its neighborhoods. Insist on ecological sustainability, health, preservation of cultural tradition, and protection of biodiversity. Keep talking, no matter what. Keep listening, no matter what. Restraint is both visionary and conservative.

Wildness is everywhere, but wilderness is a special category. Designate and preserve large wilderness areas on public land wherever possible—several in each bioregion and connected by corridors. Establish local and regional land trusts to purchase critical private lands and hold conservation easements.

One person, one passionate person speaking out stubbornly and relentlessly, can still make a difference. Hard work by one individual can start a revolution.

Arrogance is the opposite of relationship. Don't hesitate to use words like compassion and love and honor. Depoliticize and humanize the issues, and fling open the windows on bureaucracy and authority. Remove obstacles to healing.

WE ARE STUCK WITH OUR UNTIDY WEB of conflicting values. We all have our Edens, our devils, our bargains to strike. We are responsible for planning, making decisions, acknowledging duty, accepting stewardship—and for wrangling through as a community.

Start the conversation before a crisis. Share information and frustrations and dreams and anger and joy. Stomp along the riverbank together. Work together. Cook and eat together, tell stories together. Laugh together. Thrash through conflict to higher ground. Inclusivity requires trust and openness from old-timers and newcomers alike.

We call it paradise, this land of ours. We call it home. Like our nation, the West is in the middle of its arc. We must remain both vigilant and tender if we wish to preserve its authenticity. We can do this. We are not yet too old, too greedy, or too cynical to take wise action together.

NOTES

BOOK EPIGRAPH: Henry David Thoreau, "Economy," the first chapter of *Walden* (New York: North American Library, 1960), pp. 25–26 in my battered Signet paperback.

BECOMING EARL

PAGE 1: Epigraph from Hal K. Rothman, *Devil's Bargains: Tourism in the Twentieth-Century American West* (Lawrence: University Press of Kansas, 1998), p. 377. Used by permission of the publisher.

PAGE 6: Figures for the sprawl rate in America come from Eric T. Freyfogle, *The Land We Share: Private Property and the Common Good* (Washington, D.C.: Island Press/Shearwater Books, 2003), p. 2.

Each year the Wilderness Society lists its "15 Most Endangered Wildlands," American Rivers chooses "America's Most Endangered Rivers," and Scenic America picks the ten "Last Chance Landscapes" that face "imminent and potentially irrevocable harm" but also harbor a potential solution.

PAGE 7: I base my thinking about greed and generosity on Lewis Hyde's comments to Alesia Maltz in "A Conversation with Lewis Hyde," *Whole Terrain: Reflective Environmental Practice* 11 (2002/2003): 39, 45, 46.

LITTLE AMERICA

PAGE 13: Epigraph from Rob Swigart's crazy, raunchy, satirical *Little America: A Novel*, which I read with glee when I first discovered it in its 1977 original edition, and which has recently been brought back into print (New York: iUniverse.com, Inc., 2000), pp. 12, 17, 18. Used with permission.

PAGE 17: First comes William Oscar Johnson, "Earl Has Bought a Pearl," *Sports Illustrated*, November 14, 1977, pp. 93–94, 99. David Proctor and Paul Swenson, the authors of a one-page magazine profile based on generally available information ("Earl Holding: People Know Who's Boss," *Utah Holiday* [Salt Lake City], March 1986, p. 56), quote Earl's boast to the Salt Lake City Chamber of Commerce president that he hadn't given a press interview in thirteen years. A 1994 magazine article completed without his cooperation (Phyllis Berman and Alexandra Alger, "A One-Man Show," *Forbes*, February 14, 1994, p. 68) was the most extensive profile until he deigned to speak to the LDS Church-owned *Deseret News* in Salt Lake City (Lisa Riley Roche, "Holding's Olympic-Size Projects Are 'Labors of Love,'" March 23, 1997) and to the *Salt Lake Tribune* (Guy Boulton, "Buying and Holding," February 13, 2000). The *Deseret News* proudly noted that Earl had given them "nearly an hour"; the *Tribune* made similar noises.

Choosing to speak so rarely in public is an effective way for Earl to maintain control. As the 2002 Olympics approached and Earl became more newsworthy, exposure picked up, and his wall of reserve buckled slightly. He spoke at some length with a *SKI Magazine* reporter, Andrew Slough ("Earl Holding Speaks," October 2000, pp. 152–59).

Earl Holding's ownership of land in the West is discussed in the cover story by William P. Barrett, "This Land Is Their Land: The Top 100 Landowners," *Worth*, February 1997, p. 78, and in "The Land Report 100: A Comprehensive Look at the Nation's Largest Landowners," *The Land Report*, April 2007 (www.thelandreport.com/ME2/Default.asp; accessed November 12, 2007).

PAGE 19: Pat Bean, "A Look at the Man Behind Snowbasin," *Ogden Standard-Examiner*, January 24, 1999, includes Earl's quote about being "born in a bed on First Avenue." The prominent management consultant Stephen Covey, author of *The Seven Habits of Highly Effective People*, is grandson of the Stephen (S. M.) Covey who founded Little America.

PAGE 20: The quote about Carol's poor background comes from Johnson, "Earl Has Bought a Pearl." The card-playing story is in Boulton, "Buying and Holding." Carol's appearance in the "Miss Utah" contest is from Karen Bossick, "Sun Valley: In a Holding Pattern," *Wood River Journal* (Sun Valley), February 2, 2006.

Little America as "a dozen counter stools and twelve little rooms" comes from Roche, "Holding's Olympic-Size Projects."

For the Carol Holding quote about being part of the business, see Boulton, "Buying and Holding."

PAGE 21: For information on buying out Coveys, see Phyllis Berman and Alexandra Alger, "A One-Man Show."

PAGE 22: Earl spoke of "integrating backwards" in Johnson, "Earl Has Bought a Pearl," p. 94. All Earl Holding quotes in the section that follows are taken from this article, a rare description of his operating methods.

PAGE 23: Sidebar quotes on Earl appear in Roche, "Holding's Olympic-Size Projects."

PAGE 24: "Junior Achievement of Utah 2nd Utah Business Hall of Fame Induction Dinner," *Utah Business* (Salt Lake City), August 1992, pp. 45–46. For more on the Wilson Award, see "Utahns to Get Awards," *Salt Lake Tribune,* February 5, 2004, and the Woodrow Wilson International Center web site (www.wilsoncenter.org/index.cfm?fuseaction=awards.awards; accessed October 2007).

PAGE 25: Quotes come from Slough, "Earl Holding Speaks"; I also quote from the complete interview transcript that appeared on the *Ski Magazine* web site (www .skinet.com/skinet/travel/article/0,26908,327051,00.html; accessed October 2007).

PAGE 26: On Utah's being the most conservative, most Republican state, see Matthew J. Burbank, Gregory D. Andranovich, and Charles H. Heying, *Olympic Dreams: The Impact of Mega-Events on Local Politics* (Boulder, CO, and London: Lynne Rienner Publishers, 2001), p. 123.

PAGE 27: The "master salesman" quote comes from Johnson, "Earl Has Bought a Pearl," p. 94. Hatch speaks about Earl investing in Earl in Boulton, "Buying and Holding."

PAGES 27-28: Harold Bloom's *The American Religion: The Emergence of the Post-Christian Nation* (New York: Simon & Schuster, 1992) is fascinating in the parallels it allows us to draw between Bloom's version of Mormon doctrine and Earl's life; see pp. 49, 46, 58, 94, 103, 259, 264, 270. George Lakoff buttresses Bloom in *Thinking Points: Communicating Our American Vision and Values* (New York: Farrar, Straus & Giroux, 2006); the quoted passage is from p. 51.

PAGES 28-29: Alexis Kelner's *Utah's Olympics Circus* (Salt Lake City: Recreational Guidebooks, 1989), though anti-Olympics in its stance, serves as a detailed history of Olympic promotion in Utah through 1989; the John Jerome quote is taken from p. 25. For more on corporatization of the Olympics and commodification of the city, see Burbank, Andranovich, and Heying, *Olympic Dreams,* pp. 132, 153, 161; for more on the monetary amount of the bribe, see p. 3. For more on spin by other venues, see Wendy Ogata, "IOC Passes Torch to Utah," *Standard Examiner,* June

1995. The quotes from the Budapest presentation to the IOC are taken from John Keahey, "High Noon at Budapest: Salt Lake City Makes Its Pitch," *Salt Lake Tribune,* June 16, 1995.

PAGE 29: On the money for the Olympic bid raised from corporations, see Burbank, Andranovich, and Heying, *Olympic Dreams,* p. 133.

PAGE 30: Earl's quote about not being ashamed of his association with the Olympics comes from Boulton, "Buying and Holding." Andrew Jennings and Clare Sambrook provide a sharp-tongued summary of the scandals in *The Great Olympic Swindle: When the World Wanted Its Games Back* (New York: Simon & Schuster, 2000). "Labors of love" is taken from Roche, "Holding's Olympic-Size Projects."

PAGE 32: Earl's comments on retirement are in Roche, "Holding's Olympic-Size Projects." The quotes from Earl's tributes are taken from Bossick, "Sun Valley," and Megan Thomas, "Community Celebration Pays Tribute to the Holdings," *Mountain Express* (Ketchum, Idaho), February 1, 2006. Earl was described as the "patriarch of Sun Valley" in Jeff Cordes, "Sun Valley Turns Its Focus to Golf," *Idaho Mountain Express,* December 27, 2006.

MOUNTAIN OF DREAMS

PAGE 37: Epigraph from the afterword to Marc P. Reisner, *Cadillac Desert: The American West and Its Disappearing Water* (New York: Viking Penguin, 1986; rev. ed. 1993), p. 517; citation is to the revised edition. Used by permission of Viking Penguin, a division of Penguin Group (USA) Inc.

The translation of Wasatch comes from LaVan Martineau, *The Southern Paiutes* (Las Vegas: KC Publications, 1992), p. 186. See also the terrific poem by the Paiute poet Adrian Louis, "This Ends with a Frozen Penis," *Ceremonies of the Damned* (Reno and Las Vegas: University of Nevada Press, 1997), pp. 38–41. The poem is about, among other things, using "black medicine" to bewitch Burt Reynolds, making love (or trying to) with Loni Anderson in the back of a beer truck, the Mormon Tabernacle Choir, and the "bulging" Wasatch Mountains.

PAGE 38: "Births: Preliminary Data for 2002," *National Vital Statistics Reports,* vol. 51, no. 11 (June 25, 2003), recorded 90.6 births per 1,000 women aged fifteen to forty-four.

PAGE 40: Details on the Ute creator come from my book *The People: Indians of the American Southwest* (Santa Fe: School of American Research Press, 1993), p. 300. Ogden Valley was home to the "Weber Ute," who were actually Western Shoshone people and part of a culture that spanned the Great Basin from Death Valley to Pocatello, Idaho. Their close linguistic and cultural relatives, the Ute, lived in the Wasatch Range south toward Utah Lake, and in the Southern Rockies from modern Salt Lake City to Denver. See Warren L. D'Azevedo, ed., *Handbook of North American Indians: Great Basin* (Washington, D.C.: Smithsonian Institution, 1986), for extensive information about these native peoples of the area.

PAGE 41: For more on the common ownership of New England forests and wildlife, see Freyfogle, *The Land We Share: Private Property and the Common Good,* pp. 24, 31. The Brigham Young quote is taken from John B. Wright, *Rocky Mountain Divide: Selling and Saving the West* (Austin: University of Texas Press, 1993), p. 164, who in turn relies on B. H. Roberts, *History of the Church* (Salt Lake City: Desert News Press, 1930), vol. 3, p. 269.

Thomas G. Alexander traces shifting Mormon attitudes in "Stewardship and Enterprise: The LDS Church and the Wasatch Oasis Environment, 1847–1930," in George B. Handley, Terry B. Ball, and Steven L. Peck, eds., *Stewardship and the Creation: LDS Perspectives on the Environment* (Provo, UT: Religious Studies Center, Brigham Young University, 2006). Overgrazing figures were taken from Wright, *Rocky Mountain Divide,* pp. 168–69.

Early history of Cache National Forest and quotes from Logan resolution and Teddy Roosevelt come from Michael W. Johnson, "Whiskey or Water: A Brief History of the Cache National Forest," *Utah Historical Quarterly* 43, no. 4 (Fall 2005): 329–45.

PAGES 42-43: For more on DeVoto as "preeminent conservationist writer," see the introduction in Bernard DeVoto, *The Western Paradox: A Conservation Reader,* ed. Douglas Brinkley and Patricia Nelson Limerick (New Haven: Yale University Press, 2001), p. xx; the description of the Wheeler Creek flash flood appears on pp. 452–53. Used with permission. For a wonderful introduction to DeVoto and Stegner, which shaped my comments here, see John L. Thomas, *A Country in the Mind: Wallace Stegner, Bernard DeVoto, History, and the American Land* (New York: Routledge, 2002).

PAGE 43: The typhoid fever story comes from articles, editorials, and obituaries in the *Ogden Standard-Examiner* between July 16 and 30, 1929.

PAGES 45-46: About 40 percent of Wheeler Basin was purchased from the city, 35 percent was donated by the city, 10 percent was exchanged through the Chamber of Commerce, 10 percent was reserved from the public domain, and the remaining 5 percent was purchased much later.

My primary source for North American ski history is E. John B. Allen, *From Skisport to Skiing: One Hundred Years of an American Sport, 1840–1940* (Amherst: University of Massachusetts Press, 1993).

PAGE 47: Thanks to William (Bill) Klein of Ogden, the retired Forest Service remote sensing specialist, for his help with the story of the John Paul dedication. When an old Forest Service friend of Bill's, a 10th Mountain Division veteran, came to him with the idea of a memorial to John Paul, it was Bill, younger and more vital at seventy, who carried it out. He gathered statements from the old-timers to document the origin of the name for the U.S. Geological Survey and created the idea and text for the memorial plaque. He and his committee organized the dedication day event on October 1, 1999. And he brought veterans of the 10th back to Snowbasin in February 2001 to participate in the dedication of the John Paul men's downhill course.

PAGE 51: For the contributions of 10th Mountain Division veterans, see H. Benjamin Duke, "Skiing Soldiers to Skiing Entrepreneurs: Development of the Western Skiing Industry," unpublished ms., Denver Public Library, 1989.

Two recent books tell the story in much more detail: Peter Shelton, *Climb to Conquer: The Untold Story of World War II's 10th Mountain Division Ski Troops* (New York: Scribner's, 2003), and McKay Jenkins, *The Last Ridge: The Epic Story of the U.S. Army's 10th Mountain Division and the Assault on Hitler's Europe* (New York: Random House, 2003).

PAGE 52: Some of the details of the history of Snowbasin as a business come from Pat Bean, "A World Class Plan All Along," *Ogden Standard-Examiner,* December 10, 1995.

PAGE 54: Peter W. Seibert's memoir, written with William Oscar Johnson, is *Vail: Triumph of a Dream* (Boulder, CO: Mountain Sports Press, 2000). Some details of Vail's beginnings come from Rothman, *Devil's Bargains,* pp. 229–36; others are from William Philpott, "Visions of a Changing Vail: Fast-Growth Fallout in a Colorado Resort Town," master's thesis, University of Wisconsin, 1994. Further details about Pete Seibert and Earl Eaton come from Daniel Glick, *Powder Burn: Arson, Money, and Mystery on Vail Mountain* (New York: Public Affairs, 2001).

The "idea a minute" quote comes from Steve Lipsher, "Colorado Ski Pioneer Pete Seibert Dies of Cancer at 77," *Denver Post,* July 17, 2002.

PAGE 56: The cloud-seeding anecdote comes from Kit Miniclier, "Friends Recall Seibert's Vision," *Denver Post,* July 30, 2002.

PAGE 57: The Bob Chambers letter appeared in the *Ogden Standard-Examiner,* December 22, 1995.

THE PROPHETS OF PLACE

PAGE 59: Epigraph from Annie Dillard, *An American Childhood* (New York: Harper & Row, 1987), pp. 248–49. Copyright © 1987 by Annie Dillard. Reprinted by permission of HarperCollins Publishers.

Details of the early days of the Trimbles and Seifferts in North Dakota come from Leonard and Bette Lodoen, *This Land of Mine: An Early History of Westhope N.D. and Its Community* (privately published, Westhope, ND, 1976), and Earl Schell, *West of the River* (privately published, Westhope, ND, no date).

THE LAST RESORT

PAGE 69: Epigraph from John Hanson Mitchell, *Trespassing: An Inquiry into the Private Ownership of Land* (Reading, MA: Perseus Books, 1998), p. 127. Used with permission.

PAGE 71: My comments about consuming nature were inspired by Jennifer Price, "Looking for Nature at the Mall: A Field Guide to the Nature Company," in *Uncommon Ground: Rethinking the Human Place in Nature,* ed. William Cronon (New York: W. W. Norton, 1995), p. 200. The globalization metaphor comes from Thomas Friedman, *The Lexus and the Olive Tree* (New York: Farrar, Straus & Giroux, 2000).

For more on the ski area convention in 2000 in Orlando, see Hal Clifford, *Downhill Slide: Why the Corporate Ski Industry Is Bad for Skiing, Ski Towns, and the Environment* (San Francisco: Sierra Club Books, 2002), p. 61; the New Ski Village description is from p. 127.

The ski area executive who described "collective expectation" was Scott Oldakowski, a vice president for real estate and marketing at American Skiing, as quoted in Clifford, *Downhill Slide,* p. 60.

PAGE 73: Earl describes how he would like others to see him in Slough, "Earl Holding Speaks."

PAGE 74: The reference to "temples to skiing" comes from Clifford, *Downhill Slide,* p. 26.

Earl's assertion that an official had promised him a trade comes from Glenn R. Simpson, "Olympic Angle Helps Utah Ski Resort Gain U.S. Land to Expand," *Wall Street Journal,* July 9, 1998.

PAGE 75: For USFS annual land trade numbers, see Clifford, *Downhill Slide,* p. 155. On the Colorado wilderness blackmail of the Forest Service, see Kelly Hearn, "On the Offensive: Developer Tom Chapman," *High Country News,* February 16, 1998. Janine Blaeloch's comment about land deals going to Congress appears in Deborah Nelson and Rick Weiss, "Land Exchange Program Hurts Public, GAO Says," *Washington Post,* July 13, 2000.

PAGE 76: Forest and ski area statistics are from Clifford, *Downhill Slide,* p. 135. The Robert Redford quotes come from Pamela Fiori, "The Natural," *Town and Country,* November 2002, p. 236. For news of the Sundance Preserve, go to www.nf-pauta.org/sundance.html (accessed August 24, 2007).

PAGE 77: As of December 31, 1999, according to the National Park Service web site (www.nps.gov), 52 percent of the 377 NPS areas with designated acreage had less than 2,600 acres. The Art Carroll quote is taken from Christopher Smart, "Media Beat," *Salt Lake City Weekly,* July 16, 1998.

PAGE 80: For more on the Hatch-Tixier meeting and the infamous Robert Pope photograph, see Pat Bean, "Hatch Talks Tough about Decision," *Ogden Standard-Examiner,* March 14, 1990. Hatch's involvement with the pamphlet drawing a connection between drugs and the environment is noted in Paul Rauber, "Smoke Signals," *SIERRA Magazine,* January/February 1999, p. 16.

PAGE 81: Hatch's and Garn's comments about events of 1990 appear in Christopher Smith, "Politicians Paved Way for Snowbasin" and "Holding Gave Forest Service Employees Freebies," *Salt Lake Tribune,* February 13, 2000.

PAGE 87: For more on the 1996 permit "reform," see Clifford, *Downhill Slide,* p. 136.

That first *Deseret News* report that 88 percent of Utahns rejected the Olympics was based not on an objective poll but rather on a "coupon return" that favored the most passionate respondents; see Kelner, *Utah's Olympic Circus.*

PAGE 88: The reference to Earl's fighting "tooth and toenail" comes from Slough, "Earl Holding Speaks."

PAGE 90: The reference to "procedural republic" comes from Michael Sandel, as quoted in Daniel Kemmis, *This Sovereign Land: A New Vision for Governing the West* (Washington, D.C.: Island Press, 2001), p. 125.

THE RULES OF THE GAME

PAGE 93: Epigraph from William Greider, *The Soul of Capitalism: Opening Paths to a Moral Economy* (New York: Simon & Schuster, 2003), p. 35.

Earl's story of his conversation with Hansen appears in Slough, "Earl Holding Speaks"; I also quote from the complete interview transcript that appeared on the *SKI* web site at www.skinet.com/skinet/travel/article/0,26908,327051,00.html; accessed October 2007.

PAGE 94: For Hansen's record in Congress, I rely on the League of Conservation Voters scorecard of environmental votes. A proenvironment record scores 100 percent; Hansen averaged about 10 percent. The Hansen quote on saving the environment from the environmentalists comes from Lee Davidson, "Hansen's Swan Song," *Deseret News,* November 10, 2002.

The story about trips to Great Salt Lake for family home evening comes from Charles F. Trentelman, "Birds, Boating, Grandkids," *Ogden Standard-Examiner,* December 8, 2002. For more on Hansen's background, see Robert Gehrke, "It's a Time of Sunsets for Hansen," *Salt Lake Tribune,* December 1, 2002.

For Hansen's brash bills, see Jim Woolf, "Hansen: Free Ski Lifts from U.S. Grip," *Salt Lake Tribune,* September 23, 1995. Lee Davidson, "Hansen Bill Slammed as 'Land Grab,'" *Deseret News,* September 30, 1995.

PAGE 95: *Testimony: Writers of the West Speak on Behalf of Utah Wilderness,* compiled by Stephen Trimble and Terry Tempest Williams, was first published as a chapbook of 1,000 copies and distributed to Congress and the press. Milkweed Editions

(Minneapolis) published a trade edition in 1996. I tell the story of the book in David Thomas Sumner, "*Testimony,* Landscape, and the West: A Conversation with Stephen Trimble," *Weber Studies* 19, no. 3 (Spring/Summer 2002): 2–14.

A companion interview with Terry Tempest Williams, which appears in the same issue, includes her story about the effect of the project on Bill Clinton; see David Thomas Sumner, "*Testimony, Refuge,* and the Sense of Place: A Conversation with Terry Tempest Williams," *Weber Studies* 19, no. 3 (Spring/Summer 2002): 15–28. See also Terry Tempest Williams*, Red: Passion and Patience in the Desert* (New York: Pantheon, 2001), Terry's exploration of politics on the Colorado Plateau.

PAGE 96: Information on the Western Land Group's role in writing federal land exchange laws is taken from George Draffan and Janine Blaeloch, *Commons or Commodity: The Dilemma of Federal Land Exchanges* (Seattle: Western Land Exchange Project, 2000).

PAGE 97: For more on Tixier's tracking land exchange from retirement, see Smith, "Politicians Paved Way for Snowbasin" and "Holding Gave Forest Service Employees Freebies."

PAGE 99: Hatch quote from Tom Kenworthy, "Snowbasin Is Becoming a Slippery Slope," *Washington Post,* February 5, 1999.

PAGE 100: These details of Gray Reynolds's biography come from Charles F. Trentelman, "Reynolds: On Top of the Mountain," *Ogden Standard-Examiner,* January 31, 2002.

PAGE 103: Gray Reynolds testified before the subcommittee of the Senate Committee on Appropriations; see U.S. Senate, Department of the Interior and Related Agencies Appropriations for Fiscal Year 1997, April 24, 1996.

PAGES 103-4: I base my story of Jack Ward Thomas's role on conversations with him in 2003. He told a slightly different version in his book *The Journals of a Forest Service Chief,* ed. Harold K. Steen (Seattle: University of Washington Press, 2004), p. 333, where he reports that when he and Gray Reynolds went to meet with Jim Hansen "[we] made no requests . . . [and] told him that we did not know the position of the administration. We suggested that he and Senator Orrin Hatch meet with the president or vice president and reach an agreement with them as to the best legislative solution."

PAGE 105: The *Congressional Record* tracked the Senate debate on Utah Wilderness, including references to *Testimony* by Senators Bill Bradley and Russ Feingold during the filibuster of the "Presidio Properties Administration Act of 1995"; see March 25–27, 1996, pp. S2763–S2924.

PAGE 106: For details on Hansen's relentless push for Snowbasin legislation, see Mike Gorrell, "A Swap or a Steal?" *Salt Lake Tribune,* April 21, 1996.

Phrases about special perks for contributors are from Sara Fritz, "Special Interest Deals Get Stalled by Budget Battle," *Los Angeles Times,* January 30, 1996.

For more on Hatch's support for the land exchange deal and Earl Holding's help with Hatch's BCCI troubles, see Glenn R. Simpson, "Olympic Angle Helps Utah Ski Resort Gain U.S. Land to Expand," *Wall Street Journal,* July 9, 1998.

MUSEUM OF IMPROPRIETIES

PAGE 111: Epigraph from Jon Margolis, "Bush Is a Man of His Word: He's Audacious, But Should That Be Surprising?" *High Country News* (Paonia, Colorado), March 29, 2004, p. 23. Used with permission. Margolis wrote this line after noting that "Western environmentalists angry about the Bush administration weakening wilderness protection by administrative order applauded when the Clinton administration attempted the de facto creation of new wilderness areas—via the Roadless Rule—through executive order." He sees the same irony that I saw in Grand Staircase vs. Snowbasin.

PAGE 117: The land trade protest rally is covered in Pat Bean, "A Grim View of Snowbasin Land Swap," *Ogden Standard-Examiner,* June 20, 1996.

The national organizations that supported Save Our Snowbasin included the Natural Resources Defense Council, the Wilderness Society, Sierra Club, National Wildlife Federation, and the Isaak Walton League.

PAGE 119: The Bennett cloud quote appears in the Associated Press story "U.S. Senate Passes Snowbasin Land Swap as Part of Parks Bill," October 4, 1996 (www.afnews .org/newsroom/ap/oth/1996/oth/oly/feat/archive/100496/oly53509.html; accessed August 7, 1997).

PAGE 121: The William Cronon quote comes from his "Introduction: In Search of Nature," in *Uncommon Ground: Rethinking the Human Place in Nature,* ed. William Cronon (New York: W. W. Norton, 1995), p. 37.

Holding's quote on hiring Gray appeared in Mike Gorrell, "Ex-Federal Official's Job Raises Questions," *Salt Lake Tribune,* March 16, 1997.

PAGE 124: I paraphrase the idea that woodlands represented a second chance from a passage in Simon Schama, *Landscape and Memory* (New York: Knopf, 1995), pp. 191–93; the "tabernacle of liberty" quote is from p. 201; the "vegetable theology" quote is from p. 205.

Jim Wright's game of "Earl Rules" comes from his column "Huh, huh . . . This Game Is Cool," *Ogden Standard-Examiner,* August 1, 1996.

TRACK HOE

PAGE 127: Epigraph from Mormon apostle John Widtsoe's *Success on Irrigation Projects* (New York: Wiley, 1928), p. 138, as quoted by Wallace Stegner in *Where the*

Bluebird Sings to the Lemonade Springs: Living and Writing in the West (New York: Random House, 1992).

PAGE 136: Kent Matthews pleaded for snow in Pat Bean, "New Snowbasin Ski Lifts Tested for Safety's Sake," *Ogden Standard-Examiner,* December 12, 1998.

PAGE 137: Earl Holding quote about making something nice comes from Pat Bean, "Snowbasin Starts Runs," *Ogden Standard-Examiner* (June 1997; available at www .standard.net/utah_central/olympics/snowbasin.snowbase.html; accessed November 10, 1997).

PAGE 138: From Clifford, *Downhill Slide,* p. 29: electrical bill for snowmaking; "coal into snow," p. 184.

PAGE 139: For the idea of snow as a commodity, see Clifford, *Downhill Slide,* p. 53.

Information on the summit of Mount Ogden is from the Ogden Sierra Club web site (http://utah.sierraclub.org/ogden/Snowbasin/mtogden.html; accessed October 2007) and Charles Trentelman, "New Radio Tower Brings Controversy: Communications Site Needs Upgrade, but Nature May Take a Hard Hit," *Ogden Standard-Examiner,* July 4, 2000.

PNEUMONIA ROAD

PAGE 143: Epigraph from John McPhee, *The Control of Nature* (New York: Farrar, Straus & Giroux, 1989), p. 179. Copyright © 1989 John McPhee. Reprinted by permission of Farrar, Straus & Giroux, LLC.

PAGES 143-44: See Gloria Griffin Cline, *Exploring the Great Basin* (Norman: University of Oklahoma Press, 1963), for the story of Peter Skene Ogden's adventures in the Wasatch, including a confrontation with American trappers at Mountain Green in 1825 and journal descriptions of discovering the valley and seeing it five years later. See also Osborne Russell, *Journal of a Trapper* (Lincoln: University of Nebraska Press, 1965), pp. 116–17.

PAGE 146: Skier day statistics are taken from Clifford, *Downhill Slide,* p. 6.

The Clint Ensign quotes appeared in John Keahey, "Snowbasin Road Gets Big No," *Salt Lake Tribune,* February 18, 1998.

PAGE 147: On the Holding Highway to Holdingville, see Mary A. Carter's letter to the editor: "Who Does Jim Hansen Really Work For?" *Ogden Standard-Examiner,* October 31, 1998. Scott Leckman's quote is taken from Ralph Wakely, "Senate Hopeful Opposes Feds Paying for Road," *Ogden Standard-Examiner,* September 3, 1998.

For Bennett's claim that the Forest Service asked for his connector road bill, see Charles Trentelman, "Bennett: New Road Nothing Personal," *Ogden Standard-Examiner,* April 26, 1998. Senator John McCain's remarks of December 20, 2001, appear in the Congressional conference report on the Department of Defense Appropriations Act, 2002, p. S13837.

PAGE 152: Orrin Hatch is quoted in Tom Kenworthy, "Snowbasin Is Becoming a Slippery Slope," *Washington Post,* February 5, 1999.

PAGE 153: Earl's comment "all it takes is money" comes from Johnson, "Earl Has Bought a Pearl."

PUBLIC TRUST

PAGE 161: Epigraph from William Kittredge, *Who Owns the West?* (San Francisco: Mercury House, 1996), p. 7. Copyright © Mercury House. Used with permission.

PAGE 162: I based my discussion of the economics of resource value on Scott Lehmann, *Privatizing Public Lands* (Oxford, UK: Oxford University Press, 1995), p. 71.

PAGE 167: Doug Muir, the Wasatch/Cache land staff officer, spoke for the Forest Service to oppose the tram easement in Charles Trentelman, "Snowbasin's Owner's Plan Could Remove Taylor Canyon from Swap," *Ogden Standard-Examiner,* October 14, 1999.

The Forest Service's spokesman, Bob Swinford, is quoted in "Snowbasin Snag Spurs New Offers," *Salt Lake Tribune,* May 9, 2000.

PAGE 169: The $250 million figure for Earl's developments comes from Mike Gorrell, "A Twisting, Winding Road to Snowbasin," *Salt Lake Tribune,* June 21, 1998.

PAGE 170: Mitt Romney's "nice" statement is quoted in Christopher Smith and Linda Fantin, "Snowbasin Land Swap Finally Signed," *Salt Lake Tribune,* May 24, 2000. *Ogden Standard-Examiner* editorial after exchange announcement: "Snowbasin Land Swap Was a Good Bargain," May 25, 2000. *Salt Lake Tribune* editorial: "A Fair Trade at Snowbasin," May 28, 2000.

Janine Blaeloch's comments on swallowing the swap appear in Jerry Spangler, "U.S., Snowbasin Finalize Land Deal," *Deseret News,* May 24, 2000.

PAGE 172: Earl Holding's post-Olympic statements are quoted in Andrew E. Slough, "Earl's Mount Olympus," *SKI Magazine,* January 2003, p. 136.

PAGE 173: Chris Peterson's comments on the Malan's Basin proposal are quoted in Kristen Moulton, "Ogden Resort Development a Steep Climb," *Salt Lake Tribune,* June 19, 2006. The city council's 184 questions are posted at www.wcfhelp .blogspot.com/2006/08/184-council-and-citizen-questions.html. See Don Wilson, "Malan Could Be a Trail into Debt," *Ogden Standard-Examiner,* September 23, 2006, for a critique by a former ski area planner.

Chris Peterson described the "precarious state" of his plans in Scott Schwebke, "Mt. Ogden Off the Hook," *Ogden Standard-Examiner,* July 8, 2007.

For Robert Smith's comments on apples and oranges, see Charles Trentelman, "Land Swap Gets Some Grumbles," *Ogden Standard-Examiner,* May 29, 2000.

PAGE 176: For background on the evolving concepts of property and the common law of lands, see Freyfogle, *The Land We Share.* I paraphrase his language in my question about property rights being a "God-given right."

For a good discussion of the legal concept of public trust, see Michael Krauss, moderator, *Conservation and the Public Trust Doctrine: A Roundtable Discussion,* Center for Private Conservation, 1999 (www.cei.org/pdf/1578/pdf; accessed October 2007). The legal structure regarding public trust is mostly built from state law, with a strong nod toward indigenous rights. Once specific to navigable streams and fisheries as a way to protect the "interests of the Crown" from privatization, today's inclination to extend the commons beyond oyster beds and halibut fisheries to endangered species and their habitats makes conservative legal scholars nervous.

Land trusts were sparked to life by the Reagan era; for more on this history, see Richard Brewer, *Conservancy: The Land Trust Movement in America* (Hanover, NH: University Press of New England, 2003), p. 37.

Dale Bosworth (who was described to me by an approving Chip Sibbernsen as a "dirt forester") spoke of "process gridlock" in "Striking the Right Balance: Coming to Terms with Change in National Forest Management" (McClure Lecture, University of Idaho, Moscow, September 18, 2002).

I first heard the word *petroleocracy* applied to the Bush-Cheney administration by Barbara Kingsolver.

For a good introduction to Charles Wilkinson's work, see *Crossing the Next Meridian* (Washington, D.C.: Island Press, 1993).

PAGE 177: I've quoted from my interviews and correspondence with Jack Ward Thomas and from several different versions of his "stump speech" about the history and future of the Forest Service, "The Instability of Stability" (Thirty-First Annual Pacific Northwest Regional Economics Conference, Spokane, Washington, 1997); see also his statements before the U.S. House of Representatives Subcommittee on Forests and Forest Health, September 21, 2000, and October 17, 2001.

NINETY-NINE SECONDS

PAGE 183: The epigraph, though usually attributed to Goethe, actually comes from John Anster's loose 1835 translation of Goethe's *Faust;* the syntax is more Anster's than Goethe's. The quote became famous in mountaineering literature after W. H. Murray attributed Anster's paraphrase to Goethe in *The Scottish Himalaya Expedition* (New York: J. M. Dent & Sons, 1951), and the Sierra Club's David Brower later popularized the lines in his books and speeches.

Doug Lewis described the Grizzly downhill racecourse in "Grizzly's Hidden Bite," *SKI Magazine,* February 2002. Lewis also provided evocative commentary live on race day at the finish line at the 2002 Olympics. *National Geographic Adventure* magazine rated the Snowbasin men's downhill on the John Paul Ridge as number 45 of the top one hundred adventures in America.

PAGE 184: Medal winners at the Snowbasin Olympic races:

Men's downhill, February 10, 2002

1. Fritz Strobl, Austria 1:39.13

2. Lasse Kjus, Norway 1:39.35

3. Stephan Eberharter, Austria 1:39.41

Women's downhill, February 12, 2002

1. Carole Montillet, France 1:39.56

2. Isolde Kostner, Italy 1:40.01

3. Renate Goetschl, Austria 1:40.39

Men's combined, February 13, 2002

1. Kjetil Andre Aamodt, Norway 3:17.56

2. Bode Miller, USA 3:17.84

3. Benjamin Raich, Austria 3:18.26

Women's combined, February 14, 2002

1. Janica Kostelic, Croatia 2:43.28

2. Renate Goetschl, Austria 2:44.77

3. Martina Ertl, Germany 2:45.16

Men's super-G, February 16, 2002

1. Kjetil Andre Aamodt, Norway 1:21.58

2. Stephan Eberharter, Austria 1:21.68

3. Andreas Schifferer, Austria 1:21.83

Women's super-G, February 17, 2002

1. Daniela Ceccarelli, Italy 1:13.59

2. Janica Kostelic, Croatia 1:13.64

3. Karen Putzer, Italy 1:13.8

PAGE 186: See Thomas F. Hornbein, *Everest: The West Ridge,* ed. David Brower (San Francisco: Sierra Club/Ballantine Books, 1968).

For more on the Henriette d'Angeville story and quote, see Schama, *Landscape and Memory*, pp. 495–98.

FARMERS IN EDEN

PAGE 189: Epigraph from Barry Lopez, "Eden Is a Conversation," *Portland Magazine,* University of Portland, Autumn 2006. Used with permission.

PAGE 190: The quote about solitude from the twelfth-century Cistercian abbot St. Aelred of Rievaulx appears in a pamphlet published by the Holy Trinity Abbey, Huntsville, Utah.

PAGE 192: The Thomas Merton quote comes from a pamphlet published by the Holy Trinity Abbey, Huntsville, Utah.

PAGE 193: Information on the abbey's investing its own money appears in John Wright, "Monks Put Own Money on the Line," *Ogden Standard-Examiner,* June 10, 2005. Anyone who wishes to help the monks construct their new monastery may send donations to Abbey of the Holy Trinity Capital Campaign, 1250 S 9500 E, Huntsville, UT 84317–9702. See also www.holytrinityabbey.org.

The caretaker quote is taken from Charles Cummings, *Eco-Spirituality: Toward a Reverent Life* (Mahwah, NJ, and New York: Paulist Press, 1991), p. 69. See also Father Cummings's *Monastic Practices* (Kalamazoo, MI, and Spencer, MA: Cistercian Publications, 1986).

PAGE 194: The quote from Romans used by the Wolf Creek developer is mentioned in a cover article on Shanna Francis and Ogden Valley by Stephen Dark, "Paradise Lost," *Salt Lake City Weekly,* November 16, 2006; quotes from Haynes Fuller also come from this article.

Some quotes from Susan McKay come from her unpublished manuscript "The Way Home."

PAGE 198: Brett Zollinger conducted research in Ogden Valley and other northern Utah farm communities while working on his PhD in rural sociology (Utah State University, 1998). Farmland development statistics in Utah and change on the urban fringe are taken from Brett Zollinger and Richard S. Krannich, "Utah Agricultural Operators' Attitudes Toward Commonly Used Agricultural Land Preservation Initiatives," *Journal of the Community Development Society* 32, no. 1 (2001): 35–64. Farm sales in Weber County come from Brett Zollinger and Richard S. Krannich, "Factors Influencing Farmers' Expectations to Sell Agricultural Land for Non-Agricultural Uses," *Rural Sociology* 67, no. 2 (2002): 442–63.

PAGE 199: Statistics on land trusts are tallied at the extensive Land Trust Alliance web site (www.lta.org; accessed September 2007).

PAGE 200: For information on the Maine easement, see Brewer, *Conservancy,* p. 155.

The Sun Valley quotes appear in Rothman, *Devil's Bargains,* pp. 193–201, 343. Used by permission.

PAGE 202: For information on the decrease in Weber County farmland, see Brett Zollinger and Richard S. Krannich, "Factors Influencing Farmers' Expectations to Sell Agricultural Land for Non-Agricultural Uses," pp. 442–63.

For an analysis of the 2000 census in rural America, see Kenneth M. Johnson and Calvin L. Beale, "Nonmetro Recreation Counties: Their Identification and

Rapid Growth," *Rural America* 17, no. 4 (Winter 2002): 12–19; David A. Mc-Granahan and Calvin L. Beale, "Understanding Rural Population Loss," *Rural America* 17, no. 4 (Winter 2002): 2–11; and David Westphal, "Shifting Tide: Some Cities Grow Despite Flow of Residents to Rural Areas," *Sacramento Bee*, April 2, 2001.

For Park City as Hong Kong of Utah, see Wright, *Rocky Mountain Divide*, p. 236.

PAGE 204: For Handley's quotes from Mormon scripture, see *Doctrine and Covenants* 59: 18–20.

PAGE 205: For the classic statement of the "sacred plow, heroic farmer" view of the West, see Henry Nash Smith, *Virgin Land: The American West as Symbol and Myth* (New York: Vintage Books, 1970; originally published 1950), p. 123.

Quotes from Brigham Young and Joseph Smith come from Hugh W. Nibley, "Brigham Young on the Environment," in *Brother Brigham Challenges the Saints*, vol. 13, *The Collected Works of Hugh Nibley* (Salt Lake City: Deseret Books and Foundation for Ancient Research and Mormon Studies, Brigham Young University, 1994), pp. 28–29.

PAGE 206: For more on Wasatch Front communities as "population bombs," see Wright, *Rocky Mountain Divide*, p. 186.

William Smart, *New Genesis: A Mormon Reader on Land and Community*, ed. William B. Smart, Terry Tempest Williams, and Gibbs M. Smith (Salt Lake City: Gibbs Smith, 1998). See also Richard Francaviglia, *Believing in Place: A Spiritual Geography of the Great Basin* (Reno: University of Nevada Press, 2003), for further ideas about connections between place and spirituality.

For George Handley's work, see "The Environmental Ethics of Mormon Belief," *BYU Studies* 40, no. 2 (2001): 187–211; "LDS Belief and the Environment," *Salt Lake City: Save Our Canyons Newsletter*, Winter 2004/2005; and "The Desert Blossoms as a Rose: Toward a Western Conservation Aesthetic," in the important collection *Stewardship and the Creation: LDS Perspectives on the Environment*, ed. George B. Handley, Terry B. Ball, and Steven L. Peck (Provo, UT: Religious Studies Center, Brigham Young University, 2006). I quote Donald Adolphson from his "Environmental Stewardship and Economic Prosperity" from the same volume, p. 13.

Quotes from Brigham Young come from Hugh W. Nibley, "Brigham Young on the Environment," pp. 33, 42, 49, 51, and Craig D. Galli, "Stewardship, Sustainability, and Cities," *Stewardship and the Creation*, p. 51.

The quote from James Faust appeared in "Serving the Lord and Resisting the Devil," *The Ensign* 25, no. 9 (1995): 2–7. Within that quote, the scriptural citation is *Doctrine and Covenants* 104: 17. The passage he neglected is from *Doctrine and Covenants* 104: 13. Faust died in August 2007.

PAGE 207: See Dr. Seuss, *The Lorax* (New York: Random House Books for Young Readers, 1971).

CRAZY GRACE

PAGE 209: Epigraph from Edward Abbey, *Desert Solitaire: A Season in the Wilderness* (New York: Simon & Schuster, 1968), p. 42. Reprinted by permission of Don Congdon Associates, Inc.; © 1968 by Edward Abbey, renewed 1996 by Clarke Abbey.

PAGE 213: For help with Jim Kilburn's story, special thanks to Weber County Sheriff's Department Detective Coltan Johansen, as well as to Crime Scene Supervisor Russ Dean, who told me of a videotape made by a Weber State University film crew that included the crime scene unit's investigations of Jim's death at Snowbasin; I was able to track down this tape at the Weber State Library, and it brought to life the scene on the chairlift.

PAGE 214: The Vail story comes from Daniel Glick, *Powder Burn: Arson, Money, and Mystery on Vail Mountain* (New York: Public Affairs, 2001). Damage of twenty-six million dollars is mentioned in "Feds Find Eco-Terrorist Files," *Environment News Service,* June 1, 2000. Earth Liberation Front quotes come from Glick, *Powder Burn,* pp. 3, 61.

Earth Liberation Front statistics and history are taken from "Statement of James F. Jarboe, Domestic Terrorism Section Chief, FBI, on the Threat of Eco-Terrorism before the House Resources Committee Subcommittee on Forests and Forest Health, February 12, 2002" (posted on the FBI web site, www.fbi.gov/congress/ congress02/jarboe021202.htm; accessed October 2007) and "From Push to Shove: Radical Environmental and Animal-Rights Groups Have Always Drawn the Line at Targeting Humans. Not Anymore," *Southern Poverty Law Center Intelligence Report* (Fall 2002).

PAGE 215: The stories of the capture of the ELF cell and of the suicide of Bill Rogers appear in Vanessa Grigoriadis, "The Rise and Fall of the Eco-Radical Underground," *Rolling Stone,* August 10, 2006. Additional perspective comes from Matt Rasmussen, "Green Rage," *Orion Magazine,* January–February 2007. Chelsea Gerlach's statement appears in *U.S. District Court District of Oregon, Government v. No. 06– 60079 Chelsea Dawn Gerlach (Defendant),* Proceedings, Friday, July 21, 2006, Eugene, Oregon, posted at www.greenscare.org/pdfs/Gerlach_Transcript.pdf.

PAGE 216: Henry David Thoreau, *Walden* (New York: North American Library, 1960), pp. 25–26.

The Vail spokesperson asks "Who gets to decide?" in Glick, *Powder Burn,* p. 256.

PAGE 217: Carol Holding's comment about Earl's always knowing just what he wanted is from her deposition in Civil No. 000908494, *Sinclair Oil Corp. vs. RKW International, Inc./RKW International Inc. vs. Earl Holding,* 3rd Judicial District Court, Salt Lake County, Utah, 2001.

PAGE 220: National press attention came from Kirk Johnson, "Utah Olympic Committee's Local Interests Interwoven," *New York Times,* February 8, 1999. Information on Freedom, Utah, appears in John W. Van Cott, *Utah Place Names* (Salt Lake City: University of Utah Press, 1990), p. 148.

PAGE 222: For the *Salt Lake Tribune* editorial opposing RDA involvement, see "Blight for Business," December 28, 1995. The *Deseret News* covered the January 30 hearing in Marianne Funk, "S. L. Tells Sinclair, 3 Business Owners to Come to Terms," January 31/February 1, 1996.

PAGE 225: Mac and his alliance were a perfect example of what planning analysts call "social learning," in which people create "network power" through cooperative engagement. They must contend with the opposite—the "monolithic social reality" perpetuated by coldly insular policy analysis, a bureaucratic state, or a hierarchic church. Philip C. Emmi and Chris Beynon illuminate this dichotomy in "Envision Utah and the Quest for a Metro-Regional Development Consensus" (lecture presented at the Association of Collegiate Schools of Planning Conference, Atlanta, November 2–5, 2000). The survey on Utah values that yielded the "safe haven" comment also comes from this lecture. Emmi and Beynon state that 90 percent of the Utah legislature belongs to the real estate industry.

PAGE 226: Bent Flyvbjerg, a Danish specialist on the relationship of planning and power, concludes that in a world where power defines and creates reality, the only way to "enable democratic thinking and the public sphere to make a real contribution to democratic planning and action" is to encourage dialogue between planners and academics, the people, the politicians, and the powerful—that is, between all the stakeholders; everyone needs to "become a partisan, to face conflict, and to exercise power." See "Bringing Power to Planning Research: One Researcher's Praxis Story," *Journal of Planning Education and Research* 21, no. 4 (2002): 353–66.

DEVIL'S BARGAINS

PAGE 229: Epigraph from Christian Norberg-Schulz, *The Concept of Dwelling: On the Way to Figurative Architecture* (New York: Electa/Rizzoli International Publications, 1985), p. 91. Copyright © Electa Editrice, Milan.

PAGE 239: On Mary Austin, see Rothman, *Devil's Bargains,* pp. 106–7. Used with permission.

PAGE 244: For background on easements, see Julie Ann Gustanski and Roderick H. Squires, eds., *Protecting the Land: Conservation Easements Past, Present, and Future* (Washington, D.C.: Island Press, 2000).

PAGE 245: For the date of federal tax laws, see Gustanski and Squires, *Protecting the Land,* p. 56. On lack of judicial precedents, see p. 47.

PAGE 246: For comparisons of preserve and new house taxes, see Brewer, *Conservancy,* p. 73. William H. Whyte coined the term "conservation easement" in his *Se-*

curing Open Space for Urban America: Conservation Easements, Technical Bulletin 36 (Washington, D.C.: Urban Land Institute, 1959), the book that, in Brewer's words (*Conservancy,* p. 148), "lit the easement fuse." A terrific case study (and model) for creating an easement on a New Mexico ranch appears in Anthony Anella and John B. Wright's lovely book *Saving the Ranch: Conservation Easement Design in the American West* (Washington, D.C.: Island Press, 2004).

Thoreau (from *Walden,* p. 53) is quoted in Clifford, *Downhill Slide,* p. 68.

PAGES 246–47: For easement history and the case against conservation easements, see Julia D. Mahoney, "Perpetual Restrictions on Land and the Problem of the Future," *Virginia Law Review* 88, no. 4 (June 2002): 739–87. A particularly good review of the growing call for reform is Ray Ring, "Write-Off on the Range," *High Country News,* May 30, 2005, pp. 8–15.

See also the work of Nancy A. McLaughlin, who explains the doctrine of *cy pres* in her "Conservation Easements—A Troubled Adolescence," *Journal of Land Resources and Environmental Law* 26, no. 1 (2005): 47–56, and "A Constructive Reformist's Perspective on Voluntary Conservation Easements," *Wallace Stegner Center Newsletter* 2 (Salt Lake City: S. J. Quinney College of Law, University of Utah, Fall 2005): 8–9.

PAGE 248: For statistics on second homes, see Clifford, *Downhill Slide,* p. 45. See also Glick, *Powder Burn,* pp. 23–24: "According to the Social Welfare Research Institute at Boston College, baby boomers would inherit an estimated $11.6 to $17.5 *trillion* between 1998 and 2017 from their frugal Depression-era parents."

Christopher Alexander, Sara Ishikawa, and Murray Silverstein, *A Pattern Language: Towns, Buildings, Construction* (New York: Oxford University Press, 1977).

PAGE 251: Sarah Susanka, *The Not So Big House: A Blueprint for the Way We Really Live* (Newtown, CT: Taunton Press, 1998).

PAGE 253: On the philosophy of a home, see Norberg-Schulz, *The Concept of Dwelling,* p. 91.

My idea that the window frame turns wildland into "landscape" was influenced by Karal Ann Marling's "Not There But Here," in Merry A. Foresta, Stephen Jay Gould, and Karal Ann Marling, *Between Home and Heaven: Contemporary American Landscape Photography* (Washington, D.C.: National Museum of American Art, 1992), pp. 132–39.

THE WOES OF WAYNE COUNTY

PAGE 255: Epigraph from Wallace Stegner, *Wolf Willow: A History, a Story, and a Memory of the Last Plains Frontier* (New York: Viking Press, 1962), p. 282. Copyright © 1955, 1957, 1958, 1962 by Wallace Stegner; copyright renewed © 1990 by Wallace Stegner. Reprinted by permission of Brandt & Hochman Literary Agents, Inc. All rights reserved.

PAGE 256: Wayne County statistics and numbers come from county and state government web sites (www.city-data.com/county/Wayne_County-UT.html; www.waynecnty.com; www.governor.state.ut.us/Planning/usfs/4B%20County%20Profiles/4BWayneOverview.pdf) and Miriam B. Murphy, *History of Wayne County* (Salt Lake City: Utah State Historical Society, 1999). For current LDS percentages in Utah and individual counties, see Matt Canham, "Utah Less Mormon Than Ever," *Salt Lake Tribune*, November 18, 2007. For information on artists making a living in Utah, see Joe Baird, "Torrey, Utah: You Can't Stop Progress," *Salt Lake Tribune,* May 12, 2003.

PAGE 257: Thanks to Rick Krannich, Utah State University, for help with the literature of the rural sociologists, which includes Michael D. Smith and Richard S. Krannich, "Tourism Dependence and Resident Attitudes," *Annals of Tourism Research* 25, no. 1 (1998): 783–802. On common ground, see Michael D. Smith and Richard S. Krannich, "'Culture Clash' Revisited: Newcomer and Longer-Term Residents' Attitudes Toward Land Use, Development, and Environmental Issues in Rural Communities in the Rocky Mountain West," *Rural Sociology* 65, no. 3 (2000): 396–421. On community attachment, see Joan M. Brehm, Brian W. Eisenhauer, and Richard S. Krannich, "Dimensions of Community Attachment and Their Relationship to Well-Being in the Amenity-Rich Rural West," *Rural Sociology* 69, no. 3 (2004): 405–29.

Wayne County yielded remarkable numbers in a 2001 survey: 80 percent of randomly surveyed citizens felt that protecting agricultural land and open space, preserving opportunities for outdoor recreation, and preserving opportunities for traditional multiple-use activities on public lands ranked 6 or 7 (extremely important) on a scale of 1 to 7. Ninety percent said that they would be very or somewhat sorry to leave the community; and 92 percent said that natural landscapes are important to their attachment to Wayne County (again, categories 6 and 7). Less than 10 percent would like to see seasonal property owners increase by 50 percent. And yet the same two categories at the high end (where category 7 indicated "highly involved") yielded just 7 percent who felt involved in current decision making. These survey results are from Richard S. Krannich and Joan M. Brehm, *Rural Community Change in the Intermountain West* (executive report, Utah State University Institute for Social Science Research on Natural Resources, May 2003).

People feel strongly. They don't want more newcomers. And yet no one takes action.

PAGE 258: "The Radical Center" grew out of a 2003 meeting sponsored by the Quivira Coalition, a group of ranchers, environmentalists, and scientists who dreamed of "a meeting-ground where diverse parties can come to discuss their interests, instead of argue their positions"; see Barbara H. Johnson, ed., *Forging a West That*

Works: An Invitation to the Radical Center: Essays on Ranching, Conservation, and Science (Santa Fe: Quivira Coalition, 2003).

PAGE 262: My history of state school lands in Utah comes, in part, from Cyrus McKell and Dave Harward, "State School Trust Lands: A Problem in Wilderness Designation," in *Contested Landscapes: The Politics of Wilderness in Utah and the West,* ed. Doug Goodman and Daniel McCool (Salt Lake City: University of Utah Press, 1999), pp. 137–57. For a broad history and perspective, see Peter W. Culp, Andy Laurenzi, and Cynthia C. Tuell, *State Trustlands in the West: Fiduciary Duty in a Changing Landscape,* Policy Focus Report (Cambridge, MA: Lincoln Institute of Land Policy, 2006; online at www.lincolninst.edu/pubs/PubDetail .aspx?pubid=1151).

PAGE 263: In the West, only Utah and Arizona sell trust lands; the rest feel it's better to preserve their lands for the future. See Christopher Smart and Joe Baird, "Clashing over Utah's Trust Lands: Selling the Land vs. Saving the Land," *Salt Lake Tribune,* March 18, 2007.

PAGE 266: My thoughts on the problems with speechifying at public meetings were influenced by my insightful neighbor in Grover, Owen Olpin, via an interview (June 2003) and his "Toward Jeffersonian Governance of the Public Lands," *Loyola of Los Angeles Law Review* 27, no. 3 (April 1994): 959–68.

The legal scholar Eric T. Freyfogle charts the history of environmental values in the United States in his *Bounded People, Bounded Lands: Envisioning a New Land Ethic* (Washington, D.C.: Island Press, 1998). My history of the fractious environmental community in the last three decades was also influenced by Jeffrey C. Ellis, "On the Search for a Root Cause: Essentialist Tendencies in Environmental Discourse," in *Uncommon Ground: Rethinking the Human Place in Nature,* ed. William Cronon (New York: W. W. Norton, 1995), pp. 256–68.

William Cronon material is taken from his "The Trouble with Wilderness: or, Getting Back to the Wrong Nature," in Cronon, ed., *Uncommon Ground;* see pp. 72, 37, 77, 78, 79, 84–85 for background and quotes.

PAGE 274: Two published sources tell the history of Clinton's bold proclamation: Robert B. Keiter, Sarah B. George, and Joro Walker, eds., *Visions of the Grand Staircase–Escalante: Examining Utah's Newest National Monument* (Salt Lake City: Utah Museum of Natural History and Wallace Stegner Center, 1998), and Paul Larmer, ed., *Give and Take: How the Clinton Administration's Public Lands Offensive Transformed the American West* (Paonia, CO: High Country News Books, 2004); the Bob Bennett quote comes from *Give and Take,* p. 6.

PAGES 275-76: My pondering of the relationship between wealth and freedom owes much to Scott Lehmann, *Privatizing Public Lands* (New York: Oxford University Press, 1995).

PAGE 277: Predictions in ranching employment are tracked by the U.S. Department of Labor, Bureau of Labor Statistics, *Employment Projections* (www.bls.gov/emp/; accessed October 2007). Wayne County economic data comes from the Sonoran Institute's Economic Profile System, an amazing resource available as a free download at www.sonoran.org/programs/socioeconomics/si_se_downloads.html.

James D. Proctor's "Whose Nature? The Contested Moral Terrain of Ancient Forests," in Cronon, ed., *Uncommon Ground*, pp. 269–97, influenced my thinking about environmental politics in the rural West.

PAGE 278: For more on the reform of land exchange, see George Draffan and Janine Blaeloch, *Commons or Commodity? The Dilemma of Federal Land Exchanges* (Seattle: Western Land Exchange Project, 2000).

Daniel Kemmis, *This Sovereign Land: A New Vision for Governing the West* (Washington, D.C.: Island Press, 2001), offers a detailed vision for a new model of managing the West. See also Bruce Babbitt, *Cities in the Wilderness: A New Vision of Land Use in America* (Washington, D.C.: Island Press, 2005).

PAGES 278-79: The Jack Ward Thomas quotes come from my interview with him in February 2003, his talk "The Instability of Stability," and testimony before the U.S. House of Representatives Subcommittee on Forests and Forest Health on October 17, 2001.

PAGE 279: Victor B. Scheffer, "Environmentalism's Articles of Faith," *Northwest Environmental Journal* 5 (1989): 99–109.

I've paraphrased the "wise use" countermanifesto in Ron Arnold's "Overcoming Ideology" (www.cdfe.org/wiseuse.htm; accessed October 2007). The piece also appears in Philip D. Brick and R. McGreggor Cawley, eds., *A Wolf in the Garden: The Land Rights Movement and the New Environmental Debate* (Lanham, MD: Rowman & Littlefield, 1996). I also base my summary of wise use and American values on Sherry Cable and Charles Cable, *Environmental Problems/Grassroots Solutions: The Politics of Grassroots Environmental Conflict* (New York: St. Martin's Press, 1995), pp. 11–12.

CREDO: THE PEOPLE'S WEST

PAGE 281: My credo owes much to Jim Howe, Ed McMahon, and Luther Propst, *Balancing Nature and Commerce in Gateway Communities* (Washington, D.C.: Island Press, 1997).

See also Scott Russell Sanders, "A Conservationist's Manifesto," in *Coming to Land in a Troubled World,* ed. Helen Whybrow (San Francisco: A Center for Land and People Book, Trust for Public Land, 2003). Peter Forbes has become a leading spokesman for the connections between language, land, and relationship. See his web site www.wholecommunities.org and his book *What Is a Whole Community? A Letter to Those Who Care for and Restore the Land* (Fayston, VT: Center for Whole

Communities, 2006). Jim Stiles, the cranky editor of Moab's *Canyon Country Zephyr,* has thought about these issues as well. See his "Can the West Be One?" *Salt Lake Tribune,* November 14, 2004, and *Brave New West: Morphing Moab at the Speed of Greed* (Tucson: University of Arizona Press, 2007).

For detailed analysis of our challenges, see the introduction to the 176-page final report of the 2005 National Environmental Conflict Resolution Advisory Committee at www.ecr.gov/ecr.asp?link=522.

ACKNOWLEDGMENTS

THIS STORY OF MOUNT OGDEN and its Olympic downhill ski race caught my attention in the spring of 1997, when I drove up to the little ski area above Ogden to photograph for a travel article assignment about the "old" Snowbasin. Peter Shelton, who was commissioned to write the piece, wrote an elegy. Our editor at Universal Press Syndicate, Harriet Choice, from whom both of us had received years of useful and challenging mentoring, chose a title to match his tone: "Paradise Doomed."

Though I lived in Salt Lake City, I had paid only subliminal attention to the news stories about the controversial changes at Snowbasin. I had never skied there, nor had I been involved with the grassroots struggle to slow its development.

While I shadowed Peter for the next two days, I became more and more intrigued with the story he was reporting. We began with Kent Matthews, mountain manager, who turned out to be a classic character from the postwar ski industry, a man of the rural Mountain West to his core. He had grown up in Ogden Valley, the little-known jewel of a mountain valley below the ski area, and had inherited his job from his father. Kent dearly loved

"The Basin" and was thrilled with the prospect of worldwide attention that the Olympics would bring.

We met Tom Leonard, the mountain's laconic and competent avalanche expert. Leonard took us to the top of the men's downhill on a snowmobile, and we skied the John Paul Ridge as backcountry—in fresh powder—before any course-cutting or lift construction had taken place.

Snowbasin's proprietor, Earl Holding, lived in Salt Lake City, I knew, but he had the reputation of being a mysterious eccentric. He sounded like Howard Hughes. Snowbasin staff spoke of him in heavily weighted tones, circumspectly, as "Mr. Holding." We did not meet him.

———

At the time I'd been publishing nonfiction books for two decades. An apprentice at fiction, I had been working on my first novel for three and a half years. I found myself gradually grinding to a halt on the novel, not quite ready to pull it off. Then one soft summer morning in a friend's backyard in Sacramento, while reading a fine work of literary nonfiction, I had an epiphany: this Snowbasin story had a book in it—and this was a book I knew how to write. I set the novel aside and began to work on what became *Bargaining for Eden*.

When I returned to Snowbasin in the summer of 1997, Kent Matthews was generous with his time. Chip Sibbernsen and Scott Layton freely opened up the inner workings of the Forest Service. The next year, Chip invited me to observe the meetings of the connector road Partnering Team. Later, Frank Erickson did the same for the BLM planning process in southern Utah, making sure to keep me in the loop through six years of his journey from optimism to frustration. Tom Berggren loaned me his files of clippings and correspondence from years of working on Snowbasin issues as a member of the Save Our Canyons board.

Many other people who have lived part of this story revealed their dreams to me. I wish to acknowledge, especially, the family and friends of Jim Kilburn, Mac Livingston, Margot Smelzer and her sister, Maxine Bernhisel, and Susan Snow.

———

The Utah Humanities Council supported my work with the 2002 Delmont Oswald Fellowship in Utah Studies. I'm grateful for their taking a risk on a project that involved as much potential controversy as this one. The fellowship gave me just enough financial help to allow me to focus on the writing and finish a first complete draft of the text. A 2002 Artist's Grant from the Utah Arts Council helped to purchase new technology for my slide shows. The manuscript received the Utah Arts Council Literature Program Non-Fiction Book Award and Publication Grant in 2004.

Ben Altman, manager of my slide files, helped scan and organize all those track hoe pictures with efficiency and good cheer. You can find more of my photos and a schedule of appearances at www.stephentrimble.net.

———

My writing group kept me on task for years. I am honored and moved by their willingness to read draft after draft, from one millennium to the next, and repeatedly—and graciously—give me pep talks about my missed turns. Over the years the rotating members of this insightful and supportive group have been my primary readers, and I owe much to them: Michelle Baldwin, Howard Bartlett, Melissa Bond, Betsy Burton, Ann Edwards Cannon, Chris Cokinos, Bill Coles, Teresa Jordan, Margot Kadesch, Dorothee Kocks, Felicia Olivera, Stephanie Rosenfeld, Sylvia Torti, and the late Greg Totland.

Steve Baar, Mark Bailey, Carol Dayn, Jennifer Owings Dewey, Gale Dick, Bob Emrich, Frank Erickson, John Gattuso, Phyllis Geldzhaler, Brooke Hopkins, Janet Kaufman, Kate Lambert, Nancy McLaughlin, Gary Nabhan, Sarah Rabkin, Susan Snow, Fred Voros, Randy Welsh, and my father, Don Trimble, gave me helpful critiques of all or part of the manuscript. When Scott Slovic interviewed me for the collection *What's Nature Worth?* his probing and clear thinking gave me the courage to speak with a more personal voice in the book. My book group read a draft in 2003, and I thank my readers in this core group of loyal friends: Cliff Butter, Nick Carling, Andrew Dodds, Tom Melton, and Chuck Smith.

I can't imagine a better author's emissary to the publishing world than Gail Hochman. It was a privilege to work with her, and her faith in this project over many years is testimony to the warm and intelligent care she lavishes on her lucky authors.

The book found its home at the University of California Press, and I've been delighted by the support, wise counsel, and consummate professionalism of my editor, Jenny Wapner. Laura Harger and Elizabeth Berg supervised the complicated management of the project. Julie Brand read the text closely in relentless search of clarity. Thanks to this quartet of ed-

itors and to the production and marketing teams at the press for shepherding my book into the world.

———————

My wife, Joanne Slotnik, has heard me tell the story of this book more times
than she can count—as have my children, Dory and Jake, who have grown
from middle childhood to young adulthood while I worked on the project.
Thanks to Joanne for clearing the underbrush from an evolving draft with
a smart, strong edit and for her love, support, honesty, and patience.

INDEX

TEXT
11/13.5 Adobe Garamond
DISPLAY
Akzidenz Grotesk Light Condensed, Trade Gothic
COMPOSITOR
Integrated Composition Systems
CARTOGRAPHER
Bill Nelson
PRINTER AND BINDER
Thomson-Shore